THE NEW ERA IN AMERICAN FOREIGN POLICY

The New Era in American Foreign Policy

JOHN H. GILBERT, EDITOR

ST. MARTIN'S PRESS

NEW YORK

Library of Congress Catalog Card Number: 73-82634
Copyright © 1973 by St. Martin's Press, Inc.
All Rights Reserved.
Manufactured in the United States of America.
For information, write: St. Martin's Press, Inc.,
175 Fifth Avenue, New York, N.Y. 10010

AFFILIATED PUBLISHERS: Macmillan Limited, London—
also at Bombay, Calcutta, Madras and Melbourne.

p. 21: William Van Alstyne, "Congress, the President, and the
Power to Declare War: A Requiem for Vietnam," 121, *University
of Pennsylvania Law Review,* November 1972. Reprinted by
permission of *The University of Pennsylvania Law Review* and
Fred B. Rothman & Co.
p. 90: Stanley Hoffmann, "Weighing the Balance of Power." Reprinted by permission from *Foreign Affairs,* July 1972. Copyright
1972 by Council on Foreign Relations, Inc.

Preface

During the spring of 1972 a number of distinguished scholars were invited to North Carolina State University to participate in a symposium on American foreign policy in the 1970s. The essays collected in this volume, with one exception,* are based on papers originally prepared for the symposium. On the premise that the United States has entered a period calling for a fundamental reassessment of policy and of policy-making institutions, the contributors were asked to consider some of the salient issues that are likely to command the attention of both the practitioners and students of American foreign policy in the coming decade.

The 1960s were years of transition for American foreign policy, the shock of Vietnam forcing a reappraisal of the American role in the world. Although the alarms sounded by those who fear a reawakening of the isolationist impulse may be exaggerated, a move toward retrenchment seems clearly in prospect. And although the debate between the "revisionists" and the advocates of the orthodox interpretation of postwar foreign policy continues, the Cold War now occupies the historian more than the student of contemporary foreign policy. For the latter, the greater challenge is to anticipate the debates that will occupy the historians a decade or two hence. The purpose of this volume is to contribute to that effort.

Two caveats should be entered. Making projections about the future is always a risky business, and this seemed especially true during the period in which these papers were being prepared for publication. While the symposium was in progress, President Nixon made his historic trips to Peking and Moscow, the SALT agreements were signed, and the outcome of the war in Vietnam remained in doubt. And even as the immediate past poses greater problems for the historian than distant events from which he is detached, the scholar who is concerned with the immediate future may face a more difficult task than the futurist who looks far down the road. Certainly the former is more likely than the latter to be held accountable for his errors.

Second, the scope of the inquiry, coupled with the necessity in any such undertaking for limiting the number of papers, dictated the omission of essays on some important topics. The Nixon Doctrine, broadly conceived, provided an obvious frame of reference for the selection of topics on substantive issues, though only two

* Stanley Hoffmann's essay first appeared in *Foreign Affairs* in July 1972.

of the papers are specifically and directly concerned with the Nixon Doctrine. As a group the essays deal with both the substance and the conceptual foundations of policy, consider policy-making institutions as well as processes, focus on the domestic context as well as the global, and range from a traditional power-politics orientation to systemic analysis. Thus, while the topics were assigned to the authors, a single point of view was neither desired nor, as the reader will discover, assumed in these essays.

A list of the persons who contributed to the success of the symposium and who made possible the publication of this volume would be too long to print. I owe an especially large debt to colleagues at North Carolina State University. The enthusiastic support of Professors Burton F. Beers, William J. Block, Fred V. Cahill, and Robert O. Tilman helped to make the symposium a success—and a pleasure in the bargain. Jay Hurwitz, a friend and colleague in the Department of Politics, offered a number of suggestions that improved the introductory essay. Finally, I cannot in a line properly express my appreciation to my wife Susan, but she knows without the telling of it.

March 1973

John H. Gilbert
North Carolina State University

Contents

1
Introduction

JOHN H. GILBERT

I believe that it must be the policy of the United States to support free peoples who are resisting attempted subjugation by armed minorities or by outside pressures. . . .

—HARRY S. TRUMAN, MARCH 12, 1947

Let every nation know, whether it wishes us well or ill, that we shall pay any price, bear any burden, meet any hardship, support any friend, oppose any foe to assure the survival and success of liberty.

—JOHN F. KENNEDY, JANUARY 20, 1961

We will view any new commitments in the light of a careful reassessment of our own national interests and those of other countries, of the specific threats to those interests, and of our capacity to counter those threats at an acceptable risk and cost.

—RICHARD M. NIXON, FEBRUARY 18, 1970

Presidential pronouncements, considered in retrospect, are among the most visible signposts for charting the course of American foreign policy. As the Truman Doctrine marked the beginning of the postwar era, the Nixon Doctrine appears to have signaled its end, with the war in Vietnam supplanting World War II as a point of reference for students of American foreign policy in the coming years. The contrast between Kennedy's extravagance and Nixon's caution reflects the shock of Vietnam. But profound changes in the international system and a growing concern about domestic problems would have required a "careful reassessment" of policy even if the United States had never become involved in Southeast Asia, and regardless of the outcome of the election of 1968.

The domestic consensus in which American foreign policy has been rooted for the past twenty-five years has been severely strained, if not shattered. Our foreign policy had a remarkable continuity during that period, a continuity maintained by centrist administrations of both political parties. Liberal internationalists who saw the United States in the role of benevolent defender of democratic values and formerly isolationist conservatives bent on a holy war against communism shared a commitment to American involvement on a global scale. Their common sense of an American "mission" was conveyed by Dean Rusk's observation that "other nations have interests; the United States has responsibilities." But defining interests is difficult enough; basing policy on such a vague and value-laden concept as "responsibilities" is at best arrogant and at worst dangerous. That ideological distinctions tend to be blurred in the practice was surely demonstrated by the intervention in Vietnam. The decision initially commanded broad support because it was perceived, not as an aberration, but as an expression of policy that conformed to accepted doctrine—which, indeed, it did then.

As the war dragged on toward an uncertain conclusion, President Nixon was faced with the necessity of fashioning a foreign policy based on a clearer conception of interests and on a revised consensus. The policy has been labeled the "Nixon Doctrine." This policy was first articulated at a background press briefing on American policy in Vietnam at Guam in July 1969. The central thesis of the policy offered by the President at that time seemed reasonably clear and unremarkable: the commitments of the United States would be maintained, but its allies would be expected to assume a larger share of the burden for their own defense. In theory, at least, there was more of continuity than of change in the new policy. And its first application, Vietnamization, was nothing more than the acceleration of a process already under way and was, in any case, a feasible policy only because the United States had previously assumed a very large share of the burden for the defense of South Vietnam.

Subsequent elaboration of the Guam formula, however—notably in the President's annual foreign policy reports to the Congress—suggests that the Nixon Doctrine envisages not only a reduction of the American burden but, more importantly, a fundamental restructuring of the pattern of relationships between the United States and its allies and between the United States and its potential adversaries. The new pattern of relationships and its implications for American foreign policy are not yet clear. The Nixon Doctrine, as Robert Osgood reminds us, is not a blueprint but a statement of broad concepts and general directions whose full meaning will emerge only as it is applied. In that connection, it is well to recall that the containment doctrine, as conceived by George Kennan, was so variously interpreted and applied, so wrenched from its original context and intent, that its author on several occasions denied the legitimacy of his progeny.

The content of the new policy will, presumably, be shaped in part by the lessons learned from the Vietnam experience, for it is widely believed that the managers of our foreign policy in the 1970's must begin by heeding the public cry of "no more Vietnams." But this slogan is, after all, an unanalyzed abstraction. What does it mean? No more land wars in Asia? No more interventions in civil wars? Or does it mean no more "no-win" wars? It is necessary to have a common idea of what Vietnam was in order to know what "no more Vietnams" means, and there clearly is no agreement at this time.

President Nixon's public view, consistently maintained since 1954, is that the United States has an important interest in preventing a communist take-over in South Vietnam. He now maintains that the settlement to which his administration has agreed assures a reasonable prospect that the American objective will be achieved. Given his consistent advocacy of that objective, the President's minimum requirement was a settlement for which a claim of success was at least plausible. Should the policy yet prove to have failed, the failure is likely to be regarded by the Nixon administration as a failure of will and of execution, not of conception. Even though it is unlikely that American power would be re-introduced into Vietnam in any case, the distinction is crucial because of the implications for American policy in similar situations in the future. Thus, the meaning of Vietnam, viewed from the perspective of the Nixon Doctrine, is shrouded in ambiguity.

The position of the critics of American policy in Vietnam is much clearer, but the critics are by no means in agreement. There is one group which accepted the applicability of the containment doctrine to the situation in Vietnam and initially supported the intervention, but which subsequently decided that the objectives were no longer worth the costs. They concede miscalculations, but like the Nixon administration, they are not prepared to reject the conceptual bases of the policy. Another group of critics is convinced that the intervention not only was a tragic mistake but was also a symptom of the bankruptcy of the policies that spawned it. Accordingly, in view of Nixon's position on Vietnam, these critics are inclined to be skeptical of the Nixon Doctrine because they suspect that it may represent less of a change than they believe is required.

In the essay that follows, Hans Morgenthau, who opposed the intervention as early as 1961, argues that American policy in Vietnam was based on a fundamental misconception of the nature of the world in which we live and of the nature of the conflict in that country in particular. Asserting that "much of the world is in a revolutionary or pre-revolutionary state," Professor Morgenthau denies that the security of the United States is threatened by revolution *per se;* on the contrary, "to defend the status quo in a revolutionary age is to bet on the losing side." He warns that we must not allow the Soviet Union or the Chinese to co-opt the cause of revolution for their own power-political purposes; that we must learn to distinguish between their rhetoric, which has often been inflammatory, and their actions, which have generally been cautious and restrained; that, in short, we must learn to distinguish between Soviet or Chinese expansionism, which may indeed threaten our security, and indigenous revolutions which do not.

The Vietnamese conflict, Professor Morgenthau believes, was essentially a national and social revolution, an effort to rid the country of foreign domination, not the result of a conspiracy hatched in Peking or Moscow. The attempt to suppress it, therefore, was not only an inappropriate application of the containment policy, but represented a perversion of the ideals in which we profess to believe. That our policy served neither our interests nor ideals is both the irony and the tragedy of Vietnam.

There is, however, an apparent ambivalence in Morgenthau's view. Thus, he stresses the immorality of the war, but he does so in terms of the "moral discord" between the means used and the ends sought, which tends to obscure his objections to the ends themselves. And while he calls for a return to an earlier American idealism, he continues to adhere to the "realist" conception of international politics with which he has for so long been identified. From his perspective there is no necessary contradiction here, but one is left to wonder what conceptual framework is to be applied when, and if, "interests" and "ideals" diverge. This dilemma, one assumes, may be a function of the familiar problem of defining "interests," which the Realists have never resolved to the satisfaction of their critics.

In addition to questions about the substance and the conceptual foundations of American foreign policy, the war in Vietnam has also generated a debate over the constitutional powers and responsibilities of the President and Congress. This is an issue that promises to receive a great deal of attention during the 1970's, and the way in which it is resolved could have a significant effect on the role that the United States will play in the world. Repeated, though unsuccessful, efforts by members of the Congress during the past four years to restrict the President's capacity to deploy American forces in Laos and Cambodia and to accelerate the withdrawal of troops from South Vietnam not only expressed congressional impatience with American policy in Southeast Asia, but also reflected a desire to reassert congressional prerogatives in the formulation of foreign policy.

Except for the equally unsuccessful effort by congressional conservatives during the 1950's to curb presidential authority with the Bricker amendment, Congress had generally acquiesced in the strong drift toward executive domination of foreign policy during the postwar period. When President Truman took the United States into the Korean War without seeking congressional sanction —much less a declaration of war—few questioned the conventional wisdom that the constitutional power to declare war was virtually obsolete. And during the period between the wars in Korea and Vietnam, Congress showed no reluctance to pass joint resolutions —some of which were neither requested nor desired—giving broad discretionary powers to the President. Thus, when President Johnson sought a sweeping declaration of support for his policy in Vietnam in 1964, Congress hastened to adopt the Tonkin Gulf Resolution without serious debate and with only two dissenting votes. The fact that President Nixon did not oppose the repeal of that resolution in 1971, on the ground that he had ample authority as Commander-in-Chief to continue his policy, suggests the difficulty Congress will face in any new efforts to check the power of the President. While the constitutionality of the war in Vietnam is, presumably, now a moot question, the larger issue is very much alive and merits consideration.

William Van Alstyne addresses himself to the question of the "war power" in the second essay in this volume. Examining the language of the war-related provisions of the Constitution, the evidence of the intentions of the Framers, and relevant decisions by the Supreme Court, Van Alstyne concludes that

> . . . the determination as to whether circumstances at any given time in fact make it necessary and appropriate to engage in war, *however limited in scope or objectives, resides solely in Congress subject to no delegation whatever.* (Italics added.)

Professor Van Alstyne also finds that the weight of governmental practice "is not in this instance nearly as long-lived or as substantial as alleged. . . ." In any case, as Van Alstyne notes, the Supreme Court has twice within this generation specifically rejected the claim that governmental practice could confer constitutional legitimacy. Turning to the case of Vietnam, he analyzes each of the several legal bases offered by successive administrations in support of their actions. He concludes that the Tonkin Gulf

Resolution, whatever individual members of Congress may have intended, could be reasonably construed as a declaration of limited war. By the same token, with the repeal of the resolution in January 1971, the President's continuation of hostilities was in defiance of the Constitution.

Ernest May undertakes the task of forecasting the broad outlines of American foreign policy in the next decade, focusing on domestic influences on policy. The premise of Professor May's essay is that the critical short-run determinants of change or continuity in American foreign policy are domestic public opinion and domestic politics. The "public" that May has in mind is the foreign policy public, the relatively small percentage of the population which maintains an active interest in foreign affairs, and the "establishment," the small cadre of leaders both in and out of the government who play a large role in shaping public opinion. "Domestic politics" embraces the roles of the Congress, the presidency, and the bureaucracy in the formulation of foreign policy. His method is to disaggregate these causative forces in order to analyze their components, "specifying and comparing the probable causes for change or continuity in past decades."

As Professor May notes, similar undertakings from earlier vantage points in this century would frequently have proved embarrassing to the aspiring prophet. One suspects that would have been true of such predictions a decade ago. Nevertheless, on the basis of specific estimates of the effects of the different variables on past policies, May is able to identify some of the important questions that surely must be answered if one is to predict future developments. His own answers to his questions forecast a foreign policy developing along the general lines indicated by the Nixon Doctrine.

The essays by Robert Osgood and Stanley Hoffmann analyze the Nixon Doctrine and consider its relevance to conditions in the international environment with which it is designed to cope. In Osgood's view the Nixon Doctrine represents a revised consensus calling for "material retrenchment without political disengagement," thus occupying the middle ground between the withdrawal of American forces from Europe and Asia and the devolution of the defense burden to Western Europe and Japan. The basic assumptions of the Nixon Doctrine, as both Osgood and Hoffmann perceive it, are: (1) China, Japan, and Western Europe have joined the superpowers as major actors dominating international politics in a multipolar system in which the Third World countries occupy peripheral roles. (2) The central military balance of power is still bipolar, and the preservation of order and the moderation of international tensions remains dependent on the mutual restraint of the United States and the Soviet Union. (3) While Western Europe and Japan will continue to rely on the nuclear deterrent of the United States for protection, the effect of that dependence on their policy calculations has been reduced as the concomitant of their perceptions of a diminished threat. (4) The split between the Soviet Union and China, the increasing divergence of interests between the United States and each of its major allies, and the reduction of ideological conflict have produced an environment in which each of the five actors will increasingly pursue its interests through diplomatic maneuver and negotiations within the multipolar framework.

Focusing on the relatonships between the United States and each of its major allies, Professor Osgood examines some of the difficult problems which must be dealt with if the new approach is to work. Retrenchment without disengagement is a subtle and complex policy that entails significant risks and costs. But after weighing the alternatives, Osgood concludes that the Nixon approach offers a reasonable prospect for success.

Stanley Hoffmann, on the other hand, is far less inclined to accept either the diagnosis of the situation or the prescription for policy put forward by the Nixon administration. The Nixon design is, he believes, inspired by the traditional balance of power model which provided the conceptual framework for the foreign policies of the European powers during the eighteenth and nineteenth centuries. It is a doubly irrelevant model for two essential reasons: (1) the conditions necessary for the traditional balancing mechanism to function do not exist and cannot be created; (2) it addresses itself to the problem of restraining the power-political ambitions of states, but states are not the only actors in the contemporary international arena nor is war the only problem that threatens disaster. Moreover, Professor Hoffmann observes a basic discrepancy in the Nixon policy: it attempts to preserve our influence and our present advantages while reducing our burdens at the expense of our allies. Parenthetically, one should note that the dollar problem, which flared up again as this Introduction was being prepared, has led our allies to levy the same charge against the United States. Finally, Hoffmann is also concerned by the tendencies already exhibited by Nixon's diplomacy to by-pass the allies in the pursuit of détente with China and the Soviet Union. If, as Professor Hoffmann warns, our allies should refuse to play the game according to our rules, "should . . . resist our attempt to get the best of all possible worlds, we might actually get the worst."

The prospects for détente with the Soviet Union are the subject of the essay by Anatol Rapoport. He conceives the conflict in terms of three components: the ideological, the strategic, and the systemic. In Professor Rapoport's view, the foreign policies of the Soviet Union and the United States are not guided by ideological considerations, but their policies have been rationalized by ideology as a means of enlisting public support, especially during the first phase of the Cold War. In any case, the ideological conflict has already begun to subside, and that process can be expected to continue. The principal barrier to ideological détente is the fact that the Soviet elite derives its legitimacy and thus its power from the ideology and may therefore be expected to resist the sort of "revisionism" that would jeopardize its power within the Soviet Union.

On the other hand, Professor Rapoport is inclined to discount ideology as a brake on the movement toward détente in so far as American leaders are concerned. That is a judgment with which one might well take issue. Clearly, the legitimacy of American leaders would not be undermined by the reduction of ideological conflict between the United States and the Soviet Union, but it is also clear that resistance to social and economic change in the United States has often been cloaked in appeals to anticommunist sentiment. It seems reasonable to speculate, therefore, that a conservative administration such as the present one might be disposed to balance the gains from détente in the international arena against the loss of an instrument that has proved to be effective in domestic politics in the past.

But certainly the focus of the Cold War has now shifted from the ideological to the strategic-diplomatic arena, which, as we have noted, accords with the "realist" or balance of power model. If détente is conceived as "a realization by both sides that neither can extend its power beyond certain limits without evoking determined resistance by the other side," then, Rapoport contends, détente is already well advanced, if indeed it has not already been achieved. If one accepts Professor Rapoport's definition of détente in strategic-diplomatic terms, then the SALT agreement of 1972 can be cited as substantial evidence in support of his conclusion.

The most important component of the conflict, Professor Rapoport believes, is the systemic component, and he sees no encouraging signs that the autonomous dynamics of the global system will be reversed. Conflict is, after all, inherent in the system of "sovereign" nation-states; all previous efforts to establish a stable balance of power have, sooner or later, ended in failure. In this area, Rapoport shares Hoffmann's skepticism. If the systemic analysis is correct, détente may provide some temporary security, but for the longer term it is clearly a policy that is irrelevant and futile in the nuclear age. In Rapoport's imagery, pursuing détente in the age of the megawar machines is like giving a placebo to a patient who has cancer.

The beginning of a new era in Sino-American relations, marked by President Nixon's trip to China in the spring of 1972, is the subject of James Thomson's essay. There are, as Professor Thomson explains, "multiple motivations" on both sides for desiring a new relationship in the 1970's, with "the existence and the behavior of the Soviet Union" central to the calculations of both parties. The Nixon administration recognizes that a necessary pre-condition for the establishment of a stable balance of power in Asia and the Western Pacific is an accommodation with China. As we have noted, one of the assumptions of the Nixon Doctrine is that such an accommodation can be achieved.

Viewing the breakthrough in the context of the "historical legacy" of Sino-American relations, Thomson brings into focus the significance of the initial achievement and identifies some of the serious obstacles that must be surmounted if the process of détente is to continue. As to the ultimate objective of Nixon's diplomacy, Thomson agrees with Osgood that a quadrilateral balance of power in the region is both desirable and possible. In the end, coping with the delicate problem of Japan may prove as difficult for the United States as establishing stable relationships with its Cold War adversaries.

George Rathjens analyzes the nuclear policy of the Nixon administration in the context of the continuing debates over (1) "the political-military utility of nuclear weapons" and (2) "the delicacy of the strategic balance" between the United States and the Soviet Union. The evidence provided by the administration's statements and actions leads him to the conclusion that the United States has embarked on an extremely dangerous course.

Thus, restraint in the use of conventional forces, which the Nixon Doctrine anticipates, is offset by the administration's apparent assumption that nuclear weapons can be used not only to deter attack but to achieve other political-military objectives. Indeed, if the administration does consider that nuclear weapons have such utility and is determined to maintain American influence on a global scale (a conclusion that Rathjens shares with Hoffmann), a reduction in conventional capability can be perceived as leading inevitably to the adoption of a high-risk strategy. One should recall, however, that the Eisenhower administration also took the position that nuclear weapons could be substituted for conventional forces and *did* act with restraint, whereas the Kennedy administration reached the opposite conclusion but did not act with notable restraint. The fear is that Nixon may be more prepared than either Eisenhower or Kennedy to translate his rhetoric into action. The fact that he took risks in Vietnam which his predecessors had considered and rejected tends to confirm that assumption. Given President Nixon's assessment of American interests in Vietnam, one wonders what he might have done if adequate conventional forces had not been available. Still, history does not reveal its alternatives, and such speculation is probably neither fruitful nor fair.

With regard to the "delicacy" thesis, it is true that the Nixon administration has accepted the concept of quantitative parity, but it has also made clear its determination to maintain technological superiority, which means, as Professor Rathjens points out, that "the arms race is simply channeled into new dimensions." The administration has explicitly rejected the concept of "sufficiency," in the sense of assured destruction or second-strike capability, in favor of an ambiguous doctrine of "flexibility" that is consistent with a belief in the political-military utility of nuclear weapons. Again, given the administration's propensity to justify new weapons systems as "bargaining chips," Rathjens derives little comfort from the SALT agreements. On the contrary, his interpretation of Nixon's nuclear policy is that a renewed emphasis will be placed on nuclear strength.

David Singer is no more sanguine than George Rathjens about the prospects for success of the arms control policies now contemplated by the Nixon administration. While recognizing the short-term value of certain of the steps which have been taken, Professor Singer emphasizes the distinction between arms control policies and disarmament. The former "are designed to enhance our capacity to live with and exercise control over major weapon systems" and assume the continuation of deterrence policies, while the latter entails the elimination of such weapon systems. Like Rapoport, Singer is convinced that arms races are propelled by systemic forces within nation-states and within the global system. After summarizing the incentives that states have to arm and disarm, Singer attempts to show how "self-aggravating mechanisms" within the system resist efforts to control arms races and prevent wars.

Turning to the immediate problem of surviving in a world in which the arms race continues, Singer suggests a number of ways in which deterrence policies can be designed to increase not only "the probability of short-run survival, but also the probability of ever making the transition to disarmament." Finally, following the logic of his own analysis, he outlines an approach to the problem which requires radical alteration of the system, with the United Nations Organization being given a role far beyond its present capacities.

In the concluding essay, Inis Claude offers a portrait of the United Nations that does little to encourage Professor Singer's hopes. Professor Claude examines three conceptions of the Organization "in the context of its relationship with the United States." The first of these is the United Nations as a "tool" of the United States. Acknowledging the dominant role played by the United States during the Organization's early years, Claude argues that the United Nations was never controlled by the United States to the degree that either the Russians or many Americans believed; that the influence we did have was generally exercised with restraint and for praiseworthy objectives; that, in any case, American influence has obviously been substantially reduced; and, finally, that the United Nations *is* the creation of states and an instrument of states, and American policy makers in the 1970's ought not be reluctant to use the Organization instrumentally.

Second, Claude analyzes the conception of the United Nations as a "substitute" for the United States. He is concerned that both critics and defenders of the United States' global role in recent years will be tempted to try to shift a large share of the burden of that role to the United Nations. The former are convinced that the United States has been guilty of an arrogant and imperial globalism and are beguiled by the virtues of multilateralism; the latter are confident that an overburdened United States has performed necessary tasks acting from just motives, but they now accept the imperative of retrenchment.

Claude is inclined to identify with the defenders of American policy, but while he believes that some retrenchment may be unavoidable, he makes a cogent argument that it is not realistic to expect the United Nations to act as a substitute for the United States. On the contrary, he is convinced that if the United States does less, so will the United Nations. Conversely, only if the United States is prepared to reaffirm its global concerns will the United Nations be able to adopt a more vigorous role.

Finally, Claude addresses himself to the conception of the

United Nations as a potential "superstate." He reminds us that this conception of the Organization is not consistent with its origins or with the directions in which it has thus far developed. Whatever the long-range prospects, the outlook for the 1970's does not encourage reliance on the "superstate" conception. Indeed, as previously noted, Professor Claude is persuaded that, properly conceived, the United Nations is the "tool" of its members, and for the foreseeable future, it will be strengthened by increased use as such, not by yielding to the chimera of the United Nations as a basis for world government. "Somebody," Claude observes, "must make the world safe for the United Nations before the United Nations can make much headway at making the world safe for mankind." The United States, he believes, must provide the leadership if that objective is to be achieved.

As this volume goes to press, the attention of the American people has turned inward, as expected, to domestic concerns. The public opinion polls indicate that inflation and the Watergate affair have supplanted Vietnam as objects of public concern. Still, the truce in Vietnam is daily violated, and the United States continues to bomb Cambodia. "Peace with honor" may yet be revealed as the empty slogan which many observers have always believed it to be.

Whatever the eventual outcome of the American intervention in Southeast Asia, the longest and most divisive foreign war in our history already seems strangely remote, and little remains of the stirring idealism of Kennedy's inaugural but a mocking echo. But if Nixon's posture of sober realism seems more in tune with the mood and needs of the 1970's, the mundane burdens of the next decade may prove to be as onerous as the crises of the last one. After all, only a tiny fraction of the American people were touched by the war in Vietnam in a direct and personal way. On the other hand, bringing the arms race under control and coping with profoundly serious monetary and trade problems are likely to require sacrifices that will be widely shared. And a call for improving the balance of payments is not a very inspiring standard around which to rally.

We should also remind ourselves that a decade hence President Nixon may appear to have misjudged what is required for a sound foreign policy as badly as his predecessors now seem to have done. If so, a generous portion of the blame, then as now, may well and properly be assessed to scholars who shared in the miscalculations. The reader, therefore, should approach the essays that follow with an enquiring mind but a skeptical eye.

2

The Lessons of Vietnam

HANS J. MORGENTHAU

The seemingly obvious answer to the question which is implicit in the title of this essay is that we are not going to do it again. This is not, however, the universally accepted answer. The very fact that there are distinguished people in our midst who by no means advocate that we ought not do it again, but that we ought to do it better the next time, signifies that we are here faced with a general problem transcending the particular persons and reasons that brought us into Vietnam.

It is, of course, obvious even to those who advocate trying it again and doing it better that the Vietnam War is one of the great tragedies of American history—a tragedy in the political, the military, and the moral sense, a tragedy which has sapped the economic and political strength of America. It is a tragedy also in the sense that it has alienated large masses of our people, especially of our youth, and that it has led to the incipient disintegration of the government.

What is interesting and disturbing in the reactions of both government officials and academics to the Vietnam disaster is the unwillingness to face the real issues of such a disaster. I have just read this morning an article which a colleague of mine sent me because he thought I would find it amusing. I didn't find it amusing at all; I found it horrifying. He describes in great detail how he was asked by a government agency to come to Washington and participate in a seminar discussing the mistakes that led us to where we are in Vietnam. He presented a paper which showed clearly the fundamental philosophic errors in our approach to the problem. The managers of this seminar, high government officials —generals and civil servants—refused to circulate this paper because it didn't deal with the technicalities within the accepted framework, but challenged the framework itself. This is exactly the enormous danger which we face today: we are unwilling and unable to consider the fundamental errors that are not the errors of one man or one group of men and do not bear upon the details of the implementation of policy, but grow out of the very conception of the world in which we live, of the very philosophy with which we approach the issues of the contemporary world.

First of all, the fundamental mistake we have made and which we are continuing to make is the conviction that a so-called war of national liberation or a disturbance that has the appearances of a national and social revolution is the result of an outside conspiracy. What has happened in Vietnam since the end of the Second World War, what has happened in all of Southeast Asia during that period of history, is not something which has been exported from Moscow or Peking. If Lenin had died of the measles as a little boy and if Marx had died of his boils and had written nothing, there would have been a revolution in Southeast Asia. This revolution, reduced to its simplest terms, aims at getting rid of foreign domination and relieving the people of being cannon fodder in foreign wars. This is what Ho Chi Minh wanted to achieve when he started the revolution in 1945, copying in his declaration of Indo-Chinese independence the first sentences of our own Declaration of Independence. To reduce this genuine revolution to the result of a foreign conspiracy worked out in Peking or Moscow is to misunderstand completely the issue we are facing. To say, as former Secretary of State Dean Rusk said time and again, that everything would be alright in Indochina if only North Vietnam would leave its neighbor alone, if only that foreign aggression would stop, reflects a similar misunderstanding.

Not only Southeast Asia but much of the so-called underdeveloped world, especially Latin America, is in a revolutionary ferment. This ferment is due to the very moral principles which the West has brought to the former colonial or semi-colonial regions of the world. The moral principles of national self-determination and of social justice have been adopted by the great masses as well as the elites of those societies, and they are being turned against us. Indochinese fight us in the name of the very principles which we brought to them during the colonial period. In the early stage of his revolution, Ho Chi Minh wrote to the State Department five times, asking us to help him, without ever getting an answer. We rejected him because we didn't realize that in a sense he was a natural progeny of the American Revolution and its ideas, that he was a natural ally of the United States in the moral sense. So we drove him into the waiting arms of the Soviet Union and China. Since he could not get the support he wanted from us, he got it from elsewhere.

To distort this basic reality into a mere outgrowth of a communist conspiracy, to assume that what happens in South Vietnam is a result of what has been conspired in North Vietnam, and that what happens in North Vietnam has been instigated in Peking or

Moscow or both places, is of course to create a fictitious world which has only the slightest relationship to the real world. What we have here, then, is a classic psychotic situation. We embark upon a policy which has no relation or but a very slight relation to reality. We justify that policy by creating a fictitious reality, and intelligence in good measure has the function of supplying seemingly empirical rationalizations and justifications for the policy decided upon. And we never break out of that fictitious framework and face the real world. It is this refusal to face reality and to adapt our preconceptions and policies to that reality which brought us to that terrible turn in Vietnam. There are many people who still believe that we could have won the war in Vietnam if we only had pursued a different policy of pacification, if we had done only a little bit more and had been a little bit more practical than we actually were. In a very gruesome sense the argument has validity. For if you have bombed enough, if you have in the immortal words of General Curtis Lemay bombed North Vietnam back to the Stone Age, you have won the war. If in a sense the last Vietnamese bearing arms against us has been killed, we will have won the war. This is the kind of victory which is unworthy of the United States, but it is the very logic of the policy which we were pursuing. That would have been the inevitable outcome if we had not changed our objectives, if we had not broken out of those artificial chains of a fictitious reality and faced the facts of life in Indochina and elsewhere.

But it is not only that we have misunderstood reality and that we have substituted superstitions and fictions for the objective assessment of reality, it is also that we have operated with the wrong historic analogies. We all must operate with historic analogies because that is the only rational point of reference we can go on when we try to deal with contemporary events. We get our information and our judgments from what we know, or think we know, about the historic past. But there are correct analogies and there are wrong analogies. And the analogies which have constituted the intellectual capital of our policy makers with regard to Indochina have indeed been extremely defective. Consider, for instance, the Munich syndrome. In 1938 Great Britain and France made concessions to Hitler, expecting thereby to avoid war, and these concessions only whetted his appetite and made the Second World War inevitable. So appeasement is bad, and we should not appease an expansionist totalitarian dictator. The principle is indeed correct. But then to equate either Ho Chi Minh or Brezhnev or Mao Tse-tung with Hitler is, of course, to operate with an analogy which is completely devoid of any relation to reality. For whatever one may say against Brezhnev or Ho Chi Minh or Mao Tse-tung, they are certainly not half-mad dictators possessed of Wagnerian dreams which they try to put into practice at the risk of self-destruction.

The Chinese have frequently talked like madmen. Consider, for instance, the famous manifesto of Lin Piao of 1964, in which he says that the agricultural regions of the world will encircle the cities of the world and will triumph over them. Some people in high places have taken this document seriously, but in fact it is just metaphysical nonsense. While the Chinese have talked like madmen from time to time, they have been extremely cautious and restrained in the foreign policy they have pursued since 1949. They have not been cautious and restrained because they are particularly good, but because they are particularly weak and they know it.

Consider Brezhnev or Stalin, and more particularly the latter. They have been relatively restrained in their foreign policies; they have acquired control over Eastern Europe and they have tried to get control over the access to the Mediterranean and the Persian Gulf. They have, in other words, aimed at the traditional goals of Czarist imperialism. Stalin once said to the British Foreign Secretary, Anthony Eden, during the Second World War, "The trouble with Hitler is that he does not know where to stop. I know where to stop." Our containment policy helped to stop Stalin, but to confuse Stalin with Trotsky, who was indeed the advocate of permanent revolution and of world revolution is a basic mistake. Stalin used communist revolution and subversion for the purposes of the Russian state and not for their own sake. And Brezhnev, in turn, pursues a classic power-political expansionist policy on behalf of the Russian state. He methodically moves into the empty spaces left by the liquidation of the British and French Empires, and he has been very successful in this.

These thoughts point to some of the realities of the contemporary world. Thus the idea that the Russians or the Chinese or both have instigated a revolution in South Vietnam for the purpose of conquering the world for communism is a mere figment of the imagination of ignorant and frightened politicians. I am always reminded, when thinking and talking about this matter, of a statement which the great conservative sociologist William Graham Sumner made at the beginning of the century. He said that the amount of superstition in the world has not changed, only it attaches now to politics rather than to religion. No truer words have been spoken about contemporary politics, domestic and international. Many of us believe in devils, in witches, and in the exorcising of evil spirits, which may have highly scientific names, which may even be quantified and put into equations, but which nevertheless partake of the same unreality of which traditional religious superstition has been the prime example.

There is in this misadventure also a moral element of perhaps even greater importance than the intellectual element to which I have just referred. For there is something revolting in the attempt on the part of the Government of the United States to impose its will upon a country which is very far away, which, even if it wanted to, could not imperil the security of the United States, and to do this for no other than ideological reasons. We have told the South Vietnamese that they ought to be dead rather than red, and we have been making that statement come true. However, this is not the preference of the South Vietnamese who would rather be alive and red than dead under the auspices of the present Saigon regime. These are *our* preferences, and the hatred we encounter in Vietnam and the loss of prestige we have suffered throughout the world are a result of the indecency of killing a whole population, of laying waste a whole region of the world, for no purpose even remotely commensurate with the destruction and suffering we have inflicted.

This war is immoral in the profound and traditional sense in which our civilization has made a distinction between just and unjust war. The Vietnam War is the prototype of an unjust war. A war is just when the end to be achieved by the means of war— which in itself is an evil because it means the methodical killing of men—is justified by some higher moral principle. A nation attacked by another nation has a right to defend itself, that is, to preserve its security, its territory, its institutions. The Second World War against Germany and Japan was just in that sense. The war against the Vietnamese people is unjust because there is no goal of a moral character which can justify the means used. In other words, there exists a moral discord between the end aimed at and the means employed, and therein lies the injustice of this war.

It is interesting to note that this injustice, this perversion of moral principles, is a result of a very typical American quality, that is, idealism. For it is exactly because we have this conception of a mission to be performed, not only for ourselves but for mankind, that we have gone into Vietnam. In the process of saving the Vietnamese from an evil which we regard to be worse than death, we have inflicted death upon them. This is a perversion of good into evil of such a magnitude that it ought to give us pause intellectually and morally. History shows that well-meaning people, ignorant of, or oblivious to, the empirical realities, have brought as much misery to the world with the best of intentions as evil men who wanted to bring evil and did it. In other words, the Innocent abroad may be a worse scourge to the victim of our benevolence than the Machiavellian abroad.

What this war has done to the United States cannot be limited to the political, military, and economic spheres. It has done terrible harm to the standing of the United States in the world. For there has existed from the beginning of American history to this day a unique and subtle relationship between the existence of American society and the American nation, on the one hand, and certain moral principles on the other. There is a profound truth hidden in this perverted American idealism. America has been created by an act of will primarily by immigrants from abroad. What has created the cohesion of the American society has not been history or religion or dynastic rule or even geography, but a moral act of will—the decision of millions of people to become Americans and abide by the principles of America. The greatest American states-man, Lincoln, was fully aware of this. In one of his speeches con-cerning slavery he said that half of our people, that is, the first-generation immigrants, are Americans only because they adhere to the principles of the Declaration of Independence. And this is exactly the point I want to make.

The Vietnam War and the way we have been waging it and all of its implications—moral, political, military, economic—are a living denial of the very principles of the Declaration of Inde-pendence, the very principles which have formed the cohesive cement through which American society has endured for almost two hundred years. It is this cement that has been weakened, and the alienation of the youth, the disloyalty of high government officials leaking secret documents, are symptoms of the same disease. American society has begun to disintegrate because the efficacy of the basic principles upon which American society has been founded is no longer as plausible as it used to be. Stated differently, the approximation at least of those principles by American reality is no longer as great as it used to be. The gap between those American principles and American reality is today greater than it has been at least since the Civil War. This is what we call the crisis of credi-bility. That is to say, the American promise seems to be further from fulfillment than it used to be because of the outrage of the Vietnam War.

As I have indicated before, those disastrous effects of the war are not limited to American society and its cohesion; they have had a deleterious effect upon the standing of the United States in the world. I think it was in 1966 that I met at an international meeting in Sweden a famous scientist who said to me with tears in his eyes, "You have been the last best hope of mankind and look what you are doing to yourself." In other words, the power of the United States, the influence which it has had throughout the world, the attraction it has exerted upon millions of people who came to its shores to find a more decent life, this intangible moral quality has been greatly impaired by the Vietnam War. We appear to the rest of the world not as a unique experiment in statecraft as we did 150 or even 50 years ago, but as the most powerful nation on earth which has used all of its power, with the exception of nuclear weapons, to smash a small peasant nation back to the Stone Age. This, in other words, is not only a moral deficiency. Out of that moral deficiency there arise certain political and psychological consequences which are a detriment to the standing of the United States in the world.

What are the lessons to be learned from this misadventure? The first lesson which we ought to learn from Vietnam is to part company with those nightmarish superstitions which we have taken for reality and to have the courage to look at the world as it really is and adapt ourselves to it in word and deed. It is a fact, which we may or may not like, that much of the world is in a state in which Indochina was 25 years ago. That is to say, it is in a revolutionary or pre-revolutionary state, and we are not going to fight revolutions and defeat them by bombing or by sending Marines to intervene on behalf of the status quo. We have to come to terms with this basic fact, and we must conclude from this basic fact that to defend the status quo in a revolutionary age is to bet on the losing side. If we want to maintain the power and influence of the United States in the world, we have to side with those to whom the future is likely to belong. It is instructive in this respect to note that a large segment of the Catholic Church in Latin America has recognized this basic fact and is trying to adapt itself to it.

Finally, we must ask ourselves why a succession of administrations, composed of intelligent and responsible men, have for years dismissed responsible and well-founded dissent out of hand and tried to suppress it. Here we are in the presence of a moral failing in our leaders: the sin of pride.

All men naturally identify themselves with their work, and a maker of policy has a personal stake in the soundness and success of that policy. He will not easily admit that it is unsound and doomed to failure. This universal human tendency, however, differs from the stubborn pursuit of a wrong course of action in the

face of all the evidence and all the arguments pointing to its un-
soundness and the inevitability of failure. This persistence in error
does not stem from a man's pride in his work but from a man's
awareness of his insufficiency and his fear lest patent failure might
give him away. Mr. Johnson's statement to Mr. Lodge, then our
Ambassador to South Vietnam, immediately after President Kennedy's death that he was not going to be the first American president to lose a war expresses something of that mood.

Policies here are less related to objective reality than to the
impression of the policy-maker's manly qualities they convey, and
objective reality is replaced by an artificial one which is attuned
to the policy. Thus policy moves in a wonderland of the policy-
maker's creation, and the invulnerability of that creation is vitally
important to the policy-maker's ego and the policy reflecting it.
Thus the dissenter who opposes the real world to the fictitious one
of the policy maker constitutes a mortal threat not only to the
policy but to the person of the policy maker. He does not limit
himself to suggesting a different policy from the official one, but
threatens to expose the fictitious character of the reality from which
the policy is derived and upon which it is intended to act.

The policy maker might tolerate the former function, since he
must be prepared to consider different policy proposals; he cannot
countenance the latter, which threatens with destruction the very
world within which he moves and puts into doubt his competence
to understand and act upon it. Thus it is the very extremity of the
defects responsible for our failure in Vietnam which in the last
analysis accounts for the unwillingness of the policy makers to
change their course of action. To do so would be an admission not
only of the failure of a particular policy but of the invalidity of
the perception of reality and of the intellectual, political, and moral
standards of the persons who have initiated and sustained the
policy. Only great men, who are sure of themselves and think they
are sure of their place in history, are capable of such an admission.

In conclusion, let me say that the disaster of Vietnam is not
an isolated instance. It cannot be put at the door of a particular
man or even a particularly small group of men; it is a result of a
general predisposition in American society of which those men
have been effective exponents. So it is for all of us to change our
outlook toward the world, to remind ourselves of the basic principles upon which this nation has been founded, and to try to
translate those principles into practice in a world, which, whether
we like it or not, is, and is likely to remain, a revolutionary world.

3
Congress, the President, and the Power to Declare War: A Requiem for Vietnam

WILLIAM VAN ALSTYNE

> The accretion of dangerous power does not come in a day. It does come, however slowly, from the generative force of unchecked disregard of the restrictions that fence in even the most disinterested assertion of authority.[1]

1. INTRODUCTION

Far more than a decade has elapsed since the first insertion of active United States military advisers into Vietnam, and we have now passed the sabbatical of 1965, when a half-million American troops entered that war. A number of months have put behind us the anniversary of the date when new thrusts were directed into Laos and Cambodia as well, an event memorialized this year by the resumption of massive air and naval bombardment of North Vietnam. A hundred billion dollars, fifty thousand of our own dead, three hundred thousand personal casualties, the new chemistry of spoliation and the old alchemy of bombs and napalm greater than any previous war in the history of mankind: headstones of American history in the late twentieth century.

The sheer endurance of this staggering fait accompli of war overhangs the Constitution and seems to ridicule its present usefulness. Renewed inquiry into the continuing legitimacy of the Vietnam War would seem to be especially pointless, moreover, in light of the State Department's lengthy Legal Memorandum of 1966 arguing that the executive practice of war has become so well established as virtually to have been absorbed into the Constitution even in the absence of any antecedent declaration by Congress.[2] If the matter were thought doubtful and not entirely moot on that account alone, still there is but the one forum in which scholastic opinion may evidently be composed for any useful purpose, the Supreme Court, and for reasons it has declined publicly to share at all, that forum has thus far been entirely closed to the question.[3]

Yet, what was occasionally denied consideration as "nonjusticiable" in the past has been more than once subsequently considered on the merits; [4] and though the Court has yielded an almost obsequious deference to other departments of government from time to time, even upon consideration of the merits of a case, it has just as often eventually reclaimed the independence of its judgment.[5] Whatever the immediate political result, moreover, it is surely never trivial to form one's own opinion as to the legitimacy of executive authority which presumes upon the horrendous use of armed force. Perhaps the duty to do so is most pressing precisely when there is no other forum of decision. The recent practice of several presidents since World War II to draw extraordinary inferences from their powers as Chief Executive and Commander in Chief (in eclipse of the war declaration clause) is certainly not dispositive of the question unless, by thinking it so, we compound the error and invest it with the ironic power of self-fulfilling prophecy.

In addition, the claim that constitutional legitimacy may be settled by the sheer weight of an unexamined governmental practice (and the claim of practice is not in this instance nearly as long-lived or as substantial as alleged) ought not lightly be accepted. To this extent, no apology is owing for the suggestion that recent practice is perhaps the *least* instructive source of constitutional legitimacy. Twice within this generation the government's reliance upon such practice was specifically rebuked when the Supreme Court finally came to terms with the issue in controversy. In 1952, military seizure of a private steel mill by presidential directive, during the Korean War but without congressional authorization, was rested in argument by government counsel partly on the prior practice of other American presidents acting under allegedly similar emergency circumstances. Concluding that any such unexamined prior executive practice was virtually weightless in measuring the constitutional propriety of still another instance of that practice, the district court concluded:

> [I]t is difficult to follow [the government's] argument that several prior acts apparently unauthorized by law, but never questioned in the courts, by repetition clothe a later unauthorized act with the cloak of legality.[6]

Upon appeal, the Supreme Court affirmed the injunction against the Secretary of Commerce, in an opinion accompanied by the mindful dictum with which this article is prefaced.

More recently still, the Congress became embroiled in controversy respecting the entitlement of one of its members to assume his seat. Though no one had disputed that Adam Clayton Powell met the only enumerated constitutional standards for eligibility, Powell was nonetheless excluded on the determination of the House that he was unfit on other grounds. When the ensuing controversy eventually came before the Supreme Court, counsel for Congress correctly noted that since 1868 the House of Representatives had excluded a number of members on the basis of its determination of disqualifications other than those expressly listed in article I; given the ambiguity of the document (and the virtual "nonjusticiability" of this internal House matter), he argued, this practice of Congress must itself be seen as an illumination of its constitutional authority. In declaring against the use of that claim of authority, however, the Court offered an observation which will be taken to heart in this article as it relates to the use of governmental practice in aid of constitutional interpretation, a limited use restricted to inferences from practices reasonably contemporary with the Constitution itself:

> That an unconstitutional action has been taken before surely does not render that same action any less unconstitutional at a later date. . . . The relevancy of prior exclusion cases is limited largely to the insight they afford in correctly ascertaining the draftsmen's intent. Obviously, therefore, the precedental value of these cases tends to increase in proportion to their proximity to the Convention in 1787. And, what evidence we have of Congress' early understanding confirms our conclusion that the House is without power to exclude any member-elect who meets the Constitution's requirements for membership.[7]

2. THE ESSENTIAL MEANING OF THAT POWER IN CONGRESS "TO DECLARE WAR"

Article I of the Constitution provides for a Congress in whom "[a]ll legislative powers herein granted shall be vested. . . ." Included among the specific powers listed in article I, section 8, is that "[t]he Congress shall have Power . . . To declare War. . . ." Also within that section is the power to grant letters of marque and reprisal, the authority to make rules concerning captures on land and water, to raise and support armies, to provide and maintain a navy, to make rules for the government and regulation of the land and naval forces, and other associated matters.

In article II, which describes the executive power, invested in a single individual, section 2 provides that the President shall be "Commander in Chief of the Army and Navy of the United States," and that he shall have power to make treaties by and with the advice and consent of the Senate. Section 3 of the same article further provides that the President shall from time to time give to the Congress information on the state of the Union, recommend to their consideration such measures as he shall judge necessary and expedient, and that he shall take care that the laws be faithfully executed. Finally, provision is made by section 4 of article IV that the United States shall guarantee to every state in the Union a republican form of government, that it shall protect each of them against invasion and, on application of a state's legislature or of the state's executive (when its legislature cannot be convened), against domestic violence as well.

Among those interpretations consistent with the language of these several war-related provisions are at least three which offer quite different impressions of the congressional power to declare war. First, perhaps this particular clause merely confirms a ceremonial duty on the part of Congress to ratify an obvious condition of war and thus to give a certain official imprimatur of its own to events of de facto belligerency that have already taken place. Second, and more significantly, perhaps it establishes in Congress a more definite power of veto, to arrest what is otherwise an executive power to make war, to declare *against* a war and thereby to check the executive from further pursuit of specific hostilities. Or third, that in the absence of an affirmative declaration by Congress authorizing the extraterritorial use of armed force as a reasonably unmistakable exercise of this very power, the President may not pursue any national policy whatever through the use of such force. There are doubtless other possibilities as well, and certainly each of these may permit significant differences of nuance, but they do not seem unfair to the basic alternatives of construction.

The most frequently used first source in coming to terms with these and other possible interpretations and questions affected by the war declaration clause is the notes of James Madison made during the course of the discussions of the Constitutional Convention. As originally drafted, the clause provided that Congress shall have power to "make" war, but debate ensued which Madison reported as follows: [8]

"To make war"

Mr. PINCKNEY opposed the vesting this power in the Legislature. Its proceedings were too slow. It would meet but once a year. The House of Representatives would be too numerous for such deliberations. The Senate would be the best depository, being more acquainted with foreign affairs, and most capable of proper resolutions. If the States are equally represented in Senate, so as to give no advantage to large States, the power will notwithstanding be safe, as the small have their all at stake in such cases as well as the large States. It would be singular for one authority to make war, and another peace.

Mr. BUTLER. The objections against the Legislature lie in great degree against the Senate. He was for vesting the power in the President, who will have all the requisite qualities, and will not make war but when the Nation will support it.

Mr. MADISON and Mr. GERRY moved to insert *"declare,"* striking out *"make"* war; leaving to the Executive the power to repel sudden attacks.

Mr. SHERMAN thought it stood very well. The Executive should be able to repel and not to commence war. "Make" better than "declare" the latter narrowing the power too much.

Mr. GERRY never expected to hear in a republic a motion to empower the Executive alone to declare war.

Mr. ELLSWORTH [said] [t]here is a material difference between the cases of making *war* and making *peace*. It should be more easy to get out of war than into it. War also is a simple and overt declaration, peace attended with intricate and secret negotiations.

Mr. MASON was against giving the power of war to the Executive, because not safely to be trusted with it; or to the Senate, because not so constructed as to be entitled to it. He was for clogging rather than facilitating war; but for facilitating peace. He preferred *"declare"* to *"make."*

On the motion to insert *declare*—in place of *make,* it was agreed to.

N.H. no.

Mass. absent.

Conn. no (On the remark by Mr. King that "make" war might be understood to "conduct" it which was an Executive function, Mr. Ellsworth gave up his objection, and the vote of Connecticut was changed to—ay.)

Pa. ay.
Del. ay.
Md. ay.
Va. ay.
N.C. ay.
S.C. ay.
Geo. ay.

Mr. Pinckney's motion to strike out the whole clause, disagreed to without call of States.

As thus accepted—"The Congress shall have power . . . to declare War"—it was apparent that the draftsmen wished to avoid their experience under British rule where an individual alone had power to determine the alleged necessity of embarking upon a course of war and thus to draw the people into foreign adventures that required their blood, extracted their treasure, and subordinated their liberties. It was also clear that the institutions and processes of the United States should be so arranged as to make it harder to initiate war and easier to achieve peace, and yet not hamstring the executive when conducting a war already declared or deny him an interim emergency power as the Commander in Chief to repel attacks against the United States until Congress could meet to consider its will.

An examination of the Federalist Papers, those political essays which accompanied the general ratification controversy in New York, assists in clarifying what was meant by the Philadelphia Framers. Of particular significance is *Federalist Number 69,* allegedly authored by Alexander Hamilton, the ardent leader of the centralist-federalist party. In this instance, moreover, nothing is to be found in the anti-federalist tracts [9] which deny or take exception to Hamilton's view that:

> The President is to be commander-in-chief of the army and navy of the United States. In this respect his authority would be nominally the same with that of the king of Great Britain, but in substance much inferior to it. It would amount to nothing more than the supreme command and direction of the military and naval forces, as first General and admiral of the Confederacy; while that of the British king extends to the *declaring* of war and to the *raising* and *regulating* of fleets and armies,—all which, by the Constitution under consideration, would appertain to the legislature.[10]

That the war declaration clause was urged by the federalists as a highly important and wholly independent source of citizenry protection against the risk of executive commitments to war, quite aside from the separate control of Congress to raise an army and navy and to control the purse, is wholly reflected by the character of their debate with the anti-federalists with respect to the anti-federalist position that Congress should be denied authority to raise a peacetime army at all.[11]

These early discussions were soon put to the test of contemporary construction during tense relations between the United States and principalities along the Barbary Coast of North Africa, at the very turn of the nineteenth century. At that time, American merchant ships were set upon by outlaws known as the Barbary Pirates. President Jefferson's reactions in his immediate Message to Congress are illuminating:

> I sent a small squadron of frigates into the Mediterranean, with assurances to that Power of our sincere desire to remain in peace, but with orders to protect our commerce against the threatened attack. The measure was seasonable and salutary. The Bey had already declared war. His cruisers were out. Two had arrived at Gibraltar. Our commerce in the Mediterranean was blockaded and that of the Atlantic in peril. The arrival of our squadron dispelled the danger. One of the Tripolitan cruisers, having fallen in with and engaged the small schooner *Enterprise*, commanded by Lieutenant Sterret, which had gone as a tender to our larger vessels, was captured, after a heavy slaughter of her men, without the loss of a single one on our part. . . . *Unauthorized by the Constitution, without the sanction of Congress,* to go beyond the line of defense, the vessel, being disabled from committing further hostilities, was liberated with its crew. The *Legislature* will doubtless consider whether, by authorizing measures of offense also, they will place our force on an equal footing with that of its adversaries. I communicate all material information on this subject, that *in the exercise of this important function confided by the Constitution to the Legislature exclusively* their judgment may form itself on a knowledge and consideration of every circumstance of weight.[12] (Emphasis added.)

In a later message to Congress, Jefferson held the same, steady course:

> Considering that Congress alone is constitutionally invested with the power of changing our condition from peace to war, I have thought it my duty to await their authority for using force in any degree which could be avoided.[13]

With virtual unanimity, the same attitude was shared by all contemporaries of these formative years.[14]

Specifically, then, the lodgment of the power to declare war exclusively in Congress forbids the sustained use of armed force abroad in the absence of a prior, affirmative, explicit authorization by Congress, subject to the one emergency exception: an interim emergency defense power in the President to employ armed force to resist invasion or to repel a sudden armed attack until Congress can be properly convened to deliberate on the question as to whether it will sustain or expand the effort by specific declaration or, by doing nothing, require the President to disengage our forces from the theater of action.

The explanation of the use of the word "declare" rather than "make" now seems clear as well. If it is the case that the Congress has made a suitable determination to authorize the use of armed force to effectuate national policy in any given instance, then discretion concerning affiliated logistical, tactical, and strategic decisions properly reposes within the presidency, consistent always, however, with the scope of the antecedent congressional declaration. The case for ungrudging construction of the power of the President as Commander in Chief, acting within the specific war authorization of Congress, was well expressed by Hamilton:

> Of all the cares or concerns of government, the direction of war most peculiarly demands those qualities which distinguish the exercise of power by a single hand. The *direction* of war implies the direction of the common strength; and the power of directing and employing the common strength, forms a usual and essential part in the definition of the executive authority.[15] (Emphasis added.)

The Congress would be left with a flexible power of review and control by its continuing legislative authority over appropriations, levies upon manpower, and, of course, the prerogative to repeal prospectively its declaration of war.

The line between the rule and the limited exception of an interim defensive emergency use of force seems to have been respected, incidentally, in President Johnson's initial reaction to the alleged firing by PT boats of North Vietnam on American destroyers in the international waters of the Gulf of Tonkin in August, 1964. The original reaction was limited to defensive action against those particular boats and the immediate bases from which it was believed they had come.

Though the incident was unquestionably an act of war, it was within the interim emergency exception of repelling armed attack, and only a single question might fairly be raised about it in isolation. President Johnson authorized no more than the limited "hot pursuit" of the PT boats, their destruction, and an attack on their immediate bases. While it is debatable that even the authorization of attack on the immediate bases was within the executive discretion, clearly prolongation beyond that point in time when Congress had an adequate opportunity to consider its will and to ratify and authorize a continuation of armed force, would have been wholly illegitimate. Again, the situation and response is well attested by presidential practice contemporary with the Federalist Period, witnessed by Jefferson's decision with respect to our schooner, the *Enterprise,* and the Bey of Tripoli's Cruiser:

> Unauthorized by the Constitution, without the sanction of Congress, to go beyond the line of defense . . . I communicate all material information on this subject, that in the exercise of this important function confided by the Constitution to the Legislature exclusively their judgment may form itself on a knowledge and consideration of every circumstance of weight.[16]

In 1798, Hamilton was cautious in the quasi-war with France:

> In so delicate a case, in one which involves so important a consequence as that of War—my opinion is that no doubtful authority ought to be exercised by the President. . . .[17]

The declared executive position on this matter remained highly consistent for a long period of years, and the fact that one or another President may otherwise have utilized his office so to force upon Congress the manner in which it may have determined to use its own authority (as was arguably done in the Mexican-American War),[18] far from providing evidence of a different rule, rather confirms the felt necessity of securing an explicit congressional declaration as a prerequisite of any extraterritorial military action not under the pretense and limitation of repelling attack. Thus, responding to inquiry on the subject while serving as Secretary of State in 1851, Daniel Webster observed:

> In the first place, I have to say that the war-making power in this Government rests entirely with Congress; and that the President can authorize belligerent operations only in the cases expressly provided for by the Constitution and the laws. By these no power is given to the Executive to oppose an attack by one independent nation on the possessions of another. We are bound to regard both France and Hawaii as independent states, and equally independent, and though the general policy of the Government might lead it to

take part with either in a controversy with the other, still, if this interference be an act of hostile force, it is not within the constitutional power of the President; and still less is it within the power of
any subordinated agent of government, civil or military.[19]

Similarly, in his Message to Congress on December 6, 1858, President
Buchanan noted:

> The executive government of this country in its intercourse with
> foreign nations is limited to the employment of diplomacy alone.
> When this fails it can proceed no further. It can not legitimately re-
> sort to force without the direct authority of Congress, except in re-
> sisting and repelling hostile attacks. It would have no authority to
> enter the territories of Nicaragua even to prevent the destruction of
> the transit and protect the lives and property of our own citizens on
> their passage.[20]

While serving in Congress, Abraham Lincoln drew the following
sharp line conservatively rejecting the extraterritorial use of force
even under claim of the interim emergency executive power to
repel invasion:

> Allow the President to invade a neighboring nation whenever he
> shall deem it necessary to repel an invasion, and you allow him to
> do so whenever he may choose to say he deems it necessary for such
> purpose, and you allow him to make war at pleasure. Study to see if
> you can fix any limit to his power in this respect, after having given
> him so much as you propose. . . .
>   The provision of the Constitution giving the war-making power
> to Congress was dictated, as I understand it, by the following rea-
> sons: Kings had always been involving and impoverishing their peo-
> ple in wars, pretending generally, if not always, that the good of the
> people was the object. This our convention understood to be the most
> oppressive of all kingly oppressions, and they resolved to so frame
> the Constitution that no one man should hold the power of bringing
> oppression upon us. But your view destroys the whole matter, and
> places our President where kings have always stood.[21]

Three decades earlier, when Colombia had drawn upon the
newly promulgated Monroe Doctrine to request the use of military
force from President Monroe against France, the administration
denied its authority to intervene by such means. Writing to former
President Madison, Monroe noted: "The Executive has no right to
compromit the nation in any question of war. . . ." Three days
later, Secretary of State Adams formally advised the Minister of
Colombia: "[B]y the constitution of the United States, the ultimate

decision of this question belongs to the Legislative Department of the Government." [22]

While a number of additional questions remain now to be examined, the configuration of immediately relevant war-related constitutional clauses appears clearly to yield the following propositions:

1. In the absence of a declaration of war by the Congress, the President may not sustain the systematic engagement of military force abroad for any purpose whatever.

2. The interim use of military force solely to repel invasion of the United States or to relieve American citizens from an existing attack is an authorized executive war power granted by the Constitution. That power expires *ex proprio vigore* when the Congress has had reasonable opportunity immediately to convene and to authorize the continuation or enlargement of hostilities by express declaration, *i.e.*, even the constitutional authorization of emergency executive war power of immediate self-defense terminates upon opportunity and failure of Congress to sustain it by express declaration.

3. In the event that the Congress authorizes the initiation, continuation, or enlargement of military hostilities by express declaration, the constitutional initiative of logistical, tactical, and strategic decision in the conduct of those authorized hostilities belongs to the executive.

4. A residual power of review and control is vested in the Congress through its continuing authority over appropriations, levies upon manpower, and its prerogative to modify or to repeal its declaration of war.

3. THE NON-DELEGABILITY OF THE CONGRESSIONAL RESPONSIBILITY

The next level of question is to determine whether or not this responsibility and power of Congress alone to declare war, it being understood that in the absence of its exercise no executive authority in the sustained extraterritorial engagement of military force has constitutional foundation, is subject to delegation to some other office or party. The question divides itself into two parts, the first being readily answerable and the second being somewhat more doubtful: the first being directed to alleged delegations by treaty, and the second being directed to alleged prospective delegations by joint resolution.

In the current controversy, some support has been sought in the fact of the Senate's earlier ratification of the Southeast Asia Treaty combined with the constitutional provision that it is the President who shall take care that the laws be faithfully executed, *i.e.*, that he shall act to fulfill that Treaty obligation. Not dissimilar reference was made during the Korean War, conducted without declaration of war by Congress, to the Uniting for Peace Resolution of the United Nations which we were allegedly bound to support through executive action alone.

Most discussions of this subject have countered these executive claims simply by observing that the particular treaties cited in aid of the President's actions are not self-executing of their obligations; rather, they specifically do not purport prospectively to delegate the power to declare war but merely establish an international obligation that *Congress* will, when the circumstances contemplated by the treaty actually arise, then act upon its authority to fulfill that obligation insofar as the use of military force may be involved. Thus, the Southeast Asia Treaty provides that, in the event of armed attack on any member, each signatory will "act to meet the common danger in *accordance with its constitutional process.*" [23] In short, the treaty commitment, rather than empowering the President to undertake the use of military force, sets an international contractual obligation—obliging Congress to make the declaration of war if it intends to fulfill the treaty commitment. But again, the cross-reference is back to the constitutional process that Congress itself shall authorize the President to engage armed force abroad before such use of force would become legitimate under our internal law as we have deemed fit to regulate it, even in the phraseology of the treaty we have signed. It follows, therefore, that the unilateral invocation of the particular treaty responsibility by the President cannot stand as a substitute for a specific and requisite authorization by Congress upon such occasions when our assistance pursuant to that treaty may be sought.

But a conclusive answer on this score is not dependent upon the conservative parsing of particular treaty phrases, for it is clear in any event that the war power cannot constitutionally be delegated by treaty at all. Treaties become law when made under the authority of the United States merely upon ratification by two-thirds of the Senate alone. This alternative of lodging the war power in the combination of the President and the Senate—rather than in the House and the Senate as was finally done with the war power—was specifically considered in the Philadelphia Convention and explicitly rejected.[24] No case, therefore, can be made that a treaty can grant to a third party, or indeed grant to the President pursuant to that treaty, the authority to engage in systematic military hostilities abroad as a claim of faithful execution of the law of that treaty. No treaty, or anything else for that matter, can serve as a declaration of war, thus satisfying that section of the Constitution, unless shared in by the House of Representatives: the constitutional draftsmen engaged in a deliberate, determined, and successful effort to include that body, with its more popular representation, in the decision prerequisite to sustained armed hostilities.

If the treaty power does not permit Congress to delegate its war powers to the President, what then of the propriety of other means, for example, a joint resolution, whereby both Houses of Congress might attempt prospectively to shift to the President the determination of the use of war as an instrument of national policy? In favor of that reading, one might review an enormous amount of material on the general question of congressional delegation of legislative powers,[25] noting that not since the 1930's has the executive exercise of authority following even a loose prospective attempt at delegation been disfavored by the Supreme Court on constitutional grounds; [26] that the Court has waxed most eloquent in favor of congressionally-supported, quasi-legislative presidential discretion in foreign affairs; [27] that decisions sustaining prospective delegations with but the barest hint of standards can readily be found; [28] that at least the usual strong presumption of constitutionality would apply were the executive to be challenged on the validity of a clear and specific congressional statement of delegation; and that even where a "preferred freedom" was involved the furthest the Court has gone in recent decades has been to construe the scope of delegation short of the executive presumption.[29] In 1965, moreover, but a single vote could be mustered from the Supreme Court that Congress had too far abdicated its legislative responsibility in granting the President and Secretary of State power to regulate passports under a statute providing nothing more definite on its face than that it should be done "under such rules as the President shall designate and prescribe. . . ." [30]

In a characteristically literate and measured criticism of executive action in Vietnam (which he concludes went beyond the authority delegated by that portion of the Tonkin Gulf Resolution he considers), Professor Bickel of the Yale Law School finds that the power to delegate the war power to the President is granted to Congress, provided only (but importantly) that it not be "without standards [the absence of which] short circuits the lines of responsibility that make the political process meaningful." [31] I agree entirely with Professor Bickel so far as he would go, to construe congressional attempts at delegation on so momentous a subject most conservatively.

I am inclined to go considerably further, however, for it seems to me clearly the case that exclusive responsibility of Congress to resolve the necessity and appropriateness of war as an instrument of national policy at any given time is uniquely not delegable at all. The pursuit of national interest by sustained extraterritorial uses of direct force was textually reserved to Congress alone after alternative formulations were pressed on precisely the grounds that conventionally rationalize a limited power to delegate an interstitial lawmaking authority to the executive, *viz.,* superior expertise in the executive, the need for flexibility in the face of rapidly changing circumstances, the cumbersomeness of parliamentary processes, and a residual power to check the executive in the event of displeasure with the manner in which he might make war. To the extent that such arguments were considered to have merit, they were accommodated by *other* means among the several war-related clauses. To the extent that they were not thus accommodated, the conclusion seems inescapable that they were rejected and correspondingly, that no further latitude of executive control was to be permitted than that already provided for.

To express the same matter less passionately, specific contingencies which give sense and shape to the general doctrine permitting limited delegations of legislative power in other areas of congressional responsibility are *already* provided for in respect to war, *so far as it was felt safe to do so.* Thus, it was contemplated and made possible that peacetime armies might be raised under presidential discretion though this might even increase the risk of war. Similarly, an interim executive capacity to respond to outright emergencies, authorizing the President to resist invasion or repel an attack when war might be thrust upon the nation too quickly for Congress to convene to authorize even such limited defensive measures, was provided. Additionally, executive discretion to make command decisions of tactics and strategy within the express war declaration by Congress was conceded. Further, confidence was also reposed of necessity in the President in recognizing that the congressional power would be exercised or not, substantially depending upon the information and advice the President would provide in his emergency message of exigent circumstances asking for *their* decision to initiate hostilities, sustain present emergency defensive war actions he had taken, enlarge upon them, or, by doing nothing, require that our extraterritorial forces be immediately disengaged and withdrawn. Finally, although there might have been much to be said for a different view (so to make going to war especially grave and therefore desirably difficult to accomplish), the Constitution does not require that the declaration of war be an all or nothing response. In the exercise of its responsibility, it is not essential that Congress must declare a total war against one or more nations, contemplating effective occupation of their territory and capitulation by their governments. Rather, the document contemplates congressional recourse to a declaration of *limited* war with specifically designated objectives which the President may then pursue through the use of armed force once that specific declaration and circumscribed objective have been articulated by Congress.

For instance, by the Act of July 7, 1798, Congress authorized President Adams to respond to French depredations on the seas in the following very specific and limited war terms:

> That the President of the United States shall be, and he is hereby authorized to instruct the commanders of the public armed vessels which are, or which shall be employed in the service of the United States, to subdue, seize and take any armed French vessel, which shall be found within the jurisdictional limits of the United States, or elsewhere, on the high seas. . . .[32]

Without question, the President's execution of that antecedent authorization of specific armed force would have been pursuant to a declaration (*"hereby* authorized . . . to subdue, seize and take") of limited war. Similarly, in passing on the question in a case raising the issue, Mr. Justice Chase declared for the Supreme Court in 1800 that:

> Congress is empowered to declare a general war, or Congress may wage a limited war; limited in place, in objects, in time.[33]

A present and specific authorization of armed force against the territory or possessions of another country does not fail as a prerequisite congressional declaration of war, of course, simply by the nature of the objectives or extent of war that it may authorize.[34]

But precisely because of these various provisions and accommodations, it is even more clearly the case that there is no standing room left for a theory which would transfer to the executive the power to authorize war on his own initiation. When all the accommodations to shared authority otherwise provided by the several war-related clauses are thus aggregated, it becomes quite evident that the determination as to whether circumstances at any given time in fact make it necessary and appropriate to engage in war, however limited in scope or objectives, resides solely in Congress subject to no delegation whatever. Indeed, were it the case that the Constitution contemplated a capacity in Congress simply to stipulate conditions (however clearly stated) upon whose happening as subsequently determined by the President war would then be deemed to be declared, it would be a surpassingly strange departure from the concerns that gave the clause its final form:

> Mr. GERRY never expected to hear in a republic a motion to empower the Executive alone to declare war.
> . . . .
> Mr. MASON was against giving the power of war to the Executive, because not safely to be trusted with it. . . .[35]

Again, this proposition also is not without its testing early in the history of the Constitution. During the conflict with France, in 1798, Hamilton prepared legislation which would have empowered "the President 'at his discretion . . . to declare that a state of war exists between the two countries' if negotiations with France did not begin by August 1 or, if they started, should they fail." President Adams wrote to Harrison Gray Otis, Chairman of the House Committee on Defense (through whom the bill was introduced) that Hamilton was crazy. Adams and Pickering maintained that war did not exist between the two countries, given the absence of a congressional declaration to that effect.[36]

Against the background of this general discussion, it may now be appropriate to offer a personal assessment of the war in Vietnam.

4. AN APPLICATION TO VIETNAM

The interim emergency defense war power of the President, to engage in acts of war without declaration of war by Congress, did not endure beyond the moment that the attack upon American destroyers had been repelled and an opportunity was provided for Congress to deliberate. From that time forward, through the undoubted, massive, and prolonged war in Vietnam, no authority existed for the President's ever-widening uses of armed force in the absence of a declaration of war by Congress.

Such a declaration, to have been sufficient, need not have been unqualified or in any specific form. It would, however, have to have been approved by both Houses of Congress. Equally, it would also have to have expressed a specific and unequivocal commitment by Congress, clearly authorizing the President thereafter to employ armed force at the level of engagement, in the area of engagement, and against such parties involved in that engagement, as he did in fact pursue. The necessity for this extent of antecedent congressional action, not subject to correction or repair by anything that even Congress might do later on as war was to develop, is built into the declaration of war clause itself: a pause must occur following the first use of war power even in emergencies and *prior* to any further deterioration of relationships; inertial movement down the slippery face of war is momentarily arrested by the force of constitutional requirement and cannot be resumed save on deliberate choice affirmatively asserted by joint declaration of war by both Houses. For this reason, it is not possible to conjure up suitable later substitutes for any congressional action which may have failed at the time as a requisite declaration of war. On the other hand, assuming that an otherwise suitable declaration of war had been made by Congress, it would of course have remained subject to subsequent modification or repeal, just as the continuing capacity of the executive would depend upon adequate congressional support in the supply of money and manpower. In the event of an act of unqualified repeal, the President would again lack authority save only to withdraw all forces from the area of war at once.

Without conceding that any kind of declaration of war was required antecedent to its widening pursuit of war following the incident of Tonkin Gulf, the executive has at different times claimed one or more of three sets of congressional action for its presumption. Two of these, consisting of two treaties and a variety of congressional bills of conscription and appropriation, clearly do not meet the requisites of an antecedent declaration of war. The reasons for their inadequacy should now already be apparent, but I shall briefly outline them again. The third, the Tonkin Gulf Resolution of August 10, 1964,[37] may just possibly have done so, however, notwithstanding the subsequent protestations of a number of members of Congress who joined in the vote to adopt that Resolution. In retrospect, promulgation of the Tonkin Gulf Resolution as a possible declaration of war may seem ironic. Even so, the greater irony by far occurred six years, four months, and two days later: on January 12, 1971, this arguably sufficient declaration of war was repealed without qualification.[38]

In repealing the Tonkin Gulf Resolution outright, rather than amending it to preserve executive authority to persist in the use of armed force at some level, for at least some purposes—for example, as might be thought essential to negotiate the return of prisoners—Congress wholly removed the only authority which sustained the executive use of armed force in Vietnam. It matters not at all that the President (a different President, of course) may by then have disclaimed reliance upon the Tonkin Gulf Resolution or, indeed, that members of Congress may not themselves have intended the consequence of their affirmative vote for outright repeal, any more than careless misapprehension of the significance of one's vote can alter the consequence of other acts of Congress. The repeal being complete when signed by the President himself on January 12, 1971, the executive use of armed force in Vietnam since that date has been without constitutional authority.

Executive claims in respect to congressional authorization for the sustained use of armed force in Vietnam, as previously stated, rested partly upon two treaties, the Southeast Asia Treaty and, indirectly, the Charter of the United Nations, both of which the Senate had previously ratified. In answer to the objection that the ratification of these treaties can in no manner be construed as declarations of war, the claim may be offered that ratification can be understood either as the delegation of authority to the President so to declare war when in his judgment conditions triggering our treaty obligations arise and we are called upon to fulfill them, or if that view is inadmissible, that ratification of the treaty was itself an inchoate declaration of war subsequently effective upon determination of the President under circumstances that he would assess in accordance with the terms of the treaties. For each of three reasons, however, the claim utterly fails.

First, neither treaty provides any basis in fact for the claim that is made. To the contrary, each provides that commitment to the use of force must be made only "in accordance with [our] constitutional process." [39] Assuming that one such obligation may involve the actual engagement of armed force, fulfillment of a treaty obligation is thus to furnish an occasion for Congress to act under the declaration of war clause, without, however, dispensing with the constitutional necessity of that action as an essential predicate to the executive use of military force. Insofar as the President may have been placed under an independent duty of his own in this respect, i.e., faithfully to execute the obligation of the treaty consistent with our constitutional processes, it was only to take account of subsequent conditions which in his judgment called up our obligation to engage in war and thereupon urgently to convene and to address Congress that Congress should act upon its own obligation. Under no view, however, is it maintainable that either treaty attempted to dispense with the constitutional requisite of subsequent congressional declaration prior to the actual commitment of armed force.

Second, even assuming a limited power in Congress to shift the determination to embark upon war to the President, under specified conditions expressed in clear and definite guidelines, the transfer of such authority cannot be accomplished by *treaty*. The House of Representatives' prerequisite consent to this nation's involvement in war was most deliberately required by the declaration of war clause after consideration of several alternatives, including the specific proposed alternative of vesting the power jointly in the Senate and President alone which was itself rejected.[40] As the House does not consent to treaties, manifestly a treaty cannot be among the possible means of delegating its authority. To imply that the constitutional draftsmen could possibly have formulated a document so specific in its precautions against involvements of war while simultaneously creating an enormous loophole of exclusive Senate power to give it away by simple treaty ratification is wholly without logic or evidence.

Third, and more briefly still, for reasons offered earlier I believe that the declaration of war clause disallows any delegation at all, *i.e.*, that Congress not only lacks power to relieve itself of that responsibility by shifting it generally to the President, but that it may not do so even fortified with the strictest and most unequivocal guidelines "merely" enabling the President to direct the sustained use of armed force when, in *his* judgment, specific conditions have arisen to trigger a prior authorization by Congress. Consider it as one will, the requirement that *Congress* shall declare war if and when war is to be declared at all leaves no room for contingent declarations where the determination of the contingency is sought to be dislocated from Congress subject only to a power to reclaim it too late to serve the function of the clause. The congressional responsibility may not be thus diluted, no matter how eagerly Congress itself might wish to be quit of it, nor will it do at all to argue that Congress might always reclaim its authority and thereupon vote *against* the pursuit of war if in disagreement with the President's assessment that led him to trigger the use of armed force pursuant to the congressional delegation. For again, the function of the clause was to force a momentary pause upon Congress even on the brink of hostilities, that there could be no slipping into war where the slippage itself might well transfigure what would otherwise have been a congressional decision not to become engaged.

Especially for this reason, as well as for the reason that none of the subsequent "supportive" bills of appropriation or manpower even purport to direct the specific use of armed force (though many were doubtless passed with complicit understanding of how the President proposed to use the additional monies and manpower thus made available), neither can these later and related pieces of legislation repair the omission of a declaration of war required *before* hostilities had been allowed to proceed in a manner making it impossible to say how far they had trammeled the congressional choice. In short, the declaration of war clause provides no means by which Congress can reduce its responsibility to a different task than that assigned to it, *i.e.*, the qualitatively different task, rejected as an inadequate constitutional safeguard, to check "the dog of war" *after* it had already been released by executive action.[41]

There remains only the Tonkin Gulf Resolution. Part of it, the following part in section 2, seems not at all sufficient as a declaration of war:

> The United States regards as vital to its national interest and to world peace the maintenance of international peace and security in Southeast Asia. Consonant with the Constitution of the United States and the Charter of the United Nations and in accordance with its treaty obligations under the Southeast Asia Collective Defense Treaty, the United States is, therefore, prepared, as the President determines, to take all necessary steps, including the use of armed force, to assist any member or protocol state of the Southeast Asia Collective Defense Treaty requesting assistance in defense of its freedom.[42]

There is altogether lacking here a present declaration of war. On its face, the section does no more than to serve notice that the country is *prepared* to go to war in the event of that necessity as a means of fulfilling its treaty obligation. The Congress states, moreover, that it has full confidence in the President and will be guided in its actions by what the President recommends. A resolution sharply pointing up what Congress is "prepared" to do is doubtless within the power of Congress publicly to resolve and may indeed be extremely useful. That it constitutes a present declaration of even limited hostilities is manifestly unreasonable for anyone to infer. That it is an oblique and disingenuous *present* authorization to the President, that he is thereafter to utilize armed force as he deems necessary to vindicate the readiness of the country to assist any member of SEATO upon their request, surely twists the words ("[T]he United States is . . . *prepared* . . . to take all necessary steps") and cannot be preferred on a matter of such gravity.[43]

The fact that section 2 seems so clearly a notice of warning, rather than a declaration of war, doubtless lends support to an argument favoring a similar and co-ordinated construction for the balance of the whole Resolution. Yet, a contrary possibility cannot be dismissed on that basis alone, and the very different wording of the balance of the Resolution must be seen in its entirety: [44]

> Whereas naval units of the Communist regime in Vietnam, in violation of the principles of the Charter of the United Nations and of international law, have deliberately and repeatedly attacked United States naval vessels lawfully present in international waters, and have thereby created a serious threat to international peace; and
>
> Whereas these attacks are part of a deliberate and systematic campaign of aggression that the Communist regime in North Vietnam has been waging against its neighbors and the nations joined with them in the collective defense of their freedom; and
>
> Whereas the United States is assisting the peoples of Southeast Asia to protect their freedom and has no territorial, military or political ambitions in that area, but desires only that these peoples should be left in peace to work out their own destinies in their own way: Now therefore, be it
>
> *Resolved by the Senate and House of Representatives of the United States of America in Congress assembled,* That the Congress approves and supports the determination of the President, as Commander in Chief, to take all necessary measures to repel any armed attack against the forces of the United States and to prevent further aggression.
>
> . . . .
>
> Section 3. This resolution shall expire when the President shall determine that the peace and security of the area is reasonably assured by international conditions created by action of the United Nations or otherwise, except that it may be terminated earlier by concurrent resolution of the Congress.

In spite of certain language which still looks in the same mood as the "notice and warning" style of section 2, there is much here of a different tone. In section 1 of the Resolution itself, Congress formally resolves a joint and solemn approval and support for the President, as Commander in Chief, not only to take all necessary measures to repel any armed attack against the forces of the United States (which might merely evidence positive support of the executive's interim emergency power which he would possess in the

absence of congressional restriction and without declaration of war,
but which might be believed useful to relieve the executive of any
margin of doubt or anxiety of subsequent congressional criticism
in the event of its exercise); it appears also to authorize the President "to take all necessary measures . . . to prevent further aggression" which section 2 of the preamble identifies as "aggression
that the Communist regime in North Vietnam has been waging
against its neighbors," presumably South Vietnam, Laos, and Cambodia.[45] Moreover, section 3, stipulating conditions under which
the Resolution will expire, would appear to be of no purpose if
the entire Resolution is to be taken merely as a solemn declaration
of notice and warning. Rather, what is it that may subsequently be
terminated by a later concurrent resolution of the Congress unless,
indeed, it is a present declaration of war authorizing the President
to use armed force as he finds necessary to thwart "further aggression" of the kind which Congress declares North Vietnam has already undertaken against its neighbors as well as "repeatedly"
against our naval vessels as "part of a deliberate and systematic
campaign of aggression"?

The following exchange in the Senate, between Senator Fulbright, Chairman of the Foreign Relations Committee and floor
manager for the Resolution, and Senator Brewster is extremely telling:

> Mr. BREWSTER. [M]y question is whether there is anything in the
> resolution which would authorize or recommend or approve the
> landing of large American armies in Vietnam or in China.
>
> Mr. FULBRIGHT. There is nothing in the resolution, as I read it,
> that contemplates it. I agree with the Senator that that is the last
> thing we would want to do. However, the language of the resolution
> would not prevent it. *It would authorize whatever the Commander
> in Chief feels is necessary.*[46]

And, again, in response to a question from Senator Cooper:

> Mr. COOPER. Then, looking ahead, if the President decided that it
> was necessary to use such force as could lead into war, *we will give
> that authority by this resolution?*
>
> Mr. FULBRIGHT. *That is the way I would interpret it.* If a situa-
> tion later developed in which we thought the approval should be
> withdrawn, it could be withdrawn by concurrent resolution.[47]

One may faithfully attend other views of the matter, of course:
that the standards delimiting the executive use of force are too
indefinite thus to delegate the power to declare war; but is not

section 1 rather a present declaration and current authorization of executive power sufficient for its purpose, and not a delegation at all? Again, the Resolution "was passed with great speed and in the heat of emotion," at a time when "there were few American troops in Vietnam;" [48] but have not declarations of war most commonly been issued exactly under such circumstances, and are they less adequate on that account even assuming that explicit provision for the declaration of war clause may not itself adequately have reckoned with this difficulty? Additionally, it has been correctly noted that the next President foreswore any reliance on the Resolution, and that even President Johnson never relied exclusively upon it for his claim of authority; [49] but what use or interpretation can safely be made of such subsequent politics? Finally, it is true as well that not all who spoke at the time necessarily intended this consequence of their vote, a telling example being the somewhat equivocal statement by Congressman Morgan, Chairman of the House Foreign Affairs Committee that "this Resolution is definitely not an *advance* declaration of war." [50] Still, in all, it is exceedingly difficult to disagree with Senator Eagleton's own reluctant conclusion that:

> Faulty vision and political pressures cannot be permitted to minimize the legal significance of the Tonkin Gulf Resolution. . . . Although the existence of the Tonkin Gulf Resolution did not make the war we have waged in South Vietnam any wiser or any more explicable, it did make it a *legitimate* war authorized by the Congress.[51]

Were the question a different one, for instance one involving conscientious judicial determination of whether executive action ordering troops or planes into *China* would exceed the bounds of the Tonkin Gulf Resolution, then I should think it might quite sensibly be argued that so great a quantum leap in the executive escalation of the Vietnam War would have required that the President return to Congress, before taking that leap, so as to secure a modified and expanded declaration of the limited war previously declared.[52] Given the Resolution as it was framed, however (and the unabating manpower and financial support Congress subsequently provided in the prosecution of the war), we would succumb to the temptation of current remorse and an overwrought desire to find additional argument to force total disengagement to insist that Congress never really declared the war at all.

Yet, ironies are heaped up on both sides, and resort to argument torturing the original adequacy or scope of the Tonkin Gulf Resolution is surprisingly beside the point so far as the constitutional imperative of total disengagement is now concerned. As the President would have had to return to Congress to secure constitutional authority for any enlargement of the war that was declared and authorized by the Tonkin Gulf Resolution, so too, at all times Congress retained the power to amend the Resolution to reduce the scale of war or, indeed, to end it. Rather than scaling down the war by any mere amendment, however, the unalterable fact of the matter is that Congress wholly repealed the Tonkin Gulf Resolution.[53] Nothing having been left of it, and no subsequent declaration of even limited war having been substituted, the President now conducts hostilities in Vietnam utterly without constitutional authority. It is simply true that the uses of American armed force in Vietnam since January 12, 1971, defy the Constitution of the United States.

NOTES

[1] Youngstown Sheet & Tube Co. v. Sawyer, 343 U.S. 579, 594 (1952) (Frankfurter, J., concurring in the upholding of an injunction against the executive seizure of steel mills during the Korean War).

[2] OFFICE OF THE LEGAL ADVISOR, U.S. DEP'T OF STATE, THE LEGALITY OF U.S. PARTICIPATION IN THE DEFENSE OF VIETNAM, *reprinted in* 112 CONG. REC. 5504-09 1966).

[3] *See, e.g.,* Orlando v. Laird, 443 F.2d 1039 (2d Cir.), *cert. denied,* 404 U.S. 869 (1971); Mora v. McNamara, 387 F.2d 862 (D.C. Cir.), *cert. denied,* 389 U.S. 934 (1967); Luftig v. McNamara, 373 F.2d 664 (D.C. Cir.), *cert. denied,* 387 U.S. 945 (1967). It is assuredly debatable whether cases otherwise ripe, brought by parties with appropriate standing, under clearly adversary circumstances with terrific personal interests at stake, are nonetheless not "justiciable" so far as the declaration of war clause is concerned. *See* Bickel, *Congress, the President and the Power to Wage War,* 48 CHI.-KENT L. REV. 131 (1971); Henkin, *Viet-Nam in the Courts of the United States: "Political Questions,"* 63 AM. J. INT'L L. 284 (1969); Schwartz & McCormick, *The Justiciability of Legal Objections to the American Military Effort in Vietnam,* 46 TEXAS L. REV. 1033 (1968); Tigar, *Judicial Power, the "Political Question Doctrine," and Foreign Relations,* 17 U.C.L.A. L. REV. 1135 (1970). *Compare* BICKEL, *The Supreme Court 1960 Term—Foreword: The Passive Virtues,* 75 HARV. L. REV. 40 (1961), *with* Gunther, *The Subtle Vices of the "Passive Virtues"—A Comment on Principle and Expediency in Judicial Review,* 64 COLUM. L. REV. 1 (1964). Given what is at stake for those willing to risk prolonged imprisonment as a condition of being heard at least on this bare threshhold question alone, however, when all constitutional requisites, statutory criteria, and announced judicial standards for the rationing of certiorari have been satisfied, it is surely a singular indecency that the Supreme Court declines even to hear the justiciability issue on the merits: "These petitioners should be told whether their case is beyond judicial cognizance." Mora v. McNamara, 389 U.S. 934, 939 (1967) (Douglas, J., dissenting from the denial of certiorari).

[4] *Compare* Fortson v. Dorsey, 379 U.S. 433 (1965), Wesberry v. Sanders, 376 U.S. 1 (1964), *and* Baker v. Carr, 369 U.S. 186 (1962), *with* South v. Peters, 339 U.S. 276 (1950), *and* Colegrove v. Green, 328 U.S. 549 (1946) (reapportionment).

For analogous developments in judicial willingness to consider constitutional questions previously avoided, see, *e.g.*, Powell v. McCormack, 395 U.S. 486 (1969); Flast v. Cohen, 392 U.S. 83 (1968).

5 *Compare* United States v. Robel, 389 U.S. 258 (1967), *with* American Communications Ass'n, CIO v. Douds, 339 U.S. 382 (1950). *Compare* Duncan v. Kahanamoku, 327 U.S. 304 (1946), *with* Korematsu v. United States, 323 U.S. 214 (1944). *Compare Ex parte* Milligan, 71 U.S. (4 Wall.) 2 (1866), *with* Luther v. Borden, 48 U.S. (7 How.) 1 (1849).

6 Youngstown Sheet & Tube Co. v. Sawyer, 103 F. Supp. 569, 575 (D.D.C. 1952).

7 Powell v. McCormack, 395 U.S. 486, 546-47 (1969) (footnote omitted).

8 2 RECORDS OF THE FEDERAL CONVENTION OF 1789, at 318-19 (M. Farrand ed. 1911) (Friday, Aug. 17, 1787) (minor changes concerning grammar, abbreviations and appearance have been made to facilitate reading) [hereinafter cited as RECORDS].

9 *See, e.g.*, THE ANTIFEDERALISTS (C. Kenyon ed. 1966); J. MAIN, THE ANTI-FEDERALISTS—CRITICS OF THE CONSTITUTION, 1781-1788, at 119-67 (1961).

10 THE FEDERALIST No. 69, at 446 (B. Wright ed. 1961) (A. Hamilton).

11 *See, e.g.*, sources cited note 9 *supra*.

12 11 ANNALS OF CONG. 11 (1801), *reprinted in* 1 MESSAGES AND PAPERS OF THE PRESIDENTS, 1789-1897, at 326-27 (J. Richardson ed. 1898).

13 3 T. JEFFERSON, WRITINGS 400 (A. Bergh ed. 1907).

14 For example, John Marshall's opinion for the Court in Talbot v. Seeman, 5 U.S. (1 Cranch) 1 (1801), was that:
The whole powers of war being, by the constitution of the United States, vested in congress, the acts of that body can alone be resorted to as our guides in this inquiry.
Id. at 28.

15 THE FEDERALIST No. 74, at 473 (B. Wright ed. 1961) (A. Hamilton).

16 1 MESSAGES AND PAPERS OF THE PRESIDENTS, 1789-1897, at 327 (J. Richardson ed. 1898).

17 Letter from Alexander Hamilton to James McHenry, May 17, 1798, in 1 OFFICE OF NAVAL RECORDS AND LIBRARY, U.S. DEP'T OF THE NAVY, NAVAL DOCUMENTS RELATED TO THE QUASI-WAR BETWEEN THE UNITED STATES AND FRANCE 75 (1935).

18 A declaration of war was entered by Congress on May 13, 1846, declaiming that hostilities had been initiated by the other side. Even so, the House subsequently excoriated Polk for having "unnecessarily and unconstitutionally" begun that war. CONG. GLOBE, 30th Cong., 1st Sess. 95 (1848).

19 7 DIGEST OF INTERNATIONAL LAW 163-64 (J. Moore ed. 1906).

20 5 MESSAGES AND PAPERS OF THE PRESIDENTS, 1789-1897, at 516 (J. Richardson ed. 1898). The immediate next sentences in Buchanan's Message are these, and seem less clear:
It is true that on a sudden emergency of this character the President would direct any armed force in the vicinity to march to their relief, but in doing this he would act upon his own responsibility.
Id. Even assuming that in saying that by thus acting "on his own responsibility" with emergency military force solely for the immediate "relief" of American citizens caught in a war zone, Buchanan meant that the President would be utilizing a proper constitutional executive power (rather than acting simply from a sense of personal duty whether or not it is constitutionally supportable), still, in context, the most that is claimed is only the interim emergency use of such military force as would be reasonably necessary to secure the safe and

speedy removal of our citizens, unless Congress were to authorize a more ambitious undertaking.

21 2 A. LINCOLN, WRITINGS 51-52 (A. Lapsley ed. 1905). Lincoln's subsequent executive imposition of a blockade on April 27, 1861, following the firing on Fort Sumter, pending prompt convocation of an extraordinary session of Congress which approved his proclamation and other interim emergency measures on July 13, 1861 (sustained five-to-four in The Prize Cases, 67 U.S. (2 Black) 635 (1862)), are not inconsistent in the least with this view. How far they might be independently supportable under article IV powers was not examined by the Supreme Court. Even so, the majority of the Court seemed to make a distinction not only relating to the suddenness of actual civil war hostilities, the need to meet it "without waiting for Congress," and its recognition by other nations for purposes of triggering international law duties of neutrality by the time the proclamation of blockade took effect, but that civil war may be distinguishable even with respect to the declaration of war clause: "By the Constitution, Congress alone has the power to declare a national or foreign war. It cannot declare war against a State, or any number of States, by virtue of any clause in the Constitution." *Id.* at 668. *See also* 7 DIGEST OF INTERNATIONAL LAW 172 (J. Moore ed. 1906): "Civil war begins by insurrection against the lawful authority of the Government, and is never solemnly declared." In directing the use of force to suppress the alleged insurrection led by Aaron Burr, moreover, Thomas Jefferson (perhaps the most scrupulous President of all in relating the war power to Congress) did not regard the declaration of war clause to be involved.

Far from *The Prize Cases* yielding great significance regarding an uncabined executive power to sustain the engagement of major military force overseas without an antecedent declaration of war by Congress, *cf.* 2 B. SCHWARTZ, A COMMENTARY ON THE CONSTITUTION OF THE UNITED STATES—PART I, THE POWERS OF GOVERNMENT 203-06 (163), it may be more significant that even with all the distinguishing elements of the case, four of nine Justices thought the decision to be incorrect and constitutionally insupportable.

22 THE RECORD OF AMERICAN DIPLOMACY 185 (R. Bartlett ed. 1954); Robertson, *South America and the Monroe Doctrine, 1824-28,* 30 POL. SCI. Q. 89-91 (1915).

23 Southeast Asia Collective Defense Treaty, Feb. 4, 1955, art. IV, para. 1, [1955] 1 U.S.T. 81, T.I.A.S. No. 3170 (emphasis added).

24 *See* 1 RECORDS, *supra* note 8, at 292, 300; 2 *id.* 318-19.

25 *See, e.g.,* L. JAFFEE & N. NATHANSON, ADMINISTRATIVE LAW 81-122 (1968). Professor Davis, possibly the leading exponent of a liberal delegation view, disparages the importance or sufficiency of legislatively-stipulated guidelines vis-à-vis the alleged greater importance of adequate procedural safeguards, appropriate legislative supervision or reexamination, and the accustomed scope of judicial review. 1 K. DAVIS, ADMINISTRATIVE LAW TREATISE 99 (1958). As the Supreme Court has wholly failed to provide any judicial review, as there are no procedural prerequisites to the executive rendering of his authorization, and as the fait accompli of executive action appears to overwhelm the capacity for legislative supervision or reexamination at the point in time when it is most needed, however, all these alternative protections in respect to the delegation of war declarations being conspicuously weak, perhaps the delegation doctrine ought to be applied more restrictively in this area than in any other. *See also* Wright, *Beyond Discretionary Justice,* 81 YALE L.J. 575, 582-87 (1972).

26 Schechter Poultry Corp. v. United States, 295 U.S. 495 (1935); Panama Refining Co. v. Ryan, 293 U.S. 388 (1935).

27 *See, e.g.,* United States v. Curtiss-Wright Export Corp., 299 U.S. 304 (1936).

28 *E.g.,* Fahy v. Mallonee, 332 U.S. 245 (1947).

29 Kent v. Dulles, 357 U.S. 116 (1958).

30 Zemel v. Rusk, 381 U.S. 1, 20-21 (1965) (quoting 22 U.S.C. § 211 (a) (1970)) (Black, J., dissenting) (The Court was divided 6-3 on the basic questions whether the Secretary of State's refusal to validate passports for travel in Cuba was statutorily and constitutionally permissible). *See also* Professor Rostow's very forceful discussion in Rostow, *Great Cases Make Bad Law: The War Powers Act,* 50 TEXAS L. REV. 833, 885-92 (1972).

31 Bickel, *Congress, the President and the Power to Wage War,* 48 CHI-KENT L. REV. 131, 137 (1971). For similar views that the Tonkin Gulf Resolution lacked adequate standards, see Velvel, *The War in Viet Nam: Unconstitutional, Justiciable and Jurisdictionally Attackable,* in 2 THE VIETNAM WAR AND INTERNATIONAL LAW 680 (R. Falk ed. 1969), and Wormuth, *The Vietnam War: The President versus the Constitution,* in *id.* 780-90.

32 Act of July 9, 1798, ch. 68, §1, 1 Stat. 578.

33 Bas v. Tingy, 4 U.S. (4 Dall.) 37, 43 (1800).

34 Talbot v. Seeman, 5 U.S. (1 Cranch) 1, 28 (1801) (Marshall, C.J.):

The whole powers of war being, by the constitution of the United States, vested in congress, the acts of that body can alone be resorted to as our guides in this inquiry. It is not denied, nor, in the course of the argument, has it been denied, that congress may authorize general hostilities, in which case the general laws of war apply to our situation; or partial hostilities, in which case the laws of war, so far as they actually apply to our situation, must be noticed.

Even the very marginal use of force, in satisfaction of private grievances unredressed by an offending sovereign against whom the government might not wish to commit a public force as an act of war, was subjected to prerequisite and exclusive congressional control in its sole authority to issue letters of marque and reprisal. The provision was added in Convention on August 18, 1787, the day following the principal discussion of the war power, Mr. Gerry remarking that such provision should be made as it was not clear that letters of marque were subsumed in the power of war. 2 RECORDS, *supra* note 8, at 326.

35 2 *id.* 318-19.

36 A. DE CONDE, THE QUASI-WAR: THE POLITICS AND DIPLOMACY OF THE UNDECLARED WAR WITH FRANCE, 1797-1801, at 171 (1966).

37 H.R.J. Res. 1145, 88th Cong., 2d Sess., 78 Stat. 384 (1964), reproduced at text accompanying notes 42, 44 *infra.*

38 Act of Jan. 12, 1971, Pub. L. No. 91-672, § 12, 84 Stat. 2053.

39 U.N. CHARTER, art. 43, para. 3 (concerned with *ratification* of agreements). The comparable language from the Southeast Asia Collective Defense Treaty (concerned with *action* to meet a threat) is quoted at text accompanying note 23 *supra.*

40 *See* 2 RECORDS, *supra* note 8, at 318-19.

41 Letter from Thomas Jefferson to James Madison, Sept. 6, 1789, in C. WARREN, THE MAKING OF THE CONSTITUTION 481 n.1 (1928):

We have already given, in example, one effectual check to the dog of war, by transferring the power of letting him loose from the Executive to the Legislative body, from those who are to spend to those who are to pay.

Consider also Mr. Justice Brandeis' observation (dissenting in Myers v. United States, 272 U.S. 52, 293 (1926)):

The doctrine of the separation of powers was adopted by the Convention of 1787, not to promote efficiency but to preclude the exercise of arbi-

trary power. The purpose was, not to avoid friction, but, by means of the inevitable friction incident to the distribution of the governmental powers among three departments, to save the people from autocracy.
[42] H.R.J. Res. 1145, 88th Cong., 2d Sess., § 2, 78 Stat. 384 (1964).

[43] *But see*, for the view that § 2 is a present authorization of force, Note, *Congress, the President, and the Power to Commit Forces to Combat*, 81 HARV. L. REV. 1771, 1804 (1968): "This rather comprehensive language certainly supports the interpretation given it by the administration: that it is a functional equivalent of a declaration of war." Moreover, certain portions of the Senate debate favor that impression, *e.g.*, 110 CONG. REC. 18,410 (1964):

> Mr. COOPER. . . . But the power provided the President in section 2 is great.
> Mr. FULBRIGHT. This provision is intended to give clearance to the President to use his discretion. . . .
> Mr. COOPER. I understand, and believe that the President will use this vast power with judgment.

For the view that so interpreted, however, § 2 then fails as too broad a carte blanche delegation of the war power, see note 25 *supra*. Consider also the views of Senator Morse, one of but two Senators voting against the Resolution:

> I shall not support any substitute which takes the form of a predated declaration of war. In my judgment, that is what the pending joint resolution is.

110 CONG. REC. 18,139 (1964).

[44] H.R.J. Res. 1145, 88th Cong., 2d Sess., 78 Stat. 384 (1964).

[45] That the phrase extended at least to South Vietnam, and not merely to protection of other American ships from sudden attack, was explicitly acknowledged:

> Mr. MILLER. It is left open. It does not say aggression against whom. It is broad enough so that it could mean aggression against the United States, or aggression against the South Vietnamese Government. . . .
> Mr. FULBRIGHT. I believe that *both* are included in that phrase.

110 CONG. REC. 18,405 (1964) (emphasis added).

[46] *Id.* 18,403 (emphasis added).

[47] *Id.* 18,409 (emphasis added).

[48] 116 CONG. REC. S7119 (daily ed. May 13, 1970), reproducing a memorandum signed by a number of legal luminaries.

[49] 117 CONG. REC. H4342 (daily ed. May 25, 1971):
President Johnson said in a news conference: "We did not think the resolution was necessary to do what we did and what we are doing." Hearings on S. Res. 151 before the Senate Comm. on Foreign Relations, 90th Cong., 1st Sess. 126 (1967). Nor does the current administration of President Nixon rely for authority upon the Gulf of Tonkin Resolution. On March 12, 1970, in response to a letter from Senator Fulbright, H. G. Torbert, Jr. stated on behalf of the Department of State: "[T]his administration has not relied on or referred to the Tonkin Gulf resolution of August 10, 1964, as support for its Vietnam policy. . . ."

[50] 110 CONG. REC. 18,539 (1964) (emphasis added).

[51] Eagleton, *Congress and the War Powers*, 37 MO. L. REV. 1, 14-15 (1970). In full accord is Rostow, *Great Cases Make Bad Law: The War Powers Act*, 50 TEXAS L. REV. 833, 874-75 (1972).

[52] *See, e.g.*, Little v. Barreme, 6 U.S. (2 Cranch) 169 (1804).

[53] Act of Jan. 12, 1971, Pub. L. No. 91-672, § 12, 84 Stat. 2053.

4

American Foreign Policy in the Next Decade: Disaggregating the Prediction Problem

ERNEST R. MAY

The essay that follows may seem an odd exercise for a professional historian, for it attempts to deal with the future, and, by and large, historians disclaim ability to foretell what will happen. Hegel framed the maxim that we learn from history that we do not learn from history; and Santayana, that those who do not know the past are condemned to repeat it. Both were philosophers who had had no practice in reconstructing the uncertain complexities of the past. Impressed, in H. A. L. Fisher's famous phrase, with the role of the contingent and the unforeseen, professional historians tend to argue that, if history teaches anything, it is how uncertain and unpredictable are the consequences of what men do. Statesmen have often misguessed because they expected patterns of the past to repeat themselves. Most historians would agree with Arthur Schlesinger, Jr., that "Santayana's aphorism must be reversed: too often it is those who *can* remember the past who are condemned to repeat it." [1]

Yet we must all make guesses about probable future trends, and it may be that historians can guess at least as well as anyone else, for they come closer than most scholars to engaging systematically in prophecy. They predict backward. That is: they construct hypotheses about the forces that produced change or continuity in some past period. In the process, they may develop some skill in identifying questions to be asked by those who look ahead. This essay provides a test of that proposition.

The question addressed is a broad one: what will American foreign policy look like a decade hence? What will be the trend lines in courses of action adopted and pursued by the government? In the aftermath of the Vietnamese war, will the United States revert to avoiding entanglements and commitments? Alternatively, will the trauma of Vietnam quickly heal and the United States resume supporting and defending any and all nations in danger of being taken over by communists? Or will the government follow other courses not prefigured in the recent past?

Anyone writing down answers to such questions risks being proved a fool. In 1933, almost any prophet would have said that the United States was committed to avoiding any future entanglement outside the Hemisphere. A decade later Americans were waging war from North Africa to New Guinea. Similarly, in 1943, most people saw a future in which the United States played the role it had not played after World War I—cooperating in the peaceful settlement of international disputes and promoting freer trade. Only a minority foresaw anything like the Cold War, and few if any would have predicted alliance pacts such as NATO or large-scale post-war rearmament.

As of 1963, almost no one would have forecast the conditions of 1973. The two preceding years had seen Kennedy's narrow victory over Nixon, the new President's call for rededication to sacrifice for freedom, urgent efforts to close the "missile gap" and prepare for "flexible response," and bargaining at the brink of war over Berlin and the future of Laos. The year 1962 had seen the torturing crisis over Soviet missiles in Cuba. It then seemed to most Americans not only right but beyond doubt that the United States should and would defend threatened noncommunist states in Southeast Asia.

Witness that in October 1961, when President Kennedy ordered 10,000 military advisers to South Vietnam, hardly a murmur of public objection was heard; that in March 1962, when Secretary of State Dean Rusk declared that the multilateral Southeast Asia Treaty involved a unilateral U.S. commitment to defend Thailand, no congressman or senator and no editorial writer in a major newspaper raised a question; that in May 1962, when President Kennedy suddenly sent 5,000 troops into Thailand, warning publicly that they would cross the Mekong if the communists continued their offensive in Laos, indices of public opinion registered no criticism; and that, as late as August 1964, when Congress passed the Tonkin Gulf Resolution, there were only two dissenting votes in the Senate and none in the House. It would have seemed most improbable that by 1973, public opinion polls, newspaper editorials, and votes on Capitol Hill would all express strong disillusionment, inclination to withdraw from foreign commitments, and skepticism even about the value of military preponderance.

On the other hand, not all decades have been marked by unexpected turns. The posture of the United States in 1913 was not wholly unlike what close observers would have predicted in 1903, nor was 1933 so far from what could have been foreseen in 1923, even given the Great Depression; nor was 1963 so different from what most people might have predicted in 1953. One who ventures to prophesy about a decade lying ahead must try to estimate whether it will be characterized by change or by relative continuity.

In the United States, change or continuity in foreign policies has been determined by domestic public opinion and domestic politics, conceived as embracing Congress, the presidency, and the bureaucracy. Any explanation of U.S. policies in past decades must begin with explanation of change or nonchange in public opinion and politics, and any predictions should be based on a number of specific forecasts concerning likely developments among the public and in each of the places where political decisions are fabricated.

Any general estimate of the public must in turn be built upon a number of specific estimates. First, and perhaps most important, is an estimate of the size and make-up of the population particularly interested in foreign affairs. For what has been labelled the "foreign policy public" never includes the whole nation or even the whole electorate. If survey data are to be trusted, it consists of a minority located primarily in cities, relatively well-educated, relatively well-off, and given much more than the average to reading daily, weekly, and monthly periodicals.[2]

This minority seems to include not more than 15 percent of the general public. Such has been the finding of public opinion analysts.[3] And this figure, of course, includes large numbers attentive not to foreign affairs as a whole but to one particular problem, as, for example, businessmen with customers or investments only in particular countries or Americans with strong ethnic or religious loyalties to the *auld sod* or the Fatherland or the Vatican or Israel or those parts of the world where their churches support missions. At times of fierce debate, as over isolation versus intervention in 1941 or over Vietnam in 1968, the interested public expanded to include large groups concerned less about international relations than about their own draft status or that of their children or taxation or inflation or, more unselfishly, a seeming moral issue so loudly trumpeted that no literate citizen could wholly ignore it. The interested public, however, probably never remained large for more than a brief period.

Even so, the composition of this public can vary. In the first place, it can be made up of relatively fragmented groups or be dominated by a single issue. In 1932–34 it included some people who cared chiefly about tariffs, trade, and gold; others more interested in Latin America and the new "Good Neighbor policy"; others who focused on Japan, China, and the Manchurian issue; others whose eyes were on Europe; and still others for whom the League of Nations remained in one way or another a preoccupation. These groups overlapped, but not much. Each had its own profile. None was large. By 1940–41, on the other hand, most of the attentive public fixed on one issue: should the United States act against the Axis powers? And this public embraced groups that had earlier paid little heed to foreign affairs—not only men and women who had been too young but also members of religious groups horrified by Nazi pogroms and the Nazi ideology, people with roots in the various countries which Hitler or Mussolini had conquered, and others aroused by years of day-in, day-out reportage on book-burnings, concentration camps, the Gestapo, the Japanese "thought police," and the cruelties of German, Italian, and Japanese conquering forces. This was a very different public from that of a decade earlier.

Change of another order occurred between 1943 and 1953. It was, first of all, generational change. Up to the end of the 1930's, people scarred by recollections of World War I and the battle over entry into the League of Nations predominated in the public attentive to foreign affairs. By the late 1940's the majority consisted of men and women who remembered instead the crises of the 1930's. In the second place, there occurred an unexpected nonchange. Instead of drifting back into concern primarily about domestic issues, many Jews, Roman Catholics, Italian-Americans, Polish-Americans, and the like retained an interest in happenings abroad. Steadily becoming better represented among the relatively well-educated, well-read, and well-off, members of these religions and ethnic groups figured significantly in a foreign policy public which, as it turned out, clutched "no appeasement" as a shibboleth and proved as militant against Stalinism as against Hitlerism.

In the most recent decade, changes in this public have been in part like those of the 1930's and in part like those of the 1940's. With cities growing, literacy rising, and the college-educated proportion of the population skyrocketing, the pool of people potentially attentive to foreign affairs has broadened. School and college instruction on foreign areas and international affairs, together with increases in tourism and business-connected or service-connected foreign travel, has stimulated interest within a more random population. Regular reportage on the war in Vietnam, including that of television cameras, coupled with month-in, month-out draft calls, then brought into being a one-issue public larger than and somewhat different from the public of the early sixties. At the same time, a generational change occurred. A majority which remembered the 1930's was gradually diluted by newcomers who harked back only to events of the Cold War.

Anyone now attempting a forecast must try to estimate what the foreign policy public will be a decade hence. Will it have the same makeup that it has today? Will some elements preoccupied with Vietnam lose interest in international affairs once Vietnam recedes into the past? Will new groups become important components of the public? If so, which groups? Will another generational change take place by 1982?

A forecaster cannot concern himself only with the gross attributes of this public. An equally important range of questions concerns its leadership. Survey data confirm the common-sense supposition that most people do not arrive at opinions on issues by independent analysis. Instead, they borrow opinions from people whose judgment they trust. Ordinarily, the shapers of opinion of issues in international relations are a small minority within the minority, composed of government officials, politicians, and businessmen and professional men with some government experience, connections in high places, many entry and exit stamps on their passports, and the habit of reading periodicals such as the *New York Times* and *The Economist:* in short, an "establishment." [4]

The size and composition of the "foreign policy public" may be in part a function of conditions within this establishment. The late 1940's and early 1950's, for example, could have seen much more widespread public debate and division over entangling alliances, foreign commitments, and the basing of forces abroad. Very little occurred. A plausible explanation is that the establishment was more or less of one mind. With little or no leadership, no significant public opposition could take form. By contrast, Vietnam divided the establishment. Senators on the Foreign Relations Committee, former government insiders such as George Ball and Robert Kennedy, correspondents covering Southeast Asia, and scholars such as Hans Morgenthau and George Kahin led protest within the establishment. This in turn legitimized opinion leadership by others who probably could not have commanded a following against a nearly unanimous establishment.

Part of the necessary guesswork about the foreign policy public has to do with the establishment. One can assume that it will continue to consist of current and former insiders who are well-educated, well-read, well-traveled, and relatively well-to-do; but this assumption is of little use for prediction. These characteristics are shared by a million or more Americans, including ex-Senator William Knowland and Dr. Daniel Ellsberg. In the 1933–43 decade, the proportion of businessmen and bankers in the establishment probably diminished. The Depression clouded their reputations. By the end of the decade, lawyers, journalists, and intellectuals, especially European refugees, formed a relatively large part of the leadership group. From World War II into the 1960's, the establishment contained an extraordinary number of people with backgrounds in the military services or the service departments. Insofar as there was a visible hierarchy, the top places were occupied by Marshall and other wartime generals and men who had worked with Henry Stimson, notably John J. McCloy and Robert A. Lovett.[5] A significant part of the establishment's new blood came later from defense-oriented corporations and research organizations. One result of Vietnam was an erosion of public confidence in this group comparable to the erosion of confidence in business consequent upon the Depression. Some questions about the decade 1973–83 are therefore: what will be the makeup of the establishment? On what types of people will the broader foreign policy public rely for leadership? What consensus, if any, will prevail within this group? If there is no consensus, what will be the lines of division? And what will be the consequences if they do divide?

Still other questions concern variables likely to influence the composition of both the foreign policy public and its leadership cadre. Unfortunately for anyone trying to build predictions, historical experience suggests that the most important variable will be events abroad. Changes in the composition of the foreign policy public in 1933–43 were precipitated by internal developments in Italy, Japan, and Germany, the Italo-Ethiopian War, the Spanish Civil War, the Sino-Japanese War, the successive crises of 1938–39 set off by Hitler, and the outbreak and progress of World War II. The changes after 1943 probably could not have occurred in the absence of communist successes in Eastern Europe and Asia, the attempted isolation of Berlin in 1948, and the North Korean attack on South Korea in 1950. The course of the war in Vietnam actuated the changes of the 1960's. Part of a prophet's task is to imagine events that might galvanize or divide an establishment, define issues for the interested public, or pull into that public groups not now actively interested in foreign affairs. Another part of the task is to estimate the probability that such events will occur.

Turning to domestic politics, one should first try to descry probable trends in the legislative branch. While congressmen and senators respond to public opinion, most of them listen to their localized constituencies. Since the foreign policy public is not distributed evenly around the country, the segments of that public which influence particular legislators may be quite unrepresentative of the whole. Because Congress does most of its work in committee and influence within committees varies from individual to individual, the Congress as a whole may, in particular areas, be unrepresentative of the nation.

After World War I, when most observers believed that a majority of interested Americans favored U.S. membership in the League of Nations, the Senate Foreign Relations Committee consisted overwhelmingly of men opposed to or skeptical about such a step. During World War II, the committee did not mirror the change that had come over the interested public. It included a disproportionate number of senators who could be characterized as isolationists. When Roosevelt and others evidenced uncertainty about whether cooperation with England and Russia could continue into the postwar period, they doubtless had in mind not only questions about the future composition of the public but also fear that, as in 1919–20, the Senate might be guided by its own lights. In the 1960's the Foreign Relations Committee became critical of involvement in Vietnam at a time when polls showed broad support within the specially interested public and its leadership corps. On the other hand, the Armed Services committees, dominated by Southerners with conservative constituents and large military installations in their states and districts, remained backers of the war long after the public mood turned around.

Not only does the legislature not necessarily follow trends in voter opinion, it may sometimes resist currents among the public or itself provide leadership. The Senate guided the turn away from internationalism after World War I. Fulbright and the Foreign Relations Committee had a powerful role in fostering opposition to the Vietnamese war. One set of questions for a forecaster thus has to do with the makeup and mood of the legislative branch. What are likely to be the dominant committees? Will the Armed Services committees continue, as in the 1950's and 1960's, to have a voice on issues in international relations equal to or greater than that of the Foreign Relations and Foreign Affairs committees? Will the

Senate Finance Committee and the House Ways and Means Committee elect to have more say than in the past regarding international questions that might affect levels of spending, allocations of revenue, and the balance of payments? On the important committees, who will exercise leadership? What will be their prejudices and predispositions?

Bearing on these questions are others having to do with relations between the legislature and the executive. In the past, there have been swings in their relative influence. For decades after the Civil War, power and initiative lay largely with the Congress. From the late 1890's through World War I, the balance went more and more in favor of the President. Although the 1920's did not bring anything like a return to the 1880's, the decade did see the Congress regain some authority. The Depression, World War II, and the Cold War then restored leadership to the executive. These swings can be attributed partly, of course, to public attitudes. After World War I, many people tended to trust Congress rather than the President because they believed Wilson to have abused his power and made calamitous mistakes. From the eve of World War II onward, many saw Congress as a culprit for having kept the United States out of the League, improvised the fatuous Neutrality laws of the mid-1930's, and resisted Roosevelt's efforts to prepare for the assumption of new international responsibilities.

Although partially a product of public attitudes, the distribution of power between the legislature and the executive has effects in turn on the makeup of the public, its leadership, and the events to which it reacts. Apart from the fact that the population which influences Congress is divided along state and district lines, it appears to be the case that legislators deal with opinion leaders of a particular type. They talk to people who are locally prominent in business or the professions rather than to financiers or industrialists or professional men with nationwide interests, for the latter deal mostly with the executive branch.[6] This may mean that effective public opinion is somewhat different when the relative influence of Congress is greater. Also, to the extent that Congress seems in the lead, perceptions among the entire interested public may be affected. It is arguable, for example, that the prominence of Congress in the mid-1930's induced many to see the crises in Ethiopia, Spain, and China as posing essentially legal problems, the reactions to which should take form in legislation. Looking ahead to 1983, one must therefore project the relative strength of Congress and the executive and attempt to assess the probable consequences.

The presidency has to be considered apart. Even in the 1920's the executive retained some power to influence the public and control events. At all times since the late nineteenth century, the President has been by far the most important opinion leader. He has had unique access to information. Since World War II, bodies such as the Central Intelligence Agency and the National Security Agency have given him resources which neither the Congress nor the press nor any portion of the public could possibly match.

Within broad limits, Presidents have made much or little of an event and thus determined its importance for Congress and the public. It is by no means unimaginable, for example, that Kennedy could have persuaded the country to see the placement of Soviet missiles in Cuba as an occurrence of minor importance. His Secretary of Defense, after all, shrugged off their presence with the remark: "A missible is a missile. It makes no great difference whether you are killed by a missile fired from the Soviet Union or from Cuba." [7] Nor is it unimaginable that President Nixon could have whipped up a greater sense of crisis about the expansion of Soviet naval power in the Mediterranean or Soviet military aid to Egypt. Few if any members of the public can successfully challenge the President's judgment about the proportions of events; and the sense of proportion influences the size and, to some extent, the characteristics of the public prompted to develop an opinion or opinions.

Speculation about the future thus entails speculation about the dispositions and predicaments of Presidents whose identities and mandates are still mysteries. If the equilibrium does tip toward Congress, will Presidents acquiesce, as did Harding and Coolidge, or will they fight? Will their set of mind be like that of Franklin Roosevelt in 1933, so preoccupied with the domestic scene as to want to minimize foreign affairs—or like that of Roosevelt after 1937 or Truman after 1946, convinced that opportunities for domestic reform are negligible and that the only leadership is in international relations? Will they be visionary activists like Theodore Roosevelt and Woodrow Wilson, or will they be more like, say, Herbert Hoover or Dwight Eisenhower? Wrong guesses on any of these counts could invalidate otherwise well-constructed prophecies.

Lastly, one enters the maze of bureaucratic politics. What has been said thus far has minimized dynamic factors, seeming to imply that the past five or six decades can be set side by side and measured against one another. In fact, the United States has undergone changes of such a character as to make its present self quite unlike its earlier self. One can even make a case that the United States of today resembles the U.S.S.R. of today much more than the United States of thirty years ago.[8]

One noteworthy change has been the growth of government. The bureaucracy has become a great reservoir of expertise. Individuals and organizations within it have assembled knowledge about foreign areas and the manifold possibilities for action. Much of this knowledge has not been shared with the public or the Congress. In part because of the limited time that a President can give to any one area or problem, this knowledge had been shared only sparingly with the White House. Understandably, many people in the bureaucracy have developed a conviction that they are better equipped than the public or Congress or the President to decide what courses of actions the United States ought to pursue. That conviction has led them to attempt—often successfully—to manipulate both public opinion and congressional and presidential actions.

The bureaucracy has had a hand in shaping perceptions of events. In the immediate aftermath of World War II, officialdom drew public, congressional, and presidential attention to certain events and not to others—specifically, to events on the European and Middle Eastern periphery of the Soviet Union rather than to those in South Asia, former colonial territories in Southeast Asia, or even East Asia or Latin America. As time passed, the bureaucracy played a crucial role in shaping public, congressional, and presidential thought. In the 1950's, as a result, great importance was attached to happenings which in retrospect seem to have had little relevance to the safety or welfare of Americans—for example, the overthrow of the French colonial regime in Indochina, clashes between Communist and Nationalist Chinese over possession of the Quemoy and Matsu islands, border trouble between Syria and Lebanon, anarchy in the former Belgian Congo, and the civil war in Laos. Kennedy's perception of the importance of Soviet missiles in Cuba was in part a function of what the bureaucracy told him. Certainly this was the case with regard to his and Lyndon Johnson's view of Southeast Asia and Vietnam.

Also, of course, the bureaucracy has had a large role in conducting U.S. international relations. Since World War II it has become increasingly less realistic to think of the executive branch as simply following courses of action determined by the President. Often, Presidents have learned about problems too late to do anything except continue what the bureaucracy had commenced or to defend what had already been done.

To the extent that the bureaucracy independently determines policy, public opinion does not; for the public is heard indistinctly inside buildings in Washington and almost not at all in United States missions overseas. Public opinion obtains its force from the attention paid to it by Congress and the President, and when Congress and the President are impotent, so is the public. Moreover, the independent strength of the bureaucracy may cut into the relative power of public opinion even when the President is a fully engaged actor, for Presidents sometimes adopt the bureaucrat's view that statesmanship calls for following expert advice rather than taking a course of action that may be popular.

The would-be prophet must thus face up to yet another group of questions. To what extent will the international posture of the United States in the next decade be fixed by the bureaucracy, with only minimal regard for public opinion or the Congress or the President? Even if public opinion and legislative and presidential politics still determine the broad outlines of American policy, to what extent will the perceptions and agenda of other actors be influenced by the ways in which the bureaucracy reports events, creates situations, and frames options?

These are hard questions, and all the harder because it is almost as simplistic to speak of "the bureaucracy" as to speak of "the United States." The bureaucracy is made up of many components, all of which are different and all of which are subject to internal change. The White House, the State Department, the Office of the Secretary of Defense, the military services, the Treasury, and the intelligence agencies all have unique characteristics. Within the State Department, the various geographic bureaus differ from one another, and functional bureaus such as Economic Affairs, Legal Affairs, and Intelligence and Research differ from the geographic bureaus. The offices headed by different assistant secretaries of Defense are often adversaries, and the relations between the Office of the Secretary of Defense and the services sometimes resemble relations among the colonial powers in Africa in the nineteenth century. Nor are agencies, bureaus, services, and service arms the only units needing to be taken into account. There are also important distinctions to be noticed between career groups (Foreign Service Officers *versus* others in the State Department, for example) and, above all, between Washington and the missions abroad, for the interests and perspectives of, say, an Army colonel working on military assistance programs in the Pentagon and a West Point classmate heading a military aid mission can be completely divergent.

Just as with the whole polity, so with the bureaucracy, the forecaster must begin by disaggregating: that is, by separating large questions about a composite entity into smaller questions about the parts of which it is composed.

First, perhaps, one ought to ask what will be the distribution of influence among the major departments and agencies. In the 1930's those concerned with domestic affairs had greater stature than those occupied with foreign affairs or defense. After World War II the reverse was true. Presidential priorities provide part of the explanation. Also, however, the prewar crises and the war attracted first-rate talent to organizations concerned with foreign affairs and defense. Increasing in size and taking on new functions, these organizations offered ambitious men and women opportunities for responsibility and advancement. Domestic agencies by contrast seemed to have had their day, to be custodians of old programs rather than innovators, and to be crowded at the top. One question about the future is whether these trends are in process of reversal. Will domestic affairs command a larger share of presidential, congressional, and public attention? Will appointive officials and bureaucrats in domestic areas be able to hold their own, or more than hold their own, against people who attach priority to foreign and defense problems?

In the foreign and defense areas themselves, what will be the distribution of influence? From World War II through the mid-1960's, the military establishment was usually stronger than the diplomatic, aid, or information establishments or the intelligence apparatus. Its staffwork was better, even on essentially political problems; its recommendations to the President were clearer; and its presentations to Congress and public bodies were far more effective.[9] If the war in Vietnam has altered the public view of the military, has it reduced or will it reduce the stature of the military establishment within the government? The *Pentagon Papers* and other evidence suggest that the State Department showed more wisdom than the Pentagon and the C.I.A. more wisdom than either. Will the future see State or the C.I.A. acquire the commanding position that the Defense Department occupied in the early 1960's?

An inescapable related question has to do with the Executive Office and the White House. Nixon shifted to the National Security Council staff some functions once thought to be departmental. This staff assembled information, offered assessments of events, and analyzed options for action. The effect of its operation was to reduce markedly the power and influence of all departments and agencies. If this does not turn out to be a temporary phenomenon, one has to ask whether a large and complex NSC staff is not destined to develop interests of its own and internal conflicts comparable to those of the State Department or the C.I.A. If so, what forms will its divisions take?

A second major question has to do with relations between the whole Washington bureaucracy and missions abroad. Will the missions be constantly working, as in the 1950's and 1960's, to induce Washington to attach greater importance to the countries in which they are located? Or will they shift in some degree toward the pre-World War II practice of minimizing the extent of U.S. interests in local events? Within missions, will the balances shift? That is, will military representatives and C.I.A. station chiefs become less or more influential? Will aid and information officers gain a larger voice or cease to be heard altogether? Will all missions follow a single trend; will those in one geographic region differ from those in another; or will there be no pattern at all?

Third, what will be the balances within major Washington agencies? In the immediate post-World War II period it was by no means insignificant that the best-manned and most energetically led bureau in State was that led by Loy Henderson, dealing with the Near East and South Asia, for it played a key role in pulling presidential, congressional, and public attention to Iran, Greece, and Turkey and in framing the Truman Doctrine. What will be the situation in the State Department in the decade ahead?

In the Pentagon, what relationships will obtain within and between the Office of the Secretary of Defense, the Joint Chiefs of Staff, and the commands overseas? In the first Eisenhower administration, the combination of a weak Secretary of Defense and a strong Joint Chiefs chairman (Admiral Arthur Radford) played some part in making Indochina and the Formosa Straits cynosures. In the second Eisenhower administration, weakness or uncertainty in both the Office of the Secretary of Defense and the Joint Chiefs of Staff organization made it possible for a strong and confident NATO commander (General Lauris Norstad) to force to the top of the nation's foreign policy agenda the question of whether there should be a multilateral nuclear force in Europe.[10] The balances in the Defense establishment and the personalities of men in critical posts can have effects in the decade ahead.

So can the balances among services and service arms. In the years immediately after World War II, the Air Force engaged in a campaign not only to establish its independence but also to win acceptance of the twin propositions that air power would be decisive in a future war and that, because bombers could not be built overnight, the nation should spend money to keep bomber forces in being. With these interests, the Air Force naturally joined in the effort to persuade the President, Congress, and the public that the Soviet Union constituted a real and present menace to national security. Subsequently, each service so defined the Soviet or Sino-Soviet threat and the options available for meeting it as to maximize their respective claims on shares of the budget. The result was to force to the fore issues having to do with air bases and missile sites abroad, naval bases in Spain, the Mediterranean, and the Pacific, troop strength and contingency planning in Europe, and military assistance for actual or would-be allies. In trying to look ahead, one must ask how the services will interpret their interests and how, as a result, they will seek to influence perceptions of foreign policy problems.

To the extent possible, one should also speculate about other important organizations. Questions similar to those about the State Department should be asked of the Agency for International Development, the United States Information Agency, and, of course, the C.I.A. With regard to the latter, some guesswork is probably also in order regarding the balance of power between intelligence analysts on the one hand and the managers of clandestine operations on the other. With regard to the Treasury Department and perhaps also the Commerce Department, one should try to envision how officials concerned with international affairs will relate to those concerned essentially with domestic affairs. Will the heads of those agencies be persuaded, as was Franklin Roosevelt's Secretary of the Treasury, Henry Morgenthau, Jr., that the health of the American economy is largely dependent on the health of the international economy? Or will they, like most of Morgenthau's successors, see the protection of American trade and payment balances as their primary business?

As has already been implied, one's guesswork must go not only to the distribution of influence among formal organizations but also to tendencies that may manifest themselves within those organizations. The fact that Loy Henderson's bureau was relatively strong in the State Department did not itself dictate that Soviet failure to withdraw from Iran, Yugoslav aid to guerrillas in Greece, and Soviet diplomatic pressure on Turkey would be defined by that bureau as critical situations requiring strong action by the United States. That they were so defined was due in part to the fact that Henderson was a Soviet specialist long committed to the view that communist expansionism would be checked only by threats of force. And the impact of Henderson was in turn dependent on the fact that most of his associates and superiors in the State Department hierarchy happened to be Foreign Service officers who shared his attitudes. Similarly, the fact that the Chairman of the Joint Chiefs was relatively powerful in the early Eisenhower years did not itself determine that the chairman's influence would be used to promote a focus on Southeast Asia and Formosa. This grew in part out of Radford's background as a naval aviator, commander of U.S. forces in the Pacific, and a skeptic about the Europe-first orientation of wartime and post-World War II U.S. strategy. And the fact that Radford did not always prevail—that the United States did not intervene militarily in Indochina in 1954—traced in part to counterbalancing tendencies within the bureaucracy, especially opposition from the Army. Such manifestations within the bureaucracy made it easier—perhaps even made it possible—for press commentators and members of Congress to express reservations about Radford's recommendations and for the President ultimately to decide not to follow his advice.

Inspecting the future, one must therefore frame hypotheses about currents that will run within the complex organizations that make up the government. Will officials in the dominant bureaus and offices continue to see the world much as nearly all of them saw it in the 1950's and 1960's: that is, as a world around which runs a well-defined frontier which the United States must defend against aggressive communist powers? After the later 1950's there gradually developed an opposing school of thought—one hypothesizing the possibility of a modus vivendi with the U.S.S.R. and even with China. The growing strength of this school was evidenced by the limited test-ban treaty of 1963, the Strategic Arms Limitation Talks, and moves toward normalization of relations between Washington and Peking. More recently, yet another school has begun to emerge. It has seen the world as divided into areas in many of which the interests of the United States are of a precise and limited character. Predicting the future involves predicting tendencies of thought within the bureaucracy and the interplay between tendencies there and tendencies in presidential, congressional, and public opinion.

By specifying and comparing the probable causes for change or continuity in past decades, one can identify at least some of the important questions that ought to be addressed by a forecaster. Now that I have indicated how these questions emerge from contemplation of the past, I have done what I set out to do in this essay; but it would be cowardly to quit at this point, even though it may be foolhardy not to do so. So I shall work backward through the questions, setting forth my own guesses—in none of which I profess high confidence.

First, what will be tendencies of opinion within the bureaucracy? Here one must bear in mind two facts. The bureaucracy has immense intellectual inertia. In the mid-1960's, twenty years after World War II, most people in the foreign affairs establishment—including Secretary Rusk and many Assistant Secretaries of State—continued to regard the public and Congress as instinctively isolationist. Although individuals perceived the Chinese-Russian split as early as 1956, at least a dozen years passed before significant numbers stopped characterizing China as an obedient Soviet satellite or speaking in public of a "Sino-Soviet bloc." Rapid changes of opinion occur in bureaucratic organizations only when there is some large-scale change in structure or personnel, as in the State Department in 1944–46. Looking ahead, one should therefore assume that the bureaucracy will continue to think tomorrow what it thought yesterday and that such a forecast will prove wrong only if major shake-ups occur.

Among the military, there seems every reason to expect rough continuity in opinion. Because the submarine fleet has a role in nuclear deterrence, part of the Navy will retain a vested interest in having the President and Congress regard Russia and China as no less threatening than in the past. To justify carriers and carrier task forces, other elements in the Navy need the planning assumption that U.S. sea and air power may have to be utilized at any moment in any part of the world. Although some changes may be in process, one would expect Navy memoranda in 1983 to say substantially what they said in 1973 and what they said in 1963.

Air Force officers can be expected also to continue pressing for recognition of an imminent nuclear threat. Many will be engaged in the next several years in a rear-guard action against critics of the air war in Vietnam. Their official line is and will be that the mistake in Vietnam was to escalate air action gradually instead of following Air Force recommendations to wage a short all-out bombing campaign against North Vietnam. Air Force officers are likely to be the most "hawkish" bureaucrats, and, since they have not had the post in the past decade, one of them is almost certain before 1983 to be Chairman of the Joint Chiefs.

The Army is harder to predict. Although it has been more involved in the Vietnamese war than either the Navy or Air Force, its middle and upper hierarchies contain many officers who regard the war as an unqualified mistake and, moreover, as an event that has seriously injured the service. It remains uncertain whether or not these officers will gain control. If not, Army positions will resemble those of the Air Force. If so, the Army will probably in the decade ahead take a "never again" posture similar to but firmer than that of the Army after the Korean War.

In making a projection for the State Department bureaucracy, one must bear in mind not only the considerations mentioned earlier but also the fact that the Department's traditions, personnel system, and organization all put a premium on service abroad. It is Foreign Service doctrine that the man on the scene is the best judge of what should be done. Hence in speculating about State Department attitudes, one must think primarily of the attitudes apt to obtain among ambassadors, deputy chiefs of missions, political affairs officers, and the like in U.S. establishments abroad.

Among these men and women, inertia is likely to be complete. That is, one can expect the 1983 cable file from any given capital to resemble in most essentials the cable file of 1973. Communications from U.S. missions in friendly countries will continue to speak of the vital importance of the country to the United States and to predict dire consequences if the United States does not give stout assurances that it will carry out its commitments and demonstrate through aid appropriations or otherwise its regard for whatever government is currently in office. Cables from missions in unfriendly countries will call attention to evidence of lack of respect for the United States and possible hostile intentions but also to all indications that some hard bargains might be driven by skillful negotiators. American diplomats have built up a vested interest in the quasi-imperial status of the United States. They will not easily change stance, and the fact that they live so far removed from the realities of presidential and congressional politics and domestic public opinion makes change all the harder.

About the intelligence community, we have less knowledge to begin with. It seems likely, however, that C.I.A. analysts will also continue as in the past. That is, they will prepare reports reinforcing mission judgments about the importance of foreign areas but also calling attention to the complexities of events there and the difficulty of devising courses of action for the United States that have any likelihood of influencing those events for the better. Operators in the agency, on the other hand, will continue to regard the world as one where forces of good and evil are everywhere in combat and will devise and propose "dirty tricks" to abet the forces of good.

For the whole foreign affairs–national security bureaucracy, I forecast, in other words, relatively little change—a "hawkish" military establishment, possibly lacking unanimity, as in the second half of the 1950's, because of noticeable dissent among Army officers; a mission-oriented State Department exerting influence in general for maintenance of the status quo; and a somewhat schizophrenic intelligence establishment. If change occurs, it will come slowly. After all, if bureaucratic politics were the only determinant, we would probably have entered the 1970's with a million troops in Vietnam and more on the way. Change that results from change in other factors will probably be visible in bureaucratic attitudes only toward the end of the coming decade.

Relationships among bureaucratic units, on the other hand, are likely to undergo more rapid alteration. In the Pentagon it already seems the case that the Office of the Secretary of Defense has grown weaker. On the assumption that the decade ahead will be one of relatively tight defense budgets, I would predict that the Secretary of Defense will at no time be more than *primus inter pares* in relation to the chiefs of staff. Doubting that any President or Secretary of Defense will want a strong individual as Chairman of the Joint Chiefs, I also predict that the individual services will be relatively more independent.

In State the geographical bureaus will probably retain their traditional pecking order—with Europe, East Asia, and the Middle East ranking first, second, and third, and Latin America and Africa pulling up far behind. Nor does there seem any reason to suppose that functional bureaus will gain markedly higher status. On the other hand, one major structural change in State has at least some chance of occurring. The almost total eclipse of the Department after the beginning of the Nixon administration brought new awareness of its weakness in capacity for analysis as distinct from reportage. Elliot Richardson as Under Secretary commenced an effort to build a program evaluation staff. At some point such a staff may give the upper echelon of the Department the ability not only to compete with the White House staff but also to exercise some real influence over the geographic bureaus and the diplomatic missions. If so, the profile of the State Department could become quite different.

In C.I.A. there seems likely to be some shift in balance away from operators and toward analysts. For one thing, the winding down of the war in Southeast Asia will probably lead to the pensioning off of the agency's more aggressive field agents.

As for the general question of Washington–overseas mission relations, I would predict that, while mission attitudes will not significantly alter, mission influence will dwindle steadily. This trend will be accelerated if, in fact, the top level of the Department of State becomes stronger. But it will occur anyway.

One reason is that it seems also predictable that the White House apparatus will not become weaker in the next ten years. Future Presidents will probably continue to see independence of agency bureaucracies as advantageous. And my guess is that at least a decade will pass before the National Security Council organization becomes so unwieldy and routinized that a President will feel need to create something else—as Nixon felt need for a Domestic Council to do what had once been done by the Budget Bureau.

A second reason for the forecast about mission-Washington relations is a belief on my part that the coming decade will also see a continued marked rise in the relative power and influence of domestic agencies. Awareness of domestic problems has, of course, grown. New bodies such as the Office of Economic Opportunity and the Environmental Protection Agency and even older agencies such as the Department of Health, Education, and Welfare have become able to recruit talented people. By contrast the diplomatic and defense establishments have lost top-flight men and women. Of course, the prospects for solving domestic problems may prove so cheerless as to change the picture, but, in a 52–48 call, I predict otherwise.

Broadly, I thus perceive bureaucratic politics as being relatively less important in the decade 1973–83. Although the bureaucracy will not change much, it will be more fragmented; the President will be more independent of it; the national security agencies will have less influence while domestic agencies will have more; and, so long as Vietnam remains vivid in memory, Presidents, congressmen, and the public will be somewhat distrustful of diplomatic and military figures.

Venturing now into presidential politics, I offer a hesitant forecast that the men (or women) who hold the presidency during the next decade will all adopt positions regarding foreign affairs resembling less those of the Roosevelts, Wilson, Truman, Kennedy, and Johnson than those of Hoover, Eisenhower, and Nixon. Whatever clarions they sound, they will be hesitant about risking war. The memory of Vietnam will make them pessimistic about their ability to have more than marginal influence on events in other lands. They will see their principal opportunities for achieving greatness as in the domestic sphere or, if abroad, in some capacity as a healer or mediator or promoter of accord.

The legislative branch probably will have slightly more power than in the recent past. In part, however, this will be because Presidents take pains to share with Congress decisions that may be productive of public blame. The Congress cannot in any circumstances regain a role such as it played before World War II. The demands of electioneering have increased too much to leave congressmen or even senators time to master a broad range of complex issues. The seniority system, which might provide a remedy, has proved too often to put the wrong men in the wrong place for a long time. And the pressures on congressmen make it almost impossible for them to use large expert staff organizations even if such could be put together. It thus seems likely that the next decade will see continued dominance by the executive.

Within Congress itself, one can expect an increase in the influence of representatives and senators who were "doves" in the Vietnam debate. Although some elders were among them, they were, on the whole, the younger members. They came out ahead in that battle. Unless forthcoming elections go more against the "ins" than have any in recent memory, these erstwhile "doves" will gain greater and greater voice not only within the committees on Foreign Relations and Foreign Affairs but also those on Armed Services, Finance, and Ways and Means. This drift, taken together with the delayed effects of the Supreme Court's reapportionment decision, makes it likely that the decade ahead will see both houses tending toward opposition to dangerous involvement abroad, skepticism about military spending, and emphasis on domestic problems.

Turning finally to public opinion, I should commence by surveying possible events that might have dramatic effects on the shape or character of the public. It should be remarked, however, that a single event is unlikely to produce great impact. In the 1930's American public opinion was not altered by one happening but rather by a whole sequence, commencing in Asia with the Manchurian incident and in Europe with Nazi Germany's unilateral rearmament. Not the *Panay* incident or Munich or the invasion of Poland or even the fall of France could have produced the same results without much having gone before. Only Pearl Harbor could have done so, and Pearl Harbor could not have occurred except in the setting established by the past. Similarly, it took a host of events between 1944 and 1948 to forge an anti-Soviet consensus, and in all probability this consensus could not have taken shape so quickly in the absence of even earlier events such as the Nazi-Soviet pact and the Winter War with Finland. Short of a surprise attack comparable to or worse than Pearl

Harbor, a single happening is not likely to transform the character, composition, or tendency of the American foreign policy public.

The central question to be asked therefore concerns apparent tendencies abroad that might significantly affect American opinion. It can be taken as given that existing opinion tends to be isolationist. As long ago as 1969, polls showed three-quarters of the population doubting that the United States should use force even to resist overt communist aggression against Thailand, Japan, or Berlin. Since then, polls have also shown, for the first time since World War II, a majority accepting the view that the United States need not be militarily superior to its possible adversaries.[11] Although the same proportions may not hold for the public among which issues in international relations have high saliency, these survey results are certainly indicative.

One cannot discount altogether the possibility of a reversal. Chains of events influencing public attitudes need not be consecutive. The Manchurian incident reawakened fear of Japan which had been quiescent for nearly a decade. Should the Soviet Union suddenly take some aggressive action against Yugoslavia, Turkey, Iran, or some other neighbor or overtly violate arms limitation agreements alarm could quickly revive. Aggressive action by China or, for that matter, by the German Federal Republic or Japan could have a similar effect, for distrust of the Germans and Japanese has never wholly subsided. And a second or third incident following a first would undoubtedly produce a marked increase in the level of public feeling.

The public experiencing alarm would, however, be somewhat different from that of the 1930's or of the two decades after World War II. The secular trend in America has accelerated, especially among the well-off and well-educated groups from which the foreign policy public comes. Also, ethnic groups such as Italian-Americans and Polish-Americans are a generation farther removed from attachment to their ancestral lands. It seems most unlikely that at any time in the next decade passion rooted in religious convictions or transplanted nationalism would reappear in anything like its earlier form.

The "establishment," moreover, will probably consist increasingly of men and women influenced by the antiwar movement of the 1960's. Sudden changes in the scene abroad could, of course, discredit the leaders of this movement and restore the stature of others, as events of the late 1930's discredited the leading isolationists and brought back the advocates of collective security. Even so, the bulk of the establishment can be expected to remain, at the very least, resistant to revival of nonappeasement doctrines, distrustful of any row-of-dominoes metaphors, and dubious about public support for protracted conflict. While a massive change in public opinion is not inconceivable, it seems improbable.

Guessing at how bureaucratic, presidential, and legislative politics and public opinion will interact with one another, I would predict with highest confidence that there will not in the coming decade be another round of Cold War. I would predict less confidently that there will not in fact be a return to anything like the isolationism of the interwar years. Instead, the contradictory pulls of the bureaucracy and public opinion, operating on the President and Congress, will produce continued nonviolent antagonism with the communist powers, never rising to a higher pitch than, say, at the time of the Soviet march into Czechoslovakia in 1968 but never becoming more cordial than, say, at the moment of President Nixon's visit to Moscow in 1972. The same contradictory forces would lead to a gradual redefinition of U.S. commitments with a view to reducing the risk of involvement in war for any purposes other than defense of Western Europe, Japan, or Israel, but without overt withdrawal from the posture of being chief protector of the international status quo.

In other words, I foresee continued development along the lines foreshadowed in President Nixon's address at Guam in July, 1969 —the maintenance of alliance relationships with a legion of noncommunist states; continuation of military and economic aid at ever-diminishing levels (at least in relation to Gross National Product and total federal expenditures); but progressive transfer to allies of the burden of providing individually and collectively for their own non-nuclear defense. Sadly, I also foresee prolonged temporization in the face of potential issues posed by a growing U.S. economic presence in that large portion of the planet where people feel themselves relatively poor, for sometime in the decade after next or the decade after that, their reactions to that presence may very well produce events which force new shapes upon the foreign policy of the United States.

NOTES

[1] Arthur M. Schlesinger, Jr., *The Bitter Heritage: Vietnam and American Democracy* (Boston: Houghton Mifflin Co., 1966), p. 91.

[2] I have attempted to summarize the enormous literature on "the foreign policy public" in "An American Tradition in Foreign Policy: The Role of Public Opinion," in William H. Nelson (ed.), *Theory and Practice in American Politics* (Chicago: The University of Chicago Press, 1964), pp. 101-22.

3 V. O. Key, Jr., *Public Opinion and American Democracy* (New York: Alfred A. Knopf, 1961), pp. 173-74.

4 Kenneth P. Adler and Davis Bobrow, "Interest and Influence in Foreign Affairs," *Public Opinion Quarterly,* XX (Spring, 1956), 89-101.

5 Richard Rovere, "Notes on the Establishment in America," *American Scholar,* XXX (Autumn, 1961), 489-95.

6 James N. Rosenau, *National Leadership and Foreign Policy: A Case Study in the Mobilization of Public Support* (Princeton, N.J.: Princeton University Press, 1963), pp. 30-31, 331-62.

7 Elie Abel, *The Missile Crisis* (Philadelphia: J. B. Lippincott Co., 1966), p. 38.

8 I have elaborated this hypothesis in "The Cold War" in C. Vann Woodward (ed.), *The Comparative Approach to American History* (New York: Basic Books, Inc., 1968), pp. 328-45.

9 Adam Yarmolinsky, *The Military Establishment: Its Impact on American Society* (New York: Harper and Row, 1971), pp. 131-32.

10 The process is detailed in a forthcoming study by John D. Steinbruner.

11 "The Limits of Commitment: A *Time*-Louis Harris Poll," *Time,* XCIII (May 2, 1969), 16-17; "Not So Hawkish: The Results of Polls on Military Spending," *Nation,* CCXI (Oct. 19, 1970), 354.

5

How New Will the New American Foreign Policy Be?

ROBERT E. OSGOOD

1

All over the world anxious observers are wondering about the future course of American foreign policy. They are still speculating about what the Nixon Doctrine really means and wondering how it will affect their countries. This is a tribute to America's hegemonial role, which the Nixon Doctrine calls into question. But so far few of the explanations of American foreign policy add anything to what the Nixon Administration has itself said on this subject, most notably in the President's annual reports to Congress, *U.S. Foreign Policy for the 1970's*. These are remarkably substantive and analytical statements, as official expositions of policy go. But their authors are the first to deny that these documents are blueprints or recipe books; rather, they indicate only a general direction and they articulate underlying concepts, the full meaning of which will unfold in the accretion of specific policies and actions over time.

Certain gross features of American foreign policy are evident to everyone who thinks about such things. As the President has said, we are at the end of an era of expanding American power, commitments, and involvements. We are in a period of transition to an era in which the United States will exert its power and leadership much less exclusively and directly, as the self-reliance of allies increases and the pattern of international politics becomes more distinctly multipolar. These generalities seem as accurate as any predictions can be in the unpredictable arena of world politics, but they leave unanswered a number of critical questions about the future.

The most significant questions concern the international system —the structure of power and the pattern of national conflicts and alignments—that will shape America's world role as much as any other factor. Of these questions none is more important than the nature of America's relationship to its major allies: the NATO countries and Japan. Will these two giant centers of economic influence become centers of independent military power, or will they remain military dependents of the United States? What difference does it make to the United States? The answer to the first question may exert the same kind of determining effect upon American foreign policy in the next decade or so as was exerted by the bipolar structure of the international system that emerged in the aftermath of the Second World War. The answer Americans give to the second question will be no less determining, although it is bound to be even more ambiguous.

But before we can reasonably speculate about the future relationship of the United States to its allies we should take stock of the changes in the international system and American foreign policy that we can already observe. Among the most significant changes in America's international environment are the following:

1. The Western European allies and Japan, physically and psychologically weakened by war, have regained their economic vitality and political self-assurance and are increasingly inclined to assert their economic and diplomatic independence from the United States.

2. The United States, by extending formal commitments of protection to Western Europe and Japan, has helped create a stable military balance to deter Soviet military and political pressure against these vital power centers and peripheral areas.

3. The Soviet Union, after more than a decade of significant American strategic superiority, has gained parity with the United States in second-strike nuclear capability; and, after an even longer period of a virtual American monopoly in overseas naval projection, has established an impressive naval presence in the Mediterranean and other oceans.

4. The Communist world has fragmented. The deepest split is manifested in the Sino-Soviet hostility that has grown in the last fifteen years.

5. Largely as a result of these four developments, the Soviet Union has found a major interest in détente; that is, in a relaxation of tensions between it and the Western powers, in more active East-West trade and greater access to Western technology, and in arms control discussions and agreements with the United States and its allies.

6. The so-called Third World of generally poor and new nations outside the developed areas of the world has turned out to be far less vulnerable to external control, far less tractable to

great-power influence, and much more diversified in national and ethnic orientations than the prevailing images of this populous area in the late 1950's and early 1960's as a decisive arena of the Cold War or as an area in which poor nations were organized against the rich and nonaligned nations against the allied.

Each one of these developments has changed America's international environment in specific ways. Together, they have produced some distinctive features of the present international system, which shapes and is shaped by American foreign policy:

1. The relations among the major developed states dominate international politics.
2. These relations are becoming more diversified as adversaries find common interests, allies find major differences of interest, and new centers of political and diplomatic influence arise.
3. The Third World is disturbed not only by growing awareness of economic and social grievances but also by increasing national and ethnic conflicts. Some of these grievances and conflicts can be expected to impinge upon the interests of developed states and occasionally threaten to involve them—particularly the superpowers—in local disorder. But generally the developed states manage to pursue their interests in these areas without dangerously confronting one another.
4. Together, these characteristics of the international system have transformed an "era of confrontation" into an "era of negotiation," as the Nixon Administration puts it with admissible hyperbole. More accurately, they have created an international system dominated by a pluralistic pattern of diplomatic accommodation and maneuver, supplanting a more polarized system dominated by threat and counterthreat, by the assertion of deterrence and the establishment of alliances, and by superpower crises.

The major actors in this international system are still the United States and the Soviet Union, and these superpowers are still the dominant managers of the central military balance in the world. But the issues between them have grown more complicated, and the superpowers no longer determine to the same extent the political issues and the policies for dealing with them among their major allies. In this system military power remains a pervasive influence, particularly in its psychological and political effects; but the precise material distribution of power between the superpowers and among their allies does not affect international politics so clearly or directly as in the heyday of the Cold War.

2

One cannot explain or even describe the altered international system without taking into account the role of one of the principal actors in that system: the United States. The principal features of America's foreign outlook and policies have changed no less markedly than the international system. The former is both cause and effect of the latter.

The fundamental changes in America's international environment were bound to change America's foreign relations sooner or later. This change would have been delayed if we had readily achieved our objectives in the Vietnam War. It has been accelerated because we failed. The change in American policy is marked by a number of specific developments: the decline of general purpose forces to levels lower than before the beginning of the Vietnam buildup in 1964; the treaty reverting Okinawa to Japan; the withdrawal of numerous forces from Japan, Korea, Thailand, and other countries in East Asia; the Sino-American rapprochement following President Nixon's visit to Peking; the Strategic Arms Limitation Talks and the resulting treaty with the Soviet Union; American commitment to reducing forces in Europe by an East-West agreement. But underlying these developments is a more fundamental change in the prevailing consensus on foreign policy—the driving ideas about America's interests, the Communist threat to these interests, and the nature and efficacy of American power in countering these threats.

At the core of the familiar consensus underlying American foreign policy in the era of expanding power and commitments was the idea, expressed in hundreds of policy pronouncements from the announcement of the Truman Doctrine and even before to dozens of documents in the Pentagon Papers, that America's vital interests are global; that they transcend specific material or military interests in particular parts of the world; that they lie in the preservation of a modicum of international order, defined particularly as the prevention and containment of direct or indirect armed aggression by Communist states; that the United States does not want to be the World's Policeman, but that it is unavoidably the indispensable and often the only power capable of deterring or helping independent countries resist armed attacks; and that American economic, military, and technical assistance is the missing component needed to enable "free peoples" to resist subjugation by subversion and insurgency assisted from outside.

This core idea was, in part a reflection of reality. But it was also a "myth" in the sociological sense. The consensus had origins deep in the American approach to the outside world. It was rooted in the universalistic conception of American interests formulated by Woodrow Wilson; in the supposed lessons of the interwar period that followed from the failure of the Western democracies to resist the chain of aggression leading to the Second World War; in the formative and disillusioning encounter in the early postwar years with hostile Soviet probes in Europe, the Mediterranean, and the Middle East; and in the trauma of failing to prevent the Communist takeover in China, followed by Chinese intervention in the Korean War.

This consensus, once it was applied to Vietnam after the fall of China to the Communists, was never questioned until the human and political costs became extravagant. Although at every critical decision to expand American involvement in the war the President was advised, and he understood, that the chances of an expanded involvement succeeding were poor, the President always decided to follow the course—usually the middle course—of escalation because he and his advisors believed that the alternative of continuing existing policies or reducing American involvement would be far more costly and risky. Why? Primarily because to permit the Communists to conquer South Vietnam, it was thought, would have been to encourage a chain of aggression that would unravel the whole fabric of international order and undermine the core of containment: the credibility of American power and commitments.

Nevertheless, America's participation in the war eventually became so costly, while carrying so little promise of victory, that Presidents Johnson and Nixon halted the process of escalation and reversed it. On the surface, this was a pragmatic change of policy; but underneath it reflected a basic disaffection with the rationale for fighting the war. How generalized and enduring this disaffection may be, only time and unpredictable circumstances will reveal; but one can no longer reasonably doubt that it has already altered the familiar American consensus on foreign policy with a suddenness and sharpness that might otherwise have taken another decade.[1]

3

The President's annual reports to Congress not only state the nature of the change in America's foreign outlook; they also probably describe, in outline, a revised national consensus. In any case, no significant political representative or private pundit has presented an alternative to the President's comprehensive articulation of a revised foreign policy.

The United States, in the revised outlook, is still dedicated to the preservation of international order, but now the order is described as a "stable structure of relationships," based on the distribution of power and influence among five developed centers of economic power and diplomatic initiative.

Given the primarily bipolar military structure of power (which Nixon Administration spokesmen avowedly hope to preserve), international order is still conceived to depend centrally on the mutual restraint of the United States and the Soviet Union, but the American-Soviet relationship is now viewed primarily in terms of an emerging global *modus vivendi*—a complex network of understandings and agreements linked together by some common but mostly parallel interests—rather than so largely in terms of containing the leader of world communism by deterring aggression, assisting free peoples against armed subversion, and establishing alliances.

The United States, President Nixon has declared, remains pledged to protect allies against direct attacks by nuclear states, but it will consider how to respond to other forms of aggression according to the circumstances and a more complicated set of criteria; and it will rely primarily upon the nation attacked to protect itself, especially in the case of internal war. The United States will support its existing commitments but will be very reluctant to undertake new ones. It will remain politically engaged in behalf of Japan and the NATO allies and continue to manage their regional security, but it will continue a moderate retrenchment of its military presence as the allies take up a larger share of their security burden and as the achievement of negotiated mutual balanced force reductions in Europe may permit.

In short, this revised consensus envisions American material retrenchment without political disengagement—that is, continued American military preponderance at a lower level of effort and reduced risk of armed involvement—in the context of a multipolar configuration of diplomatic maneuver that restrains all the major participants. Retrenchment is presumed to be the concomitant of greater allied self-reliance, but continuing American engagement is envisioned as the condition for the moderation of international conflict in the multipolar environment.

Underlying this statement of the revised consensus there is a downgrading of the official perception of the Communist threat. One reason for this downgrading is a perceived change in the interconnectedness of things in the international system. The interwar lessons about stopping chains of aggression and falling dominoes are no longer seen as axioms to be applied automatically, because the world—particularly the Communist world—is no longer as cohesive and because peace is therefore more divisible. In a multipolar or pluralistic international system, disorder and aggression in one part of the world is less likely to create disorder and aggression in another and less likely to alter the central balance of power. Another reason for downgrading the threat is that the Soviet Union is seen to have a major interest in perpetuating détente, partly because of its fear of the People's Republic of China. But most important, the official estimate of China's military strength and of its will to project this strength beyond Chinese borders has been greatly reduced, as compared to the prevailing estimate only five to ten years ago.

At the same time, the Nixon Administration has upgraded its estimate of the capacity of other states—particularly those in the Third World that were thought to be so insecure—to take care of their own military security. "The Asia of today," says the second annual report (released on February 25, 1971), "is vastly different from the Asia which required, over the past several decades, so activist an American role. Asian nations now generally have a strong and confident sense of their own national identity and future. They have generally established healthier relationships with each other and with the outside world. They have created institutions of proven vitality. Their armed forces are stronger."

Also underlying the revised foreign policy consensus, as stated by the Nixon Administration, is a lower estimate of the efficacy of American military power to intervene effectively in local wars, especially when these wars are in large measure internal. This revised estimate, obviously induced by the frustrations of the Vietnam War, is a distinct contrast to the confidence in America's limited-war capacity and the determination to counter insurgency and "wars of national liberation" during the Kennedy Administration. It accounts for the official renunciation by President Nixon of the use of U.S. forces to cope with the entire spectrum of threats, particularly when such threats take the form of subversion and guerrilla warfare. "We may be able to supplement local efforts with economic and military assistance," the President's first annual report says. "However, a direct combat role for U.S. general purpose forces arises primarily when insurgency has shaded into external aggression or when there is an overt conventional attack. In such cases, we shall weigh our interests and our commitments, and we shall consider the efforts of our allies, in determining our response."

Finally, and more subtly, the revised consensus downgrades America's interests outside the great democratic developed centers of the world: Japan, Western Europe, and North America. This widespread re-evaluation of American interests in the so-called Third World is implicit in numerous official statements that the United States must apply more exacting criteria of national interest to future commitments and involvements, and that the enthusiasm for asserting American power in behalf of the security and independence of others, expressed in President Kennedy's oft-quoted inaugural address,[2] was excessive and is now outdated. The White House evidently shares the general opinion that American interests in Southeast Asia became inflated far beyond objective security needs simply because of the involvement of American power and prestige. In the future, therefore, it affirms, in the first and second annual reports, that "we are not involved in the world because we have commitments; we have commitments because we are involved. Our interests must shape our commitments, rather than the other way around."

4

This revised foreign policy and policy consensus, and the general strategy of retrenchment without disengagement which it supports, are in theory well adapted to an international environment of increasingly multipolar diplomatic maneuver. America's continued military preponderance over its allies in Asia and Western Europe can be made bearable economically and psychologically if international tensions are moderated by the constraints of multipolar diplomacy. American preponderance, in turn, is a major condition of moderated tensions, in that American disengagement and withdrawal or the movement of America's major allies toward full-scale military independence would disturb the international equilibrium on which détente is based. But one must wonder how stable and enduring the emerging international system will be. If, for example, it turns out to be only a relatively brief transition to a new era of confrontation, crisis, deterrence, and alliance formation in a multipolar environment, the fact that the United States is still the protector of Japan and Western Europe could lead to results quite different from the "low posture" envisioned in the revised consensus. Similarly, if the Soviet extension of its naval power and political influence to Asia should gain impressive momentum, if local conflicts in the Third World, particularly on the Sino-Soviet periphery, were to become more violent and extensive, or if Japan were to seek full-scale military independence, American policy might once again defy expectations.

But let us asume that the international environment holds no big surprises and is relatively free from big conflicts and radical changes in the balance of power for a decade or so. Then what would be the chances of retrenchment without disengagement working?

In Western Europe retrenchment without disengagement, according to the present consensus, supposes no more than a moderate reduction of American troops in Europe and the stabilization of the American presence.[3] For this stabilized presence is seen as the necessary condition, on the one hand, of East-West détente (*Ostpolitik,* the Berlin treaties, conferences on security and cooperation in Europe, mutual balanced force reduction talks, improved relations between the two Germanies, and the like) and, on the other hand, of allied strength and cohesion protecting Western Europe against Soviet diplomatic intimidation while it moves toward unity in foreign and defense policy, which in the long run may permit a safe substantial reduction of American troops. According to this strategy, not only is the stabilization of American force levels at approximately the existing level the condition for détente; but also at least one item on the agenda of détente—discussion and negotiation of mutual balanced force reductions (MBFR)—is conceived to be the condition for countering domestic pressure for substantial unilateral reductions and for eventually achieving through an international agreement an East-West military balance within which the United States may safely stabilize its contribution to European defense at a much lower level.

By the same token, however, if MBFR and *Ostpolitik* look unpromising and if domestic pressures do lead the United States to withdraw substantial numbers of troops unilaterally, this would have an adverse effect on European security, on détente, and on progress toward West European unity and self-reliance. Moreover, it can be argued that, whereas talk of MBFR will not withstand pressure for substantial unilateral withdrawals of American troops, the emphasis in Western diplomacy on seeking European security through East-West transactions, talks, and agreements practically excludes an orderly readjustment of United States-European relations within NATO to accommodate a lower American force level. For the prospect of MBFR may be held out as an argument in allied countries for not disturbing the status quo, while the status quo is actually being undermined by reciprocal tendencies within NATO toward unplanned and uncoordinated unilateral reductions. One must wonder how long the United States, in a period of détente and of probably growing differences with its allies on economic issues, will maintain more than symbolic numbers of troops in Europe. In the absence of a discernible security threat or of promising East-West arms reduction agreements, these troops must seem increasingly to be justified only by the alleged political advantages of retaining the preponderant military role that the Europeans ought to be able to assume themselves. And the only reason the allies will have to increase their share of the defense burden is to keep the United States from abandoning its role.

In East Asia, as in Western Europe, the logic of retrenchment without disengagement lies in the assumption that continued American military preponderance is the necessary condition for the moderation of international tensions and conflict, which, in turn, is the condition that permits the United States to support its security interests at a lower level of material effort and involvement. With respect to Japan, according to the present consensus, this means that the United States would continue to have exclusive responsibility for the protection of areas of Japanese security concern beyond the defense of the home islands—notably, Korea and Taiwan. Otherwise, it is feared, Japan would undertake an overseas military policy in order to protect these areas itself; and that would be profoundly disturbing to the fragile multipolar Asian equilibrium, particularly if it led to Japanese production of nuclear weapons.

For the sake of effective engagement, the United States, in the prevailing view, would maintain strong air and naval capabilities in East Asia. Retrenchment in terms of the withdrawal of American military personnel from Japanese and other bases is already fairly far advanced. Korea, however, is a special case. Barring some sort of settlement that would reliably pacify the Korean peninsula, effective American engagement probably presupposes the maintenance of some American ground forces in South Korea, since the withdrawal of these forces would not only upset the balance between the two Koreas but would also leave Japan, China, and Russia dangerously confronting each other in fear that one or the other might try to fill the vacuum left by American withdrawal.

In the foreseeable future this strategy for reducing American forces within the framework of a continued American military protectorate corresponds with the strong opposition of the Japanese government to undertaking a larger military role than close-in defense of the home islands—an opposition that springs from painful memories of the shame and suffering of World War II, from constitutional constraints (Article 9) against an overseas military policy, and from acute awareness of the domestic disruption and foreign antagonism that would result from reviving the specter of Japanese "militarism." Apparently, only a combination of Japan's complete loss of confidence in America's nuclear and conventional military protection and its perception of a serious Chinese or Soviet military threat to Taiwan or Korea or perhaps intensive intimidation by the Communist nuclear states (it strains the imagination to envision a credible threat of direct military attack against Japan) could provoke Japan to exchange the obvious economic and political advantages of the American protectorate for the costs and hazards of full military self-reliance.

On the other hand, indefinite perpetuation of America's military protectorate over Japan will not be free of political costs and risks. For one thing, this American role probably depends on much closer collaboration with Japan, if only to retain reliable access to and use of air and naval bases in Japan and Okinawa. But closer collaboration depends on a convergence of military contingency plans, foreign policy interests, and, more fundamentally, political cultures and outlooks that may exceed what one can realistically expect. If so, the political burden of trying to retain Japanese confidence and cooperation would be compounded by the burden of responsibility for Japan's military impotence in a period of increasingly differentiated Japanese and American policies. The result might be mutual frustration and irritation rather than harmonious partnership, with the consequent danger of unilateral American disengagement posing an agonizing choice for Japan between neutralism, realignment, and full military autonomy—all of which courses would disrupt the multipolar Asian diplomatic equilibrium.

5

Doubtless, retrenchment without disengagement, with all its speculative difficulties, will remain the new foreign policy consensus in the United States for the foreseeable future. It entails no radical change from the past. It promises to preserve the principal advantages of America's position in the past "era of confrontation" at a tolerable material and psychological burden and a minimal risk of armed involvement in the new "era of negotiation." Nonetheless, it is worth considering briefly the two obvious options that help define this middle way, if only to illuminate further the nature of the broad policy venture upon which we seem to be embarked. On one side of this middle option is unilateral withdrawal; on the other, devolution, or the transfer of security responsibilities from the United States to Western Europe and Japan.

If the United States were content to define its vital national interests—the interests for which it would be prepared to use its armed forces—as narrowly as the territorial security and economic welfare of the United States itself, unilateral withdrawal (that is, substantial or total withdrawal, over a period of time, of American armed forces that now protect NATO and Japan, regardless of whether the allies choose to supplant these forces with their own) would be worth considering as a serious option. In stretching the words "national security" to cover the containment of Communist armed aggression against almost any country, however intrinsically unimportant it might be to American material interests, Americans have overlooked the fact that there are very few, if any, parts of the world in which a successful Communist aggression would actually undermine American military security in the strict sense of the word. Because of America's nuclear retaliatory capability and its relative independence from overseas bases, the United States is more secure from direct aggression against other countries as well as against itself than at the time of either the First or Second World War. Even successful aggression against Japan or Western Europe, although a tremendous political blow, would not be a vital blow to American military security. In any case, it is far-fetched, though not literally inconceivable, to imagine these two great centers of modern power either incurring or succumbing to an armed attack by the Soviet Union, let alone China.

Moreover, even if unilateral withdrawal of American forces were to lead to a new American isolationist posture, it is doubtful that American economic interests would be seriously jeopardized. American military and political isolation has never presupposed American economic isolationism. Perhaps the Common Market countries and Japan would be less obliging to American monetary interests and balance of payments problems if they did not feel that they had to accommodate America's economic interests in order to keep its military protection, but there is no reason to think that American trade and investments would suffer seriously from American military withdrawal. America's investments in and trade with the developed countries are more important to those countries than to itself. And in addition to the fact that the United States does not need to preserve its military preponderance abroad in order to protect its economic interests, it is clear that the effort to protect its allies has been a major factor in the chronic American balance of payments deficit.

These considerations, however, do not come to grips with America's real conception of its interests. For a variety of intangible reasons, Americans have come to think of the security and general welfare of Western Europe as a good thing in itself, second only to the security of the United States in North America. To a lesser extent, the same thing is true of Japan. Moreover, American foreign policy elites have grown used to thinking of the United States as a global power with global responsibilities, as a nation that needs a reasonably congenial international environment to retain its own vitality, and as a country that must for reasons of pride and purpose as well as for safety preserve its influence in the major centers of power in the world. In terms of these basic criteria of national interest, American unilateral withdrawal looks a lot more costly and risky.

It is not likely that American withdrawal from Europe, even if phased over a period of five years or so, would in itself lead the European allies to form a more cohesive defense community to supplant the American presence. One need not take at face value the self-serving assertions from Europe that American withdrawal would simply convince the allies that self-defense is hopeless in order to appreciate the obstacles to the creation of an adequate Western European substitute for American ground forces. Coalescence of defense efforts and policies has always been the most difficult form of cooperation for nations that think of themselves as equal. Perhaps only if they perceive a grave military threat to their security will such nations subordinate their sovereignties to a collective defense effort with the strength and cohesiveness that would be necessary to supplant an American withdrawal from Europe. Moreover, it is hard to imagine an effective European defense organization without a joint European nuclear force that would be more impressive than the present British and French forces, if only because American ground forces would no longer serve as a trigger on the U.S. nuclear force. But combining nuclear efforts and policies would be the most difficult task of coalescence, particularly because of the problem of arranging an acceptable nuclear association for West Germany.

If the European allies were nonetheless to make a serious effort to concert their defense efforts and policies when faced with American withdrawal, they would probably incur Soviet harassment and opposition at the expense of détente. For the Soviet Union has consistently opposed Western European coalescence even in the economic realm. The prospect of West Germany associating itself with a European nuclear force would almost certainly provoke a determined Soviet effort to intimidate Germany and isolate it from the allies.

One may argue in behalf of unilateral withdrawal that the Soviet threat has subsided so substantially that no such European defense community would be needed, but this argument entails a considerable gamble that the Soviet Union would not try to take advantage of the drastically altered balance of power. Perhaps under the circumstances the Soviets would find it so easy to play upon Western weakness and divisions that armed aggression would be unnecessary. Yet previous experience with the Soviet proclivity for applying pressure to Berlin for diplomatic ends suggests that in the absence of a cohesive European defense community there would be an increased risk of another crisis, to which the West might give either a dangerously timid or a dangerously bold response.

The consequences of unilateral withdrawal from Japan, Korea, Taiwan, and the surrounding waters are even more unpredictable, yet no more comforting. Would Japan pursue a posture of armed —or possibly unarmed—neutrality and isolation? Or would the Japanese government, conscious that the conditions of its security had been drastically changed by the withdrawal of its protector, assume the full military role of which it is capable, based on the full panoply of arms, including nuclear weapons? Since Japan, unlike Sweden or Switzerland, is too powerful and seems to be too dangerous for other states to leave alone, and since the Japanese are perfectly capable of radically changing their military posture in the face of new security conditions, the latter course seems more likely. One need not evoke the specter of resurgent Japanese militarism, which springs from a misleading historical analogy and an underestimation of the constraints of the nuclear age, to appreciate the disturbing effect on the Asian diplomatic equilibrium of Japan's emergence as an overseas military power with an independent nuclear force. Moreover, under conditions of American withdrawal the maintenance of an effective American alliance and of the constraints on the ally that go with it is much less likely in the case of Japan than in the case of Western Europe, since the convergence of interests and the bonds of cooperation are much weaker between Japan and the United States.

In short, it is unrealistic to envision unilateral American withdrawal from Western Europe and Japan without an increased danger to the security of these powerful democratic countries, disruption of détente and the multipolar diplomatic equilibrium, and a loss of American influence. The adverse consequences might fall far short of jeopardizing America's physical security, but they would almost surely jeopardize interests that the United States has come to value highly. Therefore, it is not unlikely that the United States, when faced with unanticipated threats to these interests, would feel compelled to re-intervene under circumstances in which intervention would be far more costly and risky than the maintenance of preponderance would have been.

6

The other alternative to retrenchment without disengagement—planned and coordinated devolution—would entail some of the same disadvantages as unilateral withdrawal, particularly the disruption of the diplomatic equilibrium. But it would be intended to offset the temporary adverse political effects by supplanting American preponderance with new regional military balances in which a secure Western Europe and Japan would in time contribute their equitable share to a stable multipolar equilibrium less dependent upon American diplomatic and military intervention. Moreover, it would be based on the calculation that an orderly, planned transfer of power and responsibility that took place in concert with allies would preserve the mutual confidence to sustain the vitality of America's alliances, thereby not only preserving the security of the allies under the American nuclear umbrella but also retaining a modicum of American influence and restraint upon them. The objective of devolution would be not merely to relieve the United States of material burdens but, equally important, to relieve it of the political and psychological burden of bearing exclusive, direct responsibility for maintaining an international environment congenial to the mutual security interests of the United States and its allies and at the same time maintaining its allies' satisfaction and cooperation.

If it worked, devolution would fulfill the Nixon Doctrine to an extent that retrenchment without disengagement is unlikely to achieve. In Europe the United States would be a more nearly equal participant in a truly tripolar balance instead of the principal manager of a largely bipolar military balance. In East Asia the United States might retire to a peripheral role in a quadrilateral balance dominated by Japan, China, and the Soviet Union. Thus the United States would find a role truly compatible with its professed desire to encourage allied self-reliance, without jeopardizing its essential military and political interests. Having abandoned the military-political basis of its waning tutelage, the United States

would free its own energies and those of its allies for the effective
pursuit of the more differentiated set of interests that are developing in Asia and within the Atlantic community and at the same
time find in the more nearly equal partnerships a more enduring
basis for harmony.

But will devolution work? Considering all the obstacles to
the creation of a self-reliant European defense community, how
could the United States encourage and facilitate a substantial transfer of security responsibilities to its European allies? It would have
to reassure its allies that the United States would protect them
during the period of transfer and at the same time convince them
that within a specified period of years the United States would
certainly withdraw all but perhaps symbolic ground forces. It
would have to encourage and facilitate the transfer and yet not
seem to dominate the process. Meanwhile, it would risk bearing
responsibility for jeopardizing détente for the sake of transferring
an unwelcome new burden of defense to its hesitant allies. Even
with the most tactful and skillful American policy it is not clear
that the European allies could develop a coordinated nuclear force.

Japan's assumption of full military self-reliance is easier to
envision in one sense, because it is a single nation, not a coalition.
On the other hand, the domestic inhibitions against such a role
are more acute and articulate in Japan than in Western Europe.
In any case, it is clear that Japan could assume a larger military
role only after an agonizing and possibly divisive internal controversy. Moreover, even if Japan were willing to incur the internal
and external political costs of military self-reliance, it is quite
doubtful that other states in Asia would seek or accept Japanese
protection in return for American. Certainly the Koreans would
not. Therefore, if devolution were to take place before an international agreement upon a reliable Korean *modus vivendi,* a
dangerously unstable situation would be created in that troubled
peninsula.

The political task of transferring power and responsibility
would also be much more difficult with respect to Japan than in
the case of West European allies. The American government would
incur a very heavy political cost in its relations with Japan and
also in its relations with the People's Republic of China and other
Asian states if it were to press Japan to take over the regional
security tasks for which the United States had been responsible.
For then the United States would be portrayed as encouraging
"militarism" and doing so against the will of "peace-loving" Japanese. And if devolution did come about, the United States would

have to reconcile itself to a much looser alliance and much less influence with Japan than it might preserve among militarily self-reliant North Atlantic Treaty powers. Indeed, faced with a nuclear Japan pursuing its own interests in a tripolar balance with two other nuclear states, the United States might be anxious to dissociate itself from political-military ties that could implicate it in confrontations and even armed conflicts incurred by Japanese initiatives.

7

The more one ponders the speculative difficulties of withdrawal or devolution, the more one tends to be content with the known problems of the present course of retrenchment without disengagement. The hypothetical benefits of withdrawal and devolution do not seem worth the risk of relinquishing the discernible advantages of maintaining a moderated military preponderance in the great centers of democratic power. Maybe the natural preference of statesmen and nations for muddling through with familiar conditions will turn out to be regrettably short-sighted in this case, but at this moment there seems to be no alternative course nearly so appealing. The Nixon Doctrine, in all its ambiguity, represents a more solid consensus about the future of American foreign policy than has existed since the United States assumed major responsibility for fighting the Vietnam War in behalf of the old consensus. If it fails and is supplanted by another basic policy thrust, external events will probably be responsible for the change. And certainly the international environment will be as full of surprises in the era of negotiation as it was in the era of confrontation.

NOTES

1 The consensus referred to here is not primarily the views of the mass public as revealed in polls but the views of the foreign policy "elites"; that is, the "attentive" public inside and outside the government that has a consistent and informed interest in following foreign affairs.

2 From the address of January 20, 1961: "Let every nation know, whether it wishes us well or ill, that we shall pay any price, bear any burden, meet any hardship, support any friend, oppose any foe to assure the survival and the success of liberty."

3 There is some sentiment, expressed in the Senate, for a substantial reduction of American troops on the grounds that present troop levels are unnecessary for security or the support of détente, that they place a disproportionate material burden on the United States in comparison to its allies, and that they

impose a serious balance of payments deficit. Senator Mansfield's resolution of May 1971, calling for a 50 percent reduction of American troops in Europe, was supported by 36 votes and opposed by 61. But assuming that this vote represents a significant group in at least one policy elite, the extent to which this group's view departs from the consensus is not clear. The dissenters disavow any intention to diminish the American political commitment. But although some argue that U.S. troop reductions would lead to a more equitable distribution of burdens in supporting this commitment, none explicitly advocates a major transfer of security responsibilities to the allies. On the nature and significance of the troops-in-Europe controversy, see John Yochelson, "The American Military Presence in Europe: Current Debate in the United States," *Orbis*, XV (Fall, 1971), 784-807.

6
Weighing the Balance of Power

STANLEY HOFFMANN

1

"The end of the bipolar postwar world" has been acknowledged by the latest presidential State of the World message. Although it is elliptic in describing the new design for a lasting and stable "structure of peace," there is little doubt that the blueprint for the future is inspired by the past. It is the model of the balance of power which moderated, if not the aspirations at least the accomplishments, of rulers in the eighteenth and nineteenth centuries. It restrained violence (without curtailing wars). It provided enough flexibility to ensure a century of global peace after the Congress of Vienna, despite drastic changes in the relative strengths and fortunes of the main actors.

If, in the quest for international stabililty, this model is in favor again, it is not only because of the preferences of that student of nineteenth-century diplomacy, Henry Kissinger. It is also because the Yalta system is coming to an end. For many years, the world has ceased to resemble the confrontation of Athens and Sparta. Nuclear weapons have muted the rivalry. The universal drive for independence has made each rival's hegemony over, or interventions outside, his camp costly and delicate (on the communist side, it has led to the Sino-Soviet break). The very heterogeneity of a world filled with stubborn crises which do not let themselves be absorbed by the East-West conflict has made the cold war irrelevant for some areas and has dampened it in others, given the superpowers' reluctance to allow themselves to be dragged into partly alien causes and to let confrontations by proxies turn into direct clashes.

In such circumstances, the balance-of-power model is tempting. As long as the world remains a contest of actors without any supranational force, the ambitions of troublemakers have to be contained by the power of the other states; but equilibrium would be assured in a more shifting, subtle, and supple way than in the recent past of fixed blocs. In a world of several main actors, the need for a superpower to be not merely the architect but chief mason of global containment would fade away. Restraining a troublemaker would be either the joint affair of several major states, or even of merely some of them, on whom the United States could rely, just as Britain could often rely on the continental powers stalemating one another. The small nations would find security, not in submission to a leader, or in a neutralist shelter, but in the balance of power itself, which would allow them to pursue more actively their interests within its less constraining limits.

Thus, mobility would return to the scene. A new age of diplomacy (and perhaps of its traditional concomitant, international law) would begin. Muted bipolarity has subjected the United States to maximum exertions and minimum results, or at least maximum constraints. The new system would provide two remedies for frustration: the political corrective of self-restraint, and the psychological compensation of openly pursuing one's national interest without having either to subordinate it to the solidarity, or to wrap it in the priorities, of one's camp. The United States would again be able to choose when, where, and whether to intervene at all. Therefore it could concentrate on the long-range, instead of rushing from the pressing to the urgent.

The President's reports and statements point to a pentagonal system in which the United States, the Soviet Union, China, Japan, and Western Europe would be the main actors. This vision raises three sets of questions. Is the United States, as a society and as a state, willing and able to pursue such a policy? Does the world of the last third of the twentieth century lend itself to a system based on the model of European cabinet diplomacy? If the answer to these questions should be no, what ought to be the alternative? I have dealt elsewhere with the first question.[1] This article addresses itself to the second question and only inferentially to the third. Since it is a critical exercise, two preliminary caveats are in order. First, this essay does not state that the new policy is a simple resurrection of the European balance of power. It examines the features of the present world that do not lend themselves to any direct transposition. It also asks whether recent United States tactics contribute to the advent of that moderate structure called for by its leaders. Second, it does not deny that the ends of international moderation and American self-restraint are highly desirable. It wonders whether they are likely to be delivered through the means of the balance. Indeed, are these ends themselves entirely compatible?

2

To use Raymond Aron's terms, the balance of power is a model of "strategic-diplomatic behavior." The essence of international relations is seen as a contest of states on a chessboard on which the players try to maximize their power at each other's expense, and on which the possibility of war makes military potential and might the chief criteria of power. This view still fits much of the "game of nations," for it follows from the logic of a decentralized milieu, whatever the specific nature of the units of the social and economic systems which they embody.

For such a game to be played according to the rules of the balance, various conditions had, in the past, to be met. First, there had to be a number of major actors superior to two—it usually was around five or six—of comparable if not equal power. Today's distribution of power among the top actors is quite different. Only two states are actual world powers, involved in most of the globe, indispensable for all important settlements. China is still mainly a regional power, more concerned with breaking out of encirclement than with active involvement outside. While Chinese leaders assert that China will never want to become a superpower, there is no way of predicting that this will indeed be the case. Even if both dogma and growing power should push Peking toward a global role, given its internal problems the transition will be long, and China is bound to remain in the meantime a potential superpower, *i.e.* a major player presently limited in scope but exerting considerable attraction globally.

As for the other two "poles," they do not exist at all. Both Japan and Western Europe are military dependents of the United States. Neither, despite huge economic power, behaves on the strategic-diplomatic chessboard as if it intended to play a world role under the American nuclear umbrella. Japan, so far, does not have even a clear regional policy. Western Europe, so far, is a promise, not a real political entity. The current *relance* of its integration was made possible by a kind of tacit agreement to reverse the Gaullist order of priorities and to put the economic, monetary, and institutional tasks of enlarged community-building ahead of the painful and divisive ones of foreign policy and defense coordination. In the traditional arena of world politics, pentagonal polycentrism does not yet exist. It would have to be created. Can it be?

A second condition for the functioning of the balance-of-power system in the past was the presence of a central balancing mechanism: the ability of several of the main actors to coalesce in order to deter or to blunt the expansion of one or more powers. This corresponds to two fundamental realities. One was the inability of any one power to annihilate any other; the other was the usefulness of force. Aggressively, force was a productive instrument of expansion; preventively or repressively, the call to arms against a troublemaker served as the moment of truth. The invention of nuclear weapons and their present distribution have thoroughly transformed the situation. The resort to nuclear weapons can obviously not be a balancing technique. Indeed, the central mechanism's purpose is the *avoidance* of nuclear conflict, the adjournment *sine die* of the moment of nuclear truth.

The central mechanism of deterrence is likely to remain for a long time bipolar. Only the United States and the Soviet Union have the capacity to annihilate each other—a capacity distinct from that which France, Britain and China possess, of severely wounding a superpower but suffering either total or unbearable destruction in return. Only the superpowers can deter each other, not merely from nuclear but also from large-scale conventional war, and from the nuclear blackmail of third parties. Their advance over other nuclear powers remains enormous, quantitatively and qualitatively. It is doubtful that Peking could find the indispensable shortcuts to catch up with Moscow and Washington. Nor is a nuclear Japan likely to outstrip the Americans and the Russians; political and psychological inhibitions in the Japanese polity are likely to delay, for a while at least, a decision to join the nuclear race, and to limit the scope of an eventual nuclear effort. Western Europe continues to have an internal problem not unlike that of squaring a vicious circle. Mr. Heath may prudently prod Mr. Pompidou toward nuclear cooperation. But Britain's special nuclear relationship to Washington, plus Gaullist doctrine, are obstacles even to that modest proposal. A genuine "West European" deterrent would require a central political and military process of decision, of which there are no traces: nor is there a willingness by Bonn to consecrate the Franco-British nuclear duopoly or a willingness by London and Paris to include Bonn. This problem, unresolved within NATO, risks being insoluble here too.

A pentagon of nuclear powers is not desirable, and could be dangerous. It is not necessary: the deterrence of nuclear war is not a matter of coalitions. What deters Moscow, or Peking, from nuclear war is the certainty of destruction. To add the potential nuclear strength of a Japanese or of a West European strategic force to that of the United States may theoretically complicate an aggressor's calculations, but it does not change the picture. One might, of course, object with the familiar argument according to which nuclear parity between the superpowers vitiates the U.S. guarantee: would the United States risk its own destruction for the protection of Paris or Tokyo? Granted that coalitions are not important, is not the deterrence of nuclear war, nuclear blackmail, and large-scale conventional attack likely only if the most tempting targets develop their own deterrents? To this, there are three replies.

First, there is never much point in desiring the improbable. For a long time, if not forever, the inferiority of Japan's and Western Europe's nuclear forces would be such that deterrence could not be assured by them alone. At the nuclear level, the United States could not expect to play the role of non-engaged holders of the balance which theorists have described as Britain's in the past centuries. Only the two superpowers would have the capacity—if not the will—to declare that certain positions are vital to their interests, and protected by their missiles. Other *forces de frappe,* even if invulnerable, would not have a credible protective power outside of their territories.

Second, the Chinese would feel threatened by a nuclear Japan, capable of dwarfing China's costly efforts, and the Soviets would react vigorously to any formula that put a West German finger near or on the trigger of a West European integrated *force de frappe.* For the United States actually to support the nuclear development of Western Europe and Japan, in the hope of being ultimately relieved of its role as nuclear guarantor, and in the conviction that the present central balance makes any Soviet or Chinese retaliation impossible, would sacrifice, if not nuclear peace, at least the chances of moderation and détente to a distant and dubious pentagonal nuclear "balance."

Third, a world of five major nuclear powers would be of questionable stability and probably foster further proliferation. Maybe five strategic forces of comparable levels could be "stable": each would-be aggressor would be deterred, not by a coalition, or by a third party's guarantee of the victim, but by that potential victim's own force. However, we are talking about five very uneven forces. The balance of uncertainty which up to now has leaned toward deterrence and restraint could begin oscillating furiously. Even if it should never settle on the side of nuclear war, it would promote an arms race *à cinq*. It is impossible to devise a "moderate" international system under these circumstances. Moreover, the very argument which stresses the dubious nature of nuclear guarantees to others would incite more states to follow the examples of Western Europe and Japan. In such a world some would have a second-strike capacity against each other, but a first-strike capacity against others.

In this area, then, the desire for moderation and the dream of self-restraint are hardly compatible. If the United States, in order to prevent proliferation to nations which are currently its allies, acts so as to keep its nuclear guarantee credible, the tensions of over-involvement will persist, and the world will not be pentagonal. If the pursuit of a more narrowly defined national interest, if doubts about the long-run credibility of nuclear guarantees, and if the desire for "burden sharing" should lead the United States to encourage nuclear proliferation, the result would be neither very safe nor conducive to the world of the balance of power with its central multipolar mechanism. For even if global peace should remain assured by the central mechanism of bipolar deterrence, the globe would probably fragment into a series of uncertain regional nuclear balances.

What of a return to a conventional balancing mechanism comparable to that of the past? It has been asserted that the very unusability of nuclear weapons restores the conditions of traditional war. But the picture is likely to be the same. Against a nuclear power, conventional forces are simply not a sufficiently credible deterrent. Deterrence of nuclear attack, or of nuclear escalation by a "conventional" aggressor, depends on either the possession of nuclear forces, or on protection by a credible nuclear guarantor. Even if conventional war provides moments of partial truth, ultimate truth is either nuclear war or its effective, *i.e.*, nuclear, deterrence. For Japan and Western Europe to concentrate on conventional forces alone would mean consecrating a division among the "great powers." They are unlikely to want to do so. But if they should, there would still be a qualitative difference in status and influence between the three nuclear powers and the other two.

Moreover, from the viewpoint of a conventional balance, a pentagonal world would not resemble the great-powers system of the past. All its members sought a world role. It is difficult to imagine either a West European entity or a conventionally rearmed Japan seeking one. Each one could become an important part of a regional balance of power—no more. This, of course, is not an argument against a conventional effort in Western Europe, which faces the Russian armies. Any such effort would have a considerable deterrent value. But this is a different problem from that of a central, worldwide balancing mechanism.

Under the nuclear stalemate, the logic of fragmentation operates here too. Would, even at this level, the United States be able to "play Britain," *i.e.,* to contribute to a regional balance merely through its nuclear guarantee? In the West European case, nothing short of a disintegration of the Soviet Union—or the most drastic and unlikely mutual and balanced force reductions—is likely to make purely West European conventional forces comparable to Soviet and East European armies in the near future. Even if one believes that somewhat lower conventional forces in Western Europe *plus* the U.S. nuclear guarantee equal a credible deterrent, the plausibility of the guarantee will continue to depend on at least some U.S. presence, in the form of troops or tactical nuclear forces.

In the case of Japan, there is a difference, obviously. The main issue is not the deterrence of an invasion; a strong Japan could theoretically replace the United States as a balancer of Chinese or Soviet conventional designs in East Asia. But third parties—especially our former Asian outposts—may not want to be protected from one or another communist plague by what they might consider the Japanese cholera. As long as there are strong defense ties between Japan and the United States, a Japanese conventional rearmament would lead to complications for us. If we should loosen those ties in order to avoid these strains and to let an East Asian balance operate without us, we would encourage nuclear proliferation, and a loss of influence. On the conventional front, in Western Europe, the desirable is not likely; in East Asia, the likely is not desirable.

On this front, in the coming international system, three phenomena will manifest themselves. First, only the two superpowers are likely to remain, for a long time, capable of sending forces and supplies to distant parts of the globe. The world conceived as a single theater of military calculations and operations is likely to remain bipolar.

Second, as long as the fear of a nuclear disaster obliges the superpowers to avoid military provocation and direct armed clashes, and as long as China, Western Europe, and Japan remain endowed only with modest conventional means and largely neutralized militarily by their very connection to the central nuclear balance of deterrence, other states, equipped or protected by a superpower and in pursuit of objectives vital to them, will be able to provoke their own "moment of truth" and to build themselves up as regional centers of military power, as Israel has done in the Middle East, or North Vietnam in Southeast Asia. A coalition of states with great power but limited stakes is not enough to stop a local player with limited power but huge stakes. For the superpowers and for such local players, conventional force used outside their borders still has considerable productivity (although, paradoxically, the superpowers can use such force only in small doses or in limited spheres). For the other "poles" of the pentagon, however, the greatest utility of conventional force is likely to be negative: its contribution to deterrence.

Third, the fragmentation which results both from the impact of nuclear weapons on world politics and from the regional nature of two, if not three, of the points of the pentagon, suggests that a future conventional balance of power will have to be regionalized some more. A strong Japan and a strong Western Europe are unlikely to ensure a sufficient balance in the Middle East or in South Asia, or even in Southeast Asia and the Western Pacific.

Nuclear weapons have not abolished war; they have displaced it. The central mechanism of the past was aimed at the problem of large military interventions by a main actor. Now, whether they succeed depends less on a global mechanism than on a local one. No amount of coalition-building would have saved Czechoslovakia. No adversary coalition could have prevented the United States from moving into the Vietnam quagmire. Moreover, due to the fear of escalation, much of international politics on the diplomatic-strategic chessboard becomes a game of influence—less violent but more intense. There is an art of knowing how to deploy force rather than to use it, how to exploit internal circumstances in order to dislodge a rival. The traditional balancing mechanism may perhaps still function where the stakes are influence, not conquest; for military strength in an area can deter or restrict the subtle access which influence requires. A strong Western Europe associated with the United States would be guaranteed against "finlandization," for instance. However, there are complications even here. A coalition aimed at stopping a great power may actually goad it into "leaping" over the coalition, and leaning on local parties determined to preserve their own freedom of maneuver (a U.S.–Chinese coalition in Asia is not sure to stop Soviet influence). Also, if much depends on the internal circumstances in the area, neither military build-ups nor coalitions may compensate for local weakness. Anyhow, moderation at a global or even at regional levels is compatible with occasional setbacks.

The traditional mechanism is too gross for the modern variety of the old game. Also, its logic is a logic of arms races, nuclear or conventional. A game of influence partly played out with weapons supplies, in a world in which many statesmen continue to see in force the only effective way of reaching vital goals, risks leading to multiple wars. In past centuries, global moderation was compatible with such explosions; in a nuclear world, are they certain to be as limited as, and more localized than, before? Does the need for moderation not point both toward the preservation of the super-powers' nuclear stalemate and toward more arms-control agreements to prevent unilateral breakthroughs and competitive escalations into the absurd; toward both a multiplication of regional balances of power and regional arms-control systems?

3

A third requirement for an effective balance of power used to be the existence of a common language and code of behavior among the major actors. This did not mean identical régimes, or the complete insulation of foreign policy from domestic politics, or a code of cooperation. But the existence of a diplomatic *Internationale* reduced misperceptions, if not miscalculations. In the nineteenth century, it provided for congresses and conferences that proved the existence of a European Concert, however dissonant.

Today, summits too are fragmentary. To be sure, the imperative of avoiding destruction, and the need to meet internal demands inject into the major powers such a dose of "pragmatism" that the purely ideological ingredient of their diplomacy, or of their rhetoric, or both, has spectacularly declined. But we are still very far from a common language. Even a tacit code prescribing how to handle conflicts, how to avoid or resolve crises, how to climb down from high horses, and how to save one another's face remains problematic for several reasons.

First, there is one important residue of ideology: the Sino-Soviet conflict, based largely on conflicts of interest but deepened and embittered by mutual charges of heresy. The United States can enjoy friendlier relations with either communist state than Moscow can have with Peking, and our détente with one may help to improve our relations with the other. But this does not suffice to bring about a moderate balance of power. To manipulate that animosity so as to benefit from it while avoiding getting entangled in it may require diplomatic skills far in excess of ours. Moreover, however much their mutual hatred softens their tone toward us, each one is likely to try to manipulate us against the other, and neither can reduce his hostility toward us too much—especially in so far as support of third parties against us is concerned—out of fear of opening the field to his rival.

Next, however much we may congratulate ourselves on having kept great-power conflicts under control and on negotiating with Moscow and Peking without ideological blinders, neither capital subscribes to a code of general self-restraint. An effective balance of power requires either agreements on spheres of influence and dividing lines, or hands-off arrangements neutralizing or internationalizing certain areas. Today, some spheres of influence are being respected: the Soviets' in Eastern Europe, ours in Latin America. Black Africa appears to be, in effect, neutralized. But Moscow and Peking both apply to the world a conceptual framework that dictates the exploitation of capitalist weaknesses and contradictions. Régimes in which the state not only controls but molds the society are better at granting priority to foreign affairs than régimes in which the impulses of the society actually control the state's freedom of action. The heterogeneity of many nations split along ethnic, class, or ideological lines, which would make it impossible even for an angelic diplomacy dedicated to the principle of nonintervention to carry out its intentions, offers irresistible opportunities for diplomacies tied to a strategic (which does not mean necessarily warlike) vision of politics and to a dynamic reading of history. Khrushchev's proclamation of the "non-inevitability of war" was a landmark, but the less likely the use of overt force, the more subtly can influence be sought.

Those who, for years, feared a monolithic Soviet design for world subjugation were wrong, but so today are those who see in the Soviet Union merely a traditional power, or one interested mainly in the conservation of its sphere of influence. Prudence, yes; the simple preservation of the status quo, no. The very delicacy of the status quo in the one area where Moscow most assuredly tries to perpetuate it—Eastern Europe—the Soviet Union's inability, for domestic and external reasons, to separate security from domination there, the fact that the West cannot easily accept an equation which enslaves half of Europe, all this is likely to oblige the Soviet Union to keep trying to weaken the West in Europe, or at least to prevent it from strengthening itself. In the Middle East, in South Asia, on the world's oceans, the Soviets, without encouraging violence where it would backfire, and while supporting it where it works, behave as if any retreat, voluntary or not, of the United States and its allies, or any weak spot constitutes an invitation. This is not the code of behavior we would like Moscow to observe. But multipolarity is not Moscow's game, or interest.

Such tactics, if skillfully used, do not destroy moderation. But they test self-restraint. Of course, Moscow should be constrained to adjust its behavior to *our* code (and so could Peking if necessary), should we encourage other powers to fill the vacuum and to strengthen the weak spots. But we are caught between our own desire for détente and the fear that it would be compromised if we built up those of our allies whom our adversaries most suspect. Our rivals' game is to improve their relations with us in so far as we tend toward disengagement without substitution—in which case, our self-restraint could benefit them.

Two requirements for a new balance of power—relaxed relations with ex-enemies, and greater power for ex-dependents—are in conflict. Such will be America's dilemma as long as our interest in "flexible alignments" is matched by our rivals' search for clients; as long as their revolutionary ideology (not to be ignored just because their vision is, literally, millennial, and their tactics flexible), as well as their great-power fears or drives, result in a demand for security tantamount to a claim for either permanent domination where it already exists, or regional hegemony to exclude any rival. Whether or not Western Europe and Japan become major actors, Eastern Europe and East or Southeast Asia will remain potential sources of instability.

Multiple asymmetrics are at work, therefore, in so far as a common code is concerned. There is the asymmetry between the ideologies of the Communists and our conceptions, which envisage order as a self-perpetuating status quo, as a web of procedures and norms rather than as the ever-changing outcome of social struggles. There is an asymmetry between the active policies of the superpowers and the still nebulous ones of Western Europe and Japan— not so much poles of power as stakes in the contest between the United States, the Soviet Union, and China. There is an asymmetry between the untenable global involvement of the United States and a Soviet (and, potentially, Chinese) strategy that has to do little more than move into the crumbling positions on our front lines, or jump across into the rotting ones in the rear. Order and moderation used to be organic attributes of the international system, corresponding to domestic conditions within the main states, as well as to the horizontal ties between their diplomatic corps and codes. Tomorrow order and moderation will be more complex and mechanical, corresponding to the necessities of survival and to the price of opportunity.

A fourth condition for an effective balance-of-power system had to do with the international hierarchy. While the world was a much wider field in days of slow communications, the international system was simple: there were few actors, and the writ of the main ones covered the whole field. In Europe, the small powers had no other recourse but to entrust their independence to the balancing mechanism. Outside Europe, the great powers carved up the world. Today, the planet has shrunk, the superpowers are omnipresent but there are more than 130 states. The small—thanks to the nuclear stalemate, or by standing on a greater power's shoulders—have acquired greater maneuverability and often have intractable concerns. Any orderly international sytem needs a hierarchy. But the relations of the top to the bottom, and the size of the top, vary. In the future world order, these relations will have to be more democratic, and the oligarchy will have to be bigger.

Consequently, and given the asymmetrics described above, for the United States to worry almost exclusively about the central balance among the major actors, as if improved relations among them were a panacea, is an error. There are three ways of making such a mistake. One is benign neglect; we have practiced it in the Middle East for a couple of years after Israel's victory in the Six-Day War, and again in the Indian subcontinent, during the months that followed Yahya Khan's decision to suppress East Bengal. This provides one's rivals with splendid opportunities for implantation.

So could the second kind of error: reacting to a local challenge in one's traditional sphere of interest in an axiomatically "tough" way—for instance, cutting off aid to and exerting pressures on Latin American régimes intent on expanding control over their nation's resources.

Third, it is a mistake to treat issues in which third parties are embroiled as if these countries were merely pawns in a global balancing game, instead of dealing with the issues' intrinsic merits and the nations' own interests. For it is most difficult to bring a theoretical balance no longer sanctioned by the moment of truth to bear on the local situation. To be sure, some important disputes among third parties, while autonomous in their origins, have become so much a part of the great powers' contest that the balancing game makes sense, either in the direction of escalation or in that of a settlement once the risks become too high. Such have been the Middle Eastern dynamics since 1970—when first the Soviets, then the United States, displayed increasing commitments to their respective clients, but also maneuvered so as to defuse the powder keg a bit. Yet this has not been the norm.

In the India–Pakistan war of December 1971, the United States, China, and Pakistan did not "balance" India and Russia. Neither America nor China were ready to commit forces, and a verbal "tilting" toward Pakistan, aimed at safeguarding our rapprochement with Peking and at warning Moscow, merely underlined Moscow's successful exploitation of India's desire to dismantle Pakistan and strengthened unnecessarily the bonds between Moscow and Delhi. The traditional balance-of-power mechanism, while enforcing self-restraint upon ambitions, depended on the opposite of self-restraint—the readiness of the great powers to use force. If the risks are too high or the stakes too low, the balance cannot operate.

Vietnam yields a similar lesson. We have not dared escalate the war to the point of actually cutting off all Soviet and Chinese supplies to Hanoi. As a result, our attempt to coax Moscow into "restraining" Hanoi, *i.e.*, to make of Vietnam a great-power issue, was doomed. Indeed, Vietnam, turned by us first into a test of misconstrued Chinese dogmas, now into a test of Soviet assumed intentions, shows that too much emphasis on the central balance and too little on local circumstances can be, if not globally, at least regionally destabilizing and destructive.

The proliferation of nations, like the impact of nuclear weapons, suggests a fragmentation of the traditional scene. The balance-of-power system assumes that peace is ultimately indivisible—although perhaps not every minute, as pure bipolarity does; more tolerant of minor shifts, it still sees any expansion by a great power as a threat to others. Our analysis suggests a greater divisibility of peace, and the more evanescent character of influence, as long as the central nuclear equilibrium lasts. What will have to be balanced, so to speak, are that equilibrium and the regional balances. Each one of these will have its own features, its own connection with (or perhaps as, in Black Africa today—but for how long?—disconnection from) the central balance. Thus, in the traditional arena, the *model* of the balance of power provides no real prescription, however wise the the *idea* of balance remains. Five powers are not the answer. What matters is, first and still, the Big Two, in pursuit of universal influence, and in possession of global military means; second, if not all of the others, at least many more than China, Western Europe, and Japan.

4

Not only have the conditions of the old game drastically changed, but there are other games as well. The model of interstate competition under the threat of force accounts only for some of what goes on in world politics. Two distinctions which provided its bases are being eroded. One is the distinction between domestic politics and foreign policy. The latter is often the direct expression of domestic forces or the by-product of bureaucratic constellations (some of which involve transnational alliances of services or agencies) or the victim of equally transnational waves or contagions—constructive or destructive—carried by the new media. These waves both prove and promote the erosion of the distinction between public activities of states and private activities of citizens across borders.

In the nineteenth-century balance, the latter provided an underpinning for interstate moderation, but they were not the constant or primary object of states' concerns (whenever they became their concern, the system deteriorated). Today, state policies are often impaired or inspired by transnational forces that range from corporations to scientists. Partly because of the importance of economic and scientific factors in a world driven by the quest for material progress, partly because of the relative decline of the traditional arena due to nuclear weapons, transnational relations raise increasingly important issues for states, and provide many new chessboards on which states pursue their interests, compete for advantages, yet are not the only actors.[2]

The model of the balance of power is doubly irrelevant to these new games. First, the logic of behavior is not the same. Although there is a competition of players for influence (as in all politics), and there is no power above them (as in all international politics), the stakes are not those of traditional diplomacy, and there are other restraints than those which on the other chessboard the "state of war" itself creates or destroys. Here, the threat of violence (however muted or diffuse) is of no utility or rationality. In the strategic-diplomatic arena, the central assumption of the contest is that ultimately my gain is your loss. My interest consists of either preventing or eliminating your gain or, should the costs prove too high, of "splitting the difference," or extracting a concession in return for my acceptance of your gain. It is not always a zero-sum game: at times, both sides can increase their power. But the perspective is still that of the final test of strength, which requires a constant calculation of force. Two powers cannot be number one simultaneously. Unless one is a seventeenth-century mercantilist lost in the twentieth, one can see that this is not an appropriate description of rational behavior on most of the economic and technological chessboards. The rules of interdependence, which condition the competition there, are not those of strategic interaction, which structure it here. The logic of the world economy, of world science and technology is, for better (growth and welfare) or worse (population explosion, pollution, and depletion) a logic of integration. The logic of traditional international state politics is that of separateness. One may, as the communist states still partly do, refuse to play games of interdependence; but if one plays them, their logic becomes compelling.

Here, quite often, your loss risks becoming mine: there is a worldwide transmission of depression, unemployment or inflation. Even when there is a test of wills—between, say, oil-producing countries and big oil companies—there is a joint incentive, often not merely to compromise but to "upgrade the common interest." A competition in fields where solidarity prevails because of the very nature of the factors in operation consists simply of the manipulation of interdependence. Even on the traditional chessboard, as we have seen, the old rules of strategic-diplomatic warfare are modified by nuclear interdependence, and tests of strength without the ultimate sanction of war become tests of will, at least among the major powers. Why apply the balancing model to new chessboards, when it falters on the old?

Second, not only does the balance of power not provide an answer, it addresses itself to the wrong problem. A world in which the autonomy of states is curtailed by transnational trends, drives and forces which operate unevenly, unpredictably, and carry political flags and tags, a world whose states' policies reflect internal wants and bargains, is permanently threatened by "statist" reactions against global integration and outside intrusion—precisely because, however sieve-like, the state remains the final unit of decision, and the more like a sieve it becomes, the more it may try to plug the holes. Hence a curse of immoderation and instability but in an original way.

It is not the use of force which is the daily peril; it is, literally, chaos. It is not war that brings the moment of truth; it is economic or monetary or environmental disaster. It is not the failure of the balance to work and curtail excessive ambitions, or the rigidity of the balance when it splits the world into rival, frozen coalitions; it is anomie. It is not the neglect or deterioration of familiar rules. It is the failure to clarify and to understand the new rules which govern the relations between different chessboards, the transfer of power from one to the other—these have only recently become major arenas of world politics: scholars are in the dark and statesmen experiment in ignorance or by analogy. Also to be feared is the inadequacy or breakdown of those rules, not of balance but of cooperation, that were devised in the past (for instance, the law of the seas), and the absence of rules of cooperation in a variety of disruptive cases in which no state can be successful in isolation—from the environment to short-term capital movements.

To apply irrelevant concepts is dangerous for general and for historical reasons. To proclaim "the primacy of the national interest" gives a free hand to domestic forces damaged or frustrated by the way these chessboards function, and encourages an epidemic of protectionist or aggressive measures. To use the logic of separateness in fields of integration invites disintegration here and discord on the traditional chessboard. Of the five "economic blocs" among which the balancing game is supposed to go on, two—those of our strategic-diplomatic rivals—are not fully integrated into the world economy. To treat Western Europe and Japan as rivals to be contained, just as we count on them to play a growing role in balancing our adversaries on that traditional chessboard, assumes that they will draw on it no consequence from our behavior on the economic chessboards, even while we use on the latter the advantages we have on, and the strong-arm tactics appropriate to, the former. This can only be self-defeating, for while each political function of a state—defense, welfare, economic growth, etc.—has some autonomy and logic, and each corresponding international chessboard has its rules, these functions all connect again at the one level that integrates them all, *i.e.*, a state's foreign policy.

Historically, what requires a new policy is not the passing of the bipolar era but the end of a unipolar one. The rules of trade and finance prescribed at Bretton Woods and by GATT were those the United States wanted; they established a dollar-exchange standard and tended toward a liberal system of trade, which other nations accepted in return for security or aid. The United States tolerated exceptions to these rules in return for immediate military advantages (American bases in Japan) or for expected political benefits (a would-be "Atlanticist" Europe, growing out of the Common Market). It is this system which collapsed with the monetary crisis of 1971 and the acrimonious trade quarrels between the United States and its allies. The problem is to avoid a fragmentation of the world economy, which would breed chaos as surely as, in the strategic-diplomatic arena, fragmentation is likely to contribute to moderation.

A single world system must still be the goal. Of course, in the new monetary order, there should be a modicum of decentralization. A West European monetary union, with its own rules governing the relations of currencies within the EEC, would be a part of such an order; a stronger and more coherent EEC would be better able than its members in the past to bargain with the United States for world rules of commerce, investments, and money less geared to American specifications. But this is quite different from a break-up into independent economic blocs with fluctuating relations based on nothing but bargaining strength. The aggressive pursuit by the United States of national interests narrowly defined will inevitably be seen as a naked attempt at retrieving the dominating position we lost.

The United States, which is the lynchpin of the noncommunist world's transnational system, risks playing Samson in the temple. The flexibility which the world economy needs is not that of shifting alignments and reversible alliances. Even in cases where the United States has legitimate grievances, the solutions cannot be found in the functional equivalent of the strategic-diplomatic game of chicken: reprisals and protectionist threats. Given the stakes, the building of a moderate international system and the goal of a "world community" (utopian on the other chessboard) will have to be made increasingly close. Moderation is a negative goal: organizing the coexistence of hugely different players. It has, in the past, been compatible with a variety of woes—wars, assaults on the quality of life, arms races, internal massacres, a vast amount of domestic and internal inequality.

But it is difficult to conceive of a future international system remaining moderate if there is so much inequality between its members and turmoil in some of them as to incite permanent fishing in troubled waters, or recurrent violent exports of discontent. While, especially in the traditional arena, sovereignty would continue to manifest itself through unilateral moves or concerted diplomacy (although rather more for restraint than for self-assertion), there is a growing need for pooled sovereignty, shared powers, and effective international institutions in all the new realms. Of course, a precondition is the maintenance of the central political-military balance. But American policy has tended in the past, and tends more than ever, to concentrate far too much of its energy on the precondition. There are two kinds of essential tasks: those which, if neglected or bungled, could lead to the ultimate disaster; those which the very success in postponing the "moment of truth," and the realities of a materially interdependent planet push onto the daily agenda. In a world full of active self-fulfilling memories—states which behave as if, despite nuclear weapons and the increasing costs of conquest, military might were still the yardstick of achievements, and by behaving in this way keep the past present —there ought to be equally active self-fulfilling prophecies: states moving on the conviction, so frequently asserted in words only, that on the seas of interdependence we are all in the same boat, and should worry more about common benefits than about national gains.

Community-building raises formidable questions of its own. Should it be primarily the duty of the developed nations, as some advocate paternalistically? Can an international system as diverse as this one function effectively without the active participation of all its members, even if one grants both the wisdom of "decoupling" the great powers' contest from the internal tribulations of the developing countries, and the risks of paralysis, corruption, or waste present in more "democratic" world institutions? Can community-building proceed in such a way as not to seem a neocolonial device through which the rich and strong perpetuate their hold on the poor? Is it compatible with economic spheres of influence? If such questions are recognized as imperative, then an economically and financially more cohesive Western Europe and a dynamic Japan would appear, not as "poles" to be contained or pushed back when they become too strong, but as contributors.

Yesterday's dialectic was that of a central balance between a handful of powers and imperialism, which pushed back the limits of the diplomatic world. Tomorrow's dialectic will have to be that of a complex balance, both global and regional, allowing for a fragmentation of the strategic-diplomatic contest under the nuclear stalemate, and an emergent community in which competition will, of course, persist, but where mankind ought, perhaps, slowly to learn to substitute games against (or with) nature for the games between what Erik Erikson has called "pseudospecies."

5

Faced with a world of unprecedented complexity, it is normal that U.S. policy-makers should seek a familiar thread. But they display a basic ambivalence. They aspire to a world in which the United States could share with others the burdens of being a great power. But they understand that self-restraint would be safe only if the game were played according to rules advantageous to us, and they realize that our favorite models and concepts may not at all be those of our would-be partners. And so they fall back on another conceptual habit, derived from the more recent past: that of explaining that we must still be the leaders and teachers of others, even if the goal is now defined as the balance, and the lesson called collective moderation. Between the desire for national self-restraint and the ambition of shaping a system in which our influence endures, there is a tug of war.

If we define, as the President does in his moments of exuberance or in his fighting moods provoked by Vietnam, our main goal as the preservation of as much influence as possible, even limited disengagement will be hard to pursue. For it increases the chance that one or the other of our main rivals will move into the void, especially in those parts of the world where our clients are weak and have depended on our military presence or on huge injections of aid. Our extrication from Vietnam has been slowed down by this fear of a loss of influence, magnified by the belief that a victory for Hanoi would encourage anti-American forces everywhere: as if we were still in the mythical world of bipolar battle to the death. Should voids be filled by one of the new centers whose emergence we call for and should these decide to play their own game, we could find ourselves as deprived of influence as if we had been evicted by our rivals (against whom it would be more easy for us to react).

Our very concern for better relations with our chief rivals argues against disengagement in Europe and East Asia, for they may well prefer a U.S. presence in their respective neighborhoods (and the strains it creates in Washington and with our allies) to the might or magnetism of their immediate neighbors. At home, within or outside the Executive, many fear that any further disengagement would open the floodgates to "neo-isolationists" or protectionists. Influence remains an incentive for worldwide commitment, a goal to presidential rhetoric about indivisible peace and domino-shaped credibility. In Western Europe, it argues for having the Europeans contribute to the costs of American troops, rather than for a West European defense organization. This "burden-sharing" formula pleases the Treasury, reassures the military, and seems a better way of deflecting Senator Mansfield.

If, on the contrary, we define our goal as devolution—the building of new centers of power in Western Europe and Japan—we are faced with a triple problem. One is their own long habit of dependence, their concentration on their internal problems or eco-

nomic growth, which have insulated them from world responsibilities. De Gaulle's failure to create his "European Europe" resulted
even more from the resistance of his neighbors to his global concerns than from their dislike of his style. Since July 1971, we have
often appeared to kick our allies into rebellion deliberately. But
that method of injecting pride conflicts with our ambition of
having these new centers tied to us, playing our kind of game. Up
to now, Western Europe and Japan have been far more eager to
develop their power where it annoys or hurts us—in the trade and
monetary fields—than in the military realm.

Second, our policy of détente encourages the West Europeans
(some of whom preceded us) and the Japanese (who didn't dare)
to seek their own entente with their communist neighbors; the
goal of reconciliation interferes with that of a more dynamic
diplomatic-strategic entity. The result, so far, is a postponement
of the defense issue.

A third obstacle is the hostility of many of our smaller allies
to a reduction of American power. South Korea, the Philippines,
or Taiwan clearly prefer our economic and military presence to
Japan's—a distant protector is better than a close one. Even within
the Europe of the Ten, some of the smaller powers may like
America's military presence better than a European defense community dominated by the Bonn-London-Paris triangle. All three
factors lead, incidentally, to one conclusion: if devolution is our
goal, and especially if we want it safe, with partners rather than
disaffected ex-allies, its forms and timetable should be negotiated
between us and them, not between us and our chief rivals, as, in
Western Europe, the linkage between the issue of American troops
and mutual and balanced force reductions dangerously leads to,
and as, in Asia, the moment and manner of Mr. Nixon's China trip
inevitably suggest.

In our ambivalence, we have attempted to get the best of all
possible worlds. On the traditional chessboard of world politics,
this attempt has been given a name: the Nixon Doctrine. To preserve our influence, we maintain our commitments. But we expect
our allies to do more for their own defense, and to count primarily
on themselves if their fight is against subversion. A limited recipe
for devolution and self-restraint, it raises two questions. One, will
our allies continue to accept our definition of their job, *i.e.*, will
they play, in the new game, the role we assign to them? Our reinter-
pretation of our commitments provides them with a choice. They
may read our doctrine not as a redistribution of strength but as a
retreat from the contest, feel quite unqualified to take up the assign-

ment, and define their national interest in a more neutralist direction.

Two, granted that they'll need tools for the job, will it be our tools—as in Vietnamization—or theirs? Will we, for instance, encourage them to develop their own defense industries? We have been most reluctant to do so. Our balance-of-payments problem has been one of the reasons for not encouraging too much local competition for our arms producers. So has our belief that we could have better control if we were the providers. This may be quite wrong. For dependence on a nation whose policy is not always clear, and whose supply of the tools may fluctuate according to domestic whims or sudden external shifts, creates the kind of insecurity that may breed accommodation with our chief rivals instead of "balance."

On the chessboards of interdependence, we have devalued the dollar, and the President's State of the World message speaks of the need for a new international monetary system that will "remove the disproportionate burden of responsibility for the system from this country's shoulders." However, our current policies seem aimed at preserving or increasing our advantages, as if to compensate for limited disinvolvement elsewhere. We have not taken steps to restore even partial convertibility. The world is still submitted to a dollar standard, and it is not clear that we are willing to subject the dollar to the constraints imposed on ordinary currencies. We seek a commercial surplus that would allow us to develop our exports of capital as well as goods. Allusions to the link between our role as providers of security, our demands for trade concessions, and the dollar's dominant position (which serves our investments abroad) reveal the depth of our ambivalence about the emergence of other power blocs. Should we succeed, because of Japan's and West Germany's continuing need for American protection, or because of the penetration of the British economy by the United States, we would actually make it more difficult to extend the Nixon Doctrine to Western Europe and Japan. Japan, utterly dependent on exports to advanced countries, would face a crisis; Western Europe, whose integration barely begins to expand from trade and agriculture to currencies, would in effect become just a free trade area, and cease to be an entity.

Should they resist our attempt to get the best of all possible worlds, we might actually get the worst. American tactics could consolidate the EEC. A separate West European trade and monetary bloc could challenge the United States and destroy the chances of a single orderly world system for currencies and trade. But at the same time, the emergence of any West European diplomatic-strategic entity may be prevented by continuing divisions among EEC countries, the hostility of their public opinion to military and world responsibility, the desire of most leaders for a détente, and perhaps, if confidence in the United States declines, for some accommodation with Russia in anticipation of American force withdrawals. The United States would only have the choice between a military presence made even more unpopular at home by the EEC's economic separatism, and a disengagement that would spell a major loss of influence.

Japan has greater freedom of maneuver than Europe. It is under no threat of subjugation, however diffuse, and is part of a four-power game. American shock tactics and humiliation could breed two equally bad alternatives. One would be a rapprochement with China but in an anti-American context (by contrast with Brandt's *Ostpolitik*). Japan would move toward neutralism and pay the price China would demand for reconciliation. However, this price would be high in security terms, and the switch would not provide an answer to Japan's commercial needs. The other possibility is a gradual rapprochement with Russia, and an increasing militarization—conventional or nuclear—due to the fear of Chinese hostility and to a declining faith in the credibility of America's guarantee. Such a policy might help "contain" China, but in a highly unstable way, to Russia's benefit, and, again, with a considerable loss of influence for the United States.

The worst is never sure. But to avoid it, we must face two problems: of tactics and of goals. Tactics are particularly important in periods of transition from one system and policy to the next. There are two kinds of pitfalls. Sometimes one lets the past linger on too long, as in Vietnam. Vietnamization, aimed at facilitating military retreat, has also made the necessary political concessions more difficult. The stated fear of a disastrous impact of such concessions on America's other Asian allies sounds a bit hollow, given the shock to them of the way in which we undertook our rapprochement with Peking. The other pitfall consists of acting as if a desired future were already here in order to produce it. We have, especially in Asia, moved as if the era of horizontal great-power diplomacy had arrived; and our weaker allies are disconcerted. We have, both in Europe and in Asia, behaved as if our principal allies were already part friends, part rivals; and they are resentful.

Never have consultation, clarity, candor, and coordination (as distinct from mere *ex post facto* information) been more important.

Henry Kissinger, ten years ago, complained that the Kennedy administration, in its overtures to Russia, failed to consult and to reassure the West Germans sufficiently. The same could now be said about the China visits and the Japanese. To be sure, the present policy aims at having the three major competing powers establish together (or rather, at having each communist power establish with the United States) the framework within which all others would have to operate. We are trying to teach our allies to swim in the proper lanes—this may be a reaction against their past tendency to leave most of the swimming to us. But they may sink, or refuse to swim at all, or insist on choosing their own lanes.

Is this merely a contradiction between high-handed "great-power tactics" (partially explained by our concentrated policy process) and the goal of a less exposed role in world affairs? Does it not rather reflect our hope to preserve our past eminence, although at bargain prices? Does it not show that our brave talk about "breakthroughs" conceals far more continuity than change? What we seem to want bears a strong resemblance to Bismarck's system. We desire, at the same time, improved relations with the Soviet Union and with China, the continuation (in perhaps modified form) of our alliances with Western Europe and Japan, an improvement of our economic position as compared with that of our main allies-competitors. Bismarck was able to have tolerable relations with France, and defensive alliances with Austria, Russia, and Italy. But the purpose of his alliances was limited to preventing France from building a coalition for revanche against Germany. They did not impose on Berlin the burden of protecting its allies against French aggression. They existed in a world of relative equality among the main powers, and considerable disconnection between *Grosspolitik* and the economic chessboards. They occurred in a century of secret diplomacy, when alliances were known to be passing affairs, and their terms could be kept in the dark without creating panics. Moreover, even Germany soon had to choose between the Russian and the Austrian connections—a choice that marked the end of the grand Bismarckian attempt at being both master and part of the balance.

Our current equivalent amounts not to a multipolar system, but to a tripolar one, with a comparably decisive but actually far heavier role for the United States. It is the United States which, in effect, protects the weakest of the three (China) from a Soviet strike; it is the United States which tries to hold the balance between Russia and China; it is the United States which attempts to contain each of these with the help of two subordinate alliances;

it is the United States which tries to retain preponderance in the arena of interdependence. Such a vast design may be wishful thinking. Having proclaimed the primacy of the "free world" interest for 25 years, the United States can hardly make its new emphasis on the national interest the sole criterion of policy, and its way of using the power it enjoys on some chessboards in order to preserve or gain influence on other appear compatible with lasting alliances.

Our policy actually entails far less self-restraint than it promises and much less multipolarity than it pretends. World moderation will have to be pursued through other means. Neither in the strategic-diplomatic realm nor in all the others does a "pentagonal" world make sense: there are no likely or desirable five centers of comparable power in the former; and while there may well be in the latter, the issues and needs there have little to do with a balancing of poles. As for self-restraint, given the nature of our chief rivals, the responsibilities of nuclear might, and the constraining need of a nuclear umbrella over Western Europe and Japan, there will be serious limits to its scope in the traditional arena. But our tactics of influence and instruments of policy are not doomed to remain as blunt and massive as in the past. Our goal should certainly be to build up autonomous strength in the main areas of the great-power contest.

But this does not mean worrying only about the "Big Five," nor does it necessarily mean a militarization of Western Europe and Japan. Western Europe's future offers possibilities of a conventional defense organization, which it is in our interest to encourage even by reorganizing NATO's structure. Soviet opposition could hardly be effective if these moves were linked to gradual American withdrawals in a context of increasing East-West exchanges. The failure of such an organization to emerge and to grow could breed a transatlantic conflict about American troops in Europe. But even if these should leave, and if West European military cooperation remained imperfect, economic prosperity and political self-confidence would be the keys to West European strength.

In East Asia, we have nothing to gain by encouraging Japanese rearmanent, conventional or nuclear, which could revive fears of Japanese domination. But the only chance of preventing it may be to provide Japan with real productivity for the power it has—economic power. Elsewhere as well, strength need not be defined too strictly in military terms, however important military might remains as an insurance against trouble. But when no autonomous strength can be found, we should disconnect ourselves entirely—

as we should have done from Vietnam or Yahya Khan's Pakistan: then, our rivals' increase in influence has a greater chance of being fleeting. In all the other arenas of world politics, self-restraint may well be a necessity, and would assuredly be a virtue. Here, we must accept, rather than resent, the shift of power that has benefited our allies, and find ways of building a community against anarchy. But here as in the traditional sphere, self-restraint, contrary to the hopes of some, will consist of a variety of involvements, not a promise of disentanglement.

Above all, let us not confuse a set of worthy goals—the establishment of a moderate international system, new relations with our adversaries, the adjustment of our alliances to the new conditions of diplomacy and economics—with a technique—a balance of five powers—that turns out to correspond neither to the world's complex needs nor to our own ambivalent desires. A "structure of peace" cannot be brought about by restoring a bygone world. Rediscovering the "habits of moderation and compromise" requires a huge effort of imagination and innovation.

NOTES

1 See *Foreign Policy*, No. 7, Summer 1972.
2 See Robert O. Keohane and Joseph S. Nye, Jr. (eds.), "Transnational Relations and World Politics," *International Organization*, vol. XXV, no. 3, Summer 1971.

7

U. S. – U. S. S. R.:
Prospects for a Detente

ANATOL RAPOPORT

I. THREE COMPONENTS OF CONFLICT

Some twelve years ago I proposed a classification of all conflicts into three idealized categories. I will begin by briefly describing these three archetypes and then will try to assess the prospects for a détente between the United States and the Soviet Union from three points of view corresponding to bringing each of the three aspects of the conflict into focus.

The Systemic Component. The first category of conflict I call a "fight." In a way, it is the most primitive type, characterized by an absence of awareness by the participants of the goals to be achieved. A dog fight is a conflict of this sort. So is the struggle between two male bucks for a female or between two animals for a disputed territory.

It might seem to an observer that the "goal" of such a conflict is well defined, that of possessing a female or a territory, for example. But we have no evidence of such foresight in nonhumans. The course of the conflict can be parsimoniously described by noting the stimuli that impinge on the fighters and the reactions to them, as is in fact done and experimentally verified by ethologists. The reaction mechanisms are typically "built in," having evolved in the process of natural selection because of their survival value. Contests of males for females in some species facilitate the procreation of robust progeny or, at any rate, of aggressive traits in males, which may have survival value in other contexts. Contests over territory prevent overcrowding in some species. It is superfluous to assume that the individuals of these species are "conscious" of the overall "species goals" served by their behavior.

An abstract model of such a conflict can be formulated to describe certain encounters between large, massive systems devoid of awareness or goals. An attempt of this sort was made by Lewis F. Richardson, a British meteorologist, who sought to explain the phenomenon of war by an inherent dynamics of arms races. Considering two rival powers or power blocs, each "apprehensive" of the use to which the other might put its military power, Richardson assumed that the levels of armaments of the two are subject to positive feedback interactions. Specifically, the level of armaments of one power induces a proportional rate of change in the level of armaments of the other. The other interaction, a negative feedback, is internal: the level of one's own armaments induces a proportional negative rate of change of one's own level. Combining these two interactions, Richardson posits a pair of differential equations, whose solution predicts the time courses of the armament levels dependent on specified initial conditions.[1]

The interesting feature of this model is that the system can be either stable or unstable, depending on the constants of proportionality governing the positive and negative feedbacks. If the system is stable, it can be expected to reach an equilibrium at some level of armaments. If it is unstable, it cannot stay in equilibrium, for the slightest deviation from any equilibrium position will evoke forces that magnify the deviation. Consequently, such an unstable system will be propelled either into a runaway armament race, which Richardson interprets as a drive toward war, or, contrarily, in the opposite direction toward complete disarmament and even beyond to ever increasing "cooperation."

On the basis of some admittedly very crude estimates of the parameters characterizing the rival European blocs in the years immediately preceding World War I, Richardson concluded that the system was unstable. That it was driven toward World War I instead of toward disarmament and possibly a united Europe was, according to this conclusion, a consequence of the possibly accidental deviation in the "wrong" direction around the year 1908.

The Strategic Component.   The second category of conflict I call a "game." The name derives from forms of conflict in which this type is most clearly represented, namely games of strategy such as chess or poker.

Awareness of goals and their paramount importance in determining the course of the conflict is the essential characteristic of conflicts conceived as games. In contrast to fights between higher animals, such as dogs or boys, emotive components do not play an *essential* part in a game. They may, of course, enter in an actual playing of a game, as when two chess masters contend for world championship, but they are not essential to the game process *as such*. Indeed, two chess masters locked in their herculean struggle need not feel any enmity toward each other. The object of the game is not to destroy or hurt or put to flight the opponent as an individual, but rather to *outwit* the opponent so as to achieve a situation which, *by common agreement,* is defined as a victory for one's own side.

Like the fight model, the game model of conflict has also been extended to a theory of international relations. It is the underlying conception of "classical" or so-called voluntaristic theories. The political history of Europe, at least since its political pattern froze into a system of national states, is conventionally pictured as a game of strategy played by potentates or by their chancellors. The payoffs of this game are increments or decrements of power or influence as reflected in territories controlled, allies attracted, later extensions of power in colonial empires overseas. The policies of these conflicts were worked out in the chancelleries through considerations not unlike those guiding the behavior of players of a game of strategy. Until the French Revolution, popular sentiment played practically no part in these struggles. The actual fighting was done by standing armies led by specialists motivated by professional competence rather than by "hatred of the enemy." Indeed, these specialists frequently left the service of one sovereign to enter the service of another, much as modern executives or lawyers leave one corporation to serve another. Conquered provinces, together with their passive populations, came under the sovereignty of this or that prince, usually without regard for their "nationalities."

The clearest formulation of this "realist" theory of international relations, which, as we have said, is based on the game model of conflict, was given by Carl von Clausewitz. Clausewitz's theory of war rests on a single fundamental assumption, namely that war is a political act undertaken to achieve political objectives. The theory is normative rather than descriptive. "Normative" can be understood here in two senses. In one sense, a normative theory deals with how things ought to be rather than with how they are. In another sense, a normative theory depicts how things *would* be were it not for the perturbations of essentials by nonessentials. The two meanings are related. For example, game theory, when applied to the analysis of games of strategy, is normative rather than descriptive in both senses. On the one hand, game theoretic analysis confines itself to the strategic structure of the game, paying no attention to the psychological characteristics of the players, their motivations, their attitudes toward each other, etc. In this way, the theory strips away the "inessentials" since it is concerned with the game, not with the players. Game theory is also normative in the sense of being prescriptive rather than descriptive. It is in a position to *prescribe* (at least in certain types of games) the "best" decisions to any player, always assuming that all players are perfectly rational.

It is important to note the meaning of "rationality" in this sense. A rational player is one who takes full cognizance of all the information available to him by the rules of the game. This means that he is aware of the consequences of his and the others' decisions. Next, a rational player, although he is completely aware of the goals of all players, is guided only by his own goals, taking into account the goals of others only to the extent that knowledge of these goals permits inference about others' decisions, which have a bearing on his own strategies. Finally, a rational player is one who assumes that all the other players are rational.

It is as important to note what a normative theory of international relations conceived in this fashion would exclude as what it would include. It would exclude the conception of war as a "fight" governed entirely by immediate actions and interactions. Every war must have a specified goal. Clausewitz conceived such a goal to be "political" and his conception of politics derived from what international politics embodied in the immediately preceding historical period, the period of "cabinet wars" fought for modest gains—to conquer a province, to settle a dynastic squabble, to discharge an obligation to an ally in order to assure his cooperation in a future war, to gain a more easily defensible frontier, etc. All these "classical" instances of *casus belli* can be reduced to a single common denominator—the distribution of a conservative abstract commodity called power.

The Ideological Component.   In the game model of conflict, the ideological component is entirely absent. The goals of "opponents" in Clausewitz's game model of international conflict are entirely similar. "I want what my brother wants," Emperor Charles V is is said to have remarked with grim humor, "namely the City of Milan."

Emphasis on the ideological component is the essential feature of the third category of conflict, which I call a "debate." To be sure, the so-called religious wars, which would come under this category, were conducted mostly as massacres rather than as debates. But "debates" have often preceded ideologically motivated massacres, as in the numerous ecumenical congresses of the Christians in which heresies were proscribed before the "holy wars" were launched.

The essential feature of a conflict originating in ideological differences is that, at least initially, the goal of the conflict appears as that of *converting* the opponent rather than of annihilating him (as in a fight) or ascribing to him goals, which, although incompatible with one's own, are nevertheless perceived as legitimate (as in a game). In the "realist" conception of international relations, justice is not supposed to be on any one's side. All wars are seen as equally just in the same way as business competition is perceived as just by the proponents of free enterprise. Not so in the ideological conception. The source of conflict is laid not to competing acquisitiveness but to competing world views. Not territories or trade treaties, but the "minds and hearts of men" are the prizes of victory. To be sure, the conflict that can ensue from incompatible world views may well be a power contest indistinguishable from Clausewitz's conception of war as "an act of violence intended to compel our opponent to fulfull our will." However, in an ideologically dominated conflict, it is assumed that our opponent "fulfills our will" if he agrees with us on what is true or what is just. Theoretically, a heretic would be forgiven if he returned to the fold of orthodoxy. The early phase of Soviet foreign policy was based on the belief or, at least, on a declaration to the effect that when all nations became socialist there would be no more international conflicts. Similarly, United States foreign policy after World War II was based on the principle of extending aid and friendship to all nations that adopted economic systems and political institutions similar to those of the United States and of resisting, by force if necessary, the extension of "communist" systems to new areas, regardless of their strategic or economic importance.

II. PROSPECTS FOR A DETENTE.

In assessing the prospects of a détente between the United States and the Soviet Union, I shall examine separately the three components of the conflict. Like every large-scale conflict, this one is not one of the pure, idealized types described above, but a mixture of all three. I shall begin with the ideological component. First, however, we must examine the roots of that component of the Cold War and its inputs to the conflict.

Sources of American and Soviet Ideologies and Goals. To what extent the foreign policies of the Soviet Union and of the United States were actually guided instead of just rationalized by ideological considerations is a question we shall raise. For the present, we shall only note that the re-introduction of ideological features into foreign policy in the twentieth century, whether sincerely or as a rationalization of conventional power politics, can be traced to the historical origins of the Big Two.

Unlike major European powers, which evolved in the course of traditional international power politics, the United States and the Soviet Union were *declared* into existence. Both were declared to be founded on new conceptions of society. Both broke away from the European family of nations which had played the game for the two and a half centuries since the last "religious" (that is, ostensibly ideological) war of 1618–48. Both were isolationist, although for different reasons. The United States did not grow by waging wars against states of comparable power, which would have necessitated recourse to alliances and the use of diplomatic virtuosity. It grew by conquering, decimating, and incarcerating technologically primitive, indigenous inhabitants of the North American continent. The Soviet Union was, from its inception, a pariah among the nations of Europe. After the clarion calls for a world proletarian revolution failed to elicit a response, attention of the Soviet ruling elite was turned inward toward acquisition of power by a vast, painful bootstrap operation.

The United States, after the conquest of half of North America was completed, surfaced as a power with imperial ambitions at times frankly expressed. For example, Senator Albert J. Beveridge of Indiana had the following to say after the United States' victory over Spain:

> We will not repudiate our duty. . . . We will not abandon our opportunity in the Orient. We will not renounce our part in the mission of our race, trustee under God, of the civilization of the world. . . . We will move forward to our work—with gratitude and thanksgiving to Almighty God that He has marked us as His Chosen People, henceforth to lead in the regeneration of the world. . . . Our largest trade, henceforth will be with Asia. The Pacific is our ocean. The power that rules the Pacific . . . is the power that rules the world. And, with the Philippines, that power is and will forever be the American Republic." [2]

One must, nevertheless, remember that in those days the assertion of the right to civilize the heathen was not considered a symptom of militarism. Militarism was seen in America as the vice of continental powers whose monarchs habitually wore military dress, where there was compulsory peace-time military service, where general staffs often dictated foreign policy, and where countries formed alliances aimed against one another. The United States had no such trappings. Its self-image was that of a peace-loving nation. Its intervention in World War I was perceived by most Americans as ideologically motivated rather than power oriented: "to make the world safe for democracy." While the purity of this motive was subsequently questioned, hardly anyone, at least in the United States, doubted that the United States' intervention in World War II was the result of an unprovoked attack by Japan and motivated by a determination to save a civilization from a savage assault by conquerors gone berserk.

As for the Soviet Union, there was even less reason to doubt that it was forced into World War II. There is no evidence that intervention in that war was even remotely in Stalin's plans. He was completely immersed in building up the power of the Soviet state by developing its internal resources. He saw in the outbreak of World War II an opportunity to continue doing it while the two "capitalist camps" bled each other.

As is well known, the wartime alliance of the United States and the Soviet Union was wrecked in a confrontation over the political fate of Eastern Europe, in particular, of Poland. It was the intention of the United States to promote "democratic" regimes in all of Europe and, according to American understanding, the essentials of democracy are embodied in certain formal political procedures, such as elections, designed as contests among candidates representing different political parties. These essentials are also thought to be embodied in certain guarantees of "individual liberties" like freedom of speech and press. Judging from the character of some of the regimes to which the United States has tended aid and protection, one may have reason to doubt the criteria by which a regime rates a membership in the "free world." But this discrepancy between professed and practiced policy did not come to light until considerably later. The fact relevant to our discussion is that the first confrontation between the United States and the Soviet Union was presented to both populations as a struggle for the "way of life" that would one day prevail on the planet. This "ideological" phase of the Cold War was the most intense and put its stamp on the nature of subsequent developments.

The accusations leveled by the American administration against the Soviet Union at he outbreak of the Cold War were at first specific, namely that the Soviet Union did not abide by the agreements made at Yalta (February 1945) in not permitting "free elections" in Poland and in other countries of Eastern Europe. However, once the issue was cast in ideological terms involving conceptions of political freedom, "way of life," etc., it became global, especially since the war aims of the United States had been stated in global terms, as in the Atlantic Charter. Thus the assumption of the role of "protector of freedom" (as seen by some) or of a "world policeman" (as seen by others) was an inevitable consequence of the ideological orientation of the United States toward World War II.

The role of protector of freedom makes sense only in the presence of a subverter of freedom. The Soviet Union, adamant on the matter of the political organization of the states on its western borders, was easily cast into that role. There followed the Truman Doctrine, which declared Greece and Turkey to be protectorates of the United States, and eventually the Eisenhower Doctrine, which extended the "protection" to the entire world. That doctrine very sharply defined the role of subverter of freedom ascribed to the Soviet Union. In a speech of January 12, 1954, John Foster Dulles (then Secretary of State) declared that local defenses ". . . must be reinforced by the further deterrent of massive retaliating power. . . . The way to deter aggression is for the free community to be willing and able to respond vigorously at places and means of its own choosing."

This could be interpreted to mean that if a group declared by the United States to be dominated by Communists attempted to seize power in, say, Honduras, or Ceylon, or Egypt, the United States might attack Moscow with nuclear weapons.

Stalin's foreign policy, on the other hand, was predominantly "consolidationist." Soviet ruling groups were overwhelmingly preoccupied with internal problems, not global ones. On that basis, the political conquest of the bordering countries can be explained in terms of old-fashioned security-mindedness, a concern for the "safety of frontiers." If American fears of expanding Soviet domination were genuine and if Stalin had genuinely wanted to forestall the wrecking of wartime cooperation, it would have made some sense for the Soviet Union to pursue a policy of reconciliation; for example, to bid for a compromise in Eastern Europe or otherwise to give assurances of noninterference in politics outside its borders. Stalin although frequently willing to retreat under pressure, was not the sort of man to make conciliatory gestures. With him, "attitudes," "impressions," "images"—feelings of either good will or hostility—were assigned weight zero in political matters. To him, power was the only legal tender of political deals. "How many divisions has the Vatican?" he is said to have asked when the Vatican was mentioned in a discussion of international affairs.

The successors of Stalin, especially Khrushchev, had more imagination, but the pattern of the Cold War had been too firmly set by the time that Stalin's death provided an opportunity for exorcising it. Thus Stalin's successors, too, were severely limited in their options for counteracting the effects of America's ideological crusade. I am now referring not to the actual activities of the United States that the Soviets perceived as threats (such as the encirclement of Soviet territory with air bases and missile sites) but to the sustained level of hostility maintained in American public opinion, which facilitated the maintenance of the menacing posture and of the burgeoning war machine. There were, to be sure, brave attempts, particularly on Khrushchev's part, to emphasize "peaceful coexistence" even to the extent of admitting that in some countries a "peaceful transition to socialism" was possible. In view of the tremendous importance assigned to ideological "purity" by orthodox Communists, one must appreciate the enormity of this concession, which, among other heresies, earned for Khrushchev the contempt of the Chinese.

In ideological matters, the Soviet elite can go only so far and no further. Every protestation of acceptance of "peaceful coexistence" *must* be coupled with an immediate disclaimer that on the ideological front there can be no peace. The ideologies of the "socialist" and the "capitalist" worlds must remain irreconcilable and the struggle must go on until one of them is utterly and irrevocably defeated. And, of course, there is no question in their minds as to which one will pass into oblivion. This is the meaning of Khrushchev's most often quoted remarks: "We shall bury you," and "Your grandchildren will live under Communism." Pronouncements of this sort, together with the endless vituperative repetitions of dogma, provided the most effective ammunition for the American propaganda machine and so helped maintain the climate of the Cold War.

It seems that the maintenance of the Cold War on the level of ideology, that is, with reference to "gut issues," served different purposes in the United States and in the Soviet Union. In the United States, it helped to perpetuate a political climate in which it was easy to undertake adventures and, at times, military operations abroad by justifying them in terms of America's self-appointed role as the protector of freedom. Also, anti-Communist hysteria was a reliable source of political ammunition for the Republicans, who were preparing for return to power ever since Truman's surprise victory in 1948. Recall that the crucial crises of the Cold War occurred during those years—the "loss of China," the Berlin blockade, the Korean War, the spy scares (the Russians "stole" the secret of the atomic bomb), etc. In the Soviet Union the situation was different. There was no need for political ammunition because there were no political contests. Nor was there any need to justify to the Soviet public the necessity for maintaining and building up the war machine. The public had nothing to say about it. The anti-Western hysteria, initiated shortly after the end of the war (actually in 1946 under the leadership of Andrei Zhdanov), was an attempt to exorcise the incubus of free-thinking introduced through the wartime contacts, however limited, with the West.

Prospects for an Ideologic Détente. What would it take to achieve "peaceful coexistence" on the ideological level? Assume for the moment (we need not be bound by this assumption) that both Soviet and American leaders really believe the rhetoric of their respective ideologies. That is, the Soviet leaders are convinced that the Russian Revolution ushered in a new era in human history, the beginning of man's emancipation, a leap from the "realm of necessity into the realm of freedom" made through abolition of the last exploitative economic system; that eventually the "working classes" of all nations will become aware of their destiny and will follow the Soviet example, after which mankind will be unified into a universal, cooperative commonwealth. Assume, likewise, that American leaders feel that theirs is a political system founded on individual liberty and the dignity of man and, therefore, embodies the most valuable achievement of civilization.

Suppose further (we continue to make suppositions that cannot be convincingly supported) that representatives of those two social philosophies confront each other in what I have called an "ethical debate." An ethical debate is one wherein the participants direct their arguments at each other instead of at third parties. Such debates hardly ever occur in real life. The formalized debates in court rooms, legislative bodies, and the like, are not intended to convince the opponent but rather to convince others—juries or constituencies, for example. How, then, should one proceed if one's object is really to convince the *opponent* of the justness of one's own views or, at least, to modify the views of the opponent so as to bring them closer to one's own?

The procedure I proposed for such a debate was originally formulated by Carl Rogers in the context of psychotherapy. The main problem is to create in the opponent an inclination to at least listen to what one is saying. The surest way of doing this is to state the *opponent's* position rather than one's own; indeed, to state it as eloquently as possible—better, perhaps, than the opponent himself could state it.

The role reversal is to be built into the rules of "ethical debate." Before being allowed to state one's own position, each party is required to state the position of the opponent *to the satisfaction of the opponent;* that is, until the opponent agrees that his case has been understood and well presented. Next, before presenting his own case, each party is required to state conditions under which the opponent's position would be justified. This can usually be done, because there is hardly a belief or an assertion that cannot be made reasonable or valid *under certain conditions.* If someone asserts that "white is black," one can make the statement appear valid by saying "Yes, if you are referring to a photographic negative." If someone maintains that the United States is a democracy, one can say "Yes, if contested elections are a crucial criterion of democracy." If one insists that the Soviet Union is a democracy, one can say "Yes, if total mobilization of effort aimed at increasing the future standard of living of the whole population is a criterion of democracy." And so on. Only after the contentions of the opponent have been "validated" by pointing out conditions under which they are justifiable can one proceed to the controversy proper.

This program guides the controversy into "constructive" channels. For the only grounds that now remain on which to criticize the opponent's position are that the conditions which justify it do not in fact obtain, or obtain only partially, or only within a specific social or historical context. If the attempt to reach an understanding is genuine, each may be induced to broaden his horizon, to appreciate the nonuniversality of his beliefs and convictions, once the validity *in the sphere of his concern* has been admitted.

If the basic idea of psychoanalysis (insight through awareness of the roots of motivations) contains a kernel of truth, then exercises of this sort could be extermely salutary. Ideological tolerance could eventually be taken as much for granted as, say, religious tolerance (in the context of ritual and sectarian identification) is in the Western world today. The question before us is whether "debates" of this sort could improve the prospects of a détente between the Soviet Union and the United States. The answer is, I believe, yes and no. Critical examination of ideological beliefs would, in my opinion, have no discernible effect on the state of mind of the leaders of the Big Two, because their foreign policies have long ceased to be guided by consciously formulated beliefs.

Wilson and Lenin were believers. John Foster Dulles and Nikita Khrushchev may have been believers. But neither Richard Nixon nor Leonid Brezhnev gives evidence of believing the clichés in which their statements are couched, and it is unlikely that their successors will be different. This judgment does not constitute support of the notion advanced in the fifties by some American sociologists to the effect that the age of ideology is ended. Every policy rests in the last analysis on an ideology. All I am saying is that the present leaders of the United States and the Soviet Union are no longer guided by ideologies that at one time made their respective societies and political systems what they are.

There are, however, still believers on both sides, although their numbers may be rapidly dwindling. A critical examination of the sources of ideological beliefs may further relax the tenacity with which these beliefs are held, and this may contribute to the prospects of détente, not because the present conflict between the Big Two is based on a clash of ideologies but because *the old beliefs are a source of support for the policies that keep the Cold War going.* The role of public opinion in keeping a policy going may be considerably overrated, but no policy can be kept going indefinitely without *some* public support, even in totalitarian states where, incidentally, public policies usually *do* command very impressive public support.

In summary, the benefits to be expected from a searching re-examination of ideologies are not those of reducing the levels of hostilities between the publics (these are already considerably reduced and can be expected to be reduced further) but in the deterioration of the bonds of unswerving loyalty of the populations to their elites. This is, in my opinion, a prerequisite for a genuine détente. The Soviet elite, however, is likely to offer most emphatic resistance to any exchange of ideas that may facilitate the sort of "revisionism" envisaged as a result of an ethical debate. As I have said, that elite considers purity of ideology the main source of its power and will not readily risk jeopardizing it. The American elite, on the other hand, would view exercises of this sort with equanimity because it does not consider ideological purity to be an essential pillar in the structure that keeps it in power.

Prospects for a Strategic Détente. In the last decade we have witnessed a change in the focus of the Cold War, away from the ideological to the strategic. It has become increasingly a game-like conflict with the consequent reduction of emotive and messianic components and the intensification of "rational" components.

Criticism of the initial ideological orientation of the Cold War was especially vociferous in the United States toward the end of the fifties. There was a shift (theoretically rationalized) away from the doctrine of massive retaliation espoused by John Foster Dulles to a doctrine of measured response. In view of the rapid acquisition by the Soviet Union of a capacity to counter-retaliate the massive retaliation, the shift of emphasis is understandable: now it appeared that the Communists, still supposed to be carrying out the Kremlin's orders, had little to fear from massive retaliation. Since it could not be used with impunity, it ceased to be a credible threat. The Communists could safely "nibble" at the edges of the Free World. The doctrine of measured response emphasized the importance of a capacity to wage "limited wars" which were pictured as putting out brush fires. Doubtless, the U.S. intervention in Vietnam was originally conceived as an operation of this sort.

Compared to the crusaders, the game-oriented strategists appeared as reasonable men, mainly because they raised for the first time the question of the limits of American power. Henry Kissinger advocated, in effect, a return to a Clausewitzian conception of foreign policy. Thomas Schelling, borrowing on ideas developed in game theory, called attention to the neglected theory of non-zerosum games in assessing strategic possibilities. A non-zerosum game is one in which the interests of the players are only partially opposed. To put it in another way, while in a two-person zerosum game the preferences of the two players for the possible outcomes of the game are strictly in reverse order (the more one wins, the more the other loses), this is not the case in non-zerosum games. Some possible outcomes may be preferred to others by both players.

A typical example of a simple non-zerosum game is the so-called Game of Chicken. In this game, each of two players must choose between two available strategies which can be labeled, respectively, "yield" and "do not yield." The choices of strategy must be made simultaneously. Thus there are four possible outcomes to this game, to which the following payoffs are assigned respectively. If both yield, each wins a modest amount. If one yields while the other does not, the player who yields loses a modest amount while the player who did not yield wins a larger amount than he would have won had both yielded. If neither yields, both lose a very large amount. The relevance of this model to "eyeball-to-eyeball" confrontations, of which the Cuban missile crisis was a dramatic example, is obvious.

A purely strategic analysis of this game leads to certain ambiguities. For instance, one cannot answer definitively the question, which is the "rational" strategy: to yield or not to yield? If "to yield" is the rational choice, it must be rational also for the opponent who, recall, is always assumed to be rational in game-theoretic analysis. But, if the opponent is "rational" and, therefore, is expected to yield, then clearly it is safe *not* to yield and thereby win more. On the other hand, if this conclusion is correct, the opponent may also have arrived at it. If both decide that "not to yield" is the rational choice, the outcome is disaster for both.

Another, even more often cited, example is the game called Prisoner's Dilemma, which can be taken as the simplest paradigm of the disarmament problem. The two strategies are "to disarm" or "not to disarm." It is to the advantage of *each* player not to disarm *regardless* of whether the other disarms or not. For, if the other does not disarm, then clearly one must remain armed in self defense. On the other hand, if the other does disarm, then one has an advantage over him if one remains armed. Here it is clearly "rational" to remain armed in either case. But, if we assume that two disarmed powers are equally safe from each other as two armed ones and that the cost of armaments is an economic burden, then it is clear that, although it is to the advantage of *each* not to disarm, it is to the advantage of *both* to disarm. The paradox is the consequence of the fact that in non-zerosum games *individually* rational choices are often *collectively* irrational, and vice versa. The advantages of collective rationality can be reaped only if either of the following two conditions is fulfilled: (1) it is possible to make an enforceable agreement to choose a strategy *jointly* and adhere to it, or (2) each of the two parties *trusts* the other to make the collectively rational decision and is himself trustworthy, that is, does not take advantage of the other's trust.

The notion of "trust" is absent from the conceptual repertoire of the "realists." Therefore, the second condition does not even come into consideration. There remains the possibility of "enforceable agreements" on matters where both parties can benefit. This is the principle theme in all the discussions of the past decade on the subject of arms control. It turns out that very few areas offer opportunities for making enforceable agreements. For instance, Herman Kahn, in his book *On Escalation,* has this to say about the problem of arms control:

> Assume there are two individuals who are going to fight a duel to the death with blow torches. The duel is to be conducted in a warehouse filled with dynamite. One might conjecture that they could agree to leave the lights on. There is undoubtedly powerful motivation for them to do so. While both are agreed that only one is to

survive, they would each like some chance of being that one; neither prefers an effective certainty of both being killed. Yet they might still disagree on: How many lights? Where? How bright? Should the one with greater acuity handicap himself in other ways?

Working out problems of this sort is what is most commonly understood by "détente" in diplo-military circles where United States policy is made. This is what the SALT talks are about. In addition, détente is pictured as a series of agreements on dividing the world into spheres of influence. Because of connotations relating it to a more frankly imperial past, the phrase is not often used explicitly. But whatever crises did *not* occur can be credited to the implicit recognition of "spheres of influence." Soviet interventions in Hungary and Czechoslovakia did not produce crises, nor did American interventions in Latin America. On the other hand, the extension of Soviet influence to Cuba did produce a crisis, and so did the NATO outpost in Berlin (maintained deliberately as an irritant).

It seems that the prevailing opinion in diplo-military circles is that a détente between the United States and the Soviet Union in the sense described is already in effect, perhaps has been in effect since the Cuban missile crisis of 1962, now more than 10 years in the past. It is natural for "realists" to attribute this apparent stabilization to the success of a "firm but flexible" policy. The role of the weapons of total destruction as deterrents has apparently been demonstrated: we have survived for a quarter of a century without nuclear war. The Communist world is no longer monolithic and, therefore, opportunities exist for some diplomatic finesse. The important thing is to tailor the extent of American domination (or influence, to use a more polite word) to a realistic appraisal of power relations and to limit it to areas where it would be foolhardy to challenge it. "Realism" demands also a recognition of where the *opponent* is going to draw the line. It is inevitable, therefore, that some portions of the world will remain under Soviet domination. The nature of relations among powerful states being what it is (and always has been), this is about the most one can expect in the way of "assuring peace in our time" by a simple standoff—a recognition by either side that it cannot destroy the other without itself perishing.

Prospects for a Reversal of System Dynamics.   Let us now look at the "systemic" component of the conflict between the United States and the Soviet Union.

Recall that from the systemic point of view a conflict is pictured as a process propelled by its own dynamics without awareness of "goals" by the interacting systems, or, at any rate, a process not guided by strategic calculations of "optimal" strategies. An analogy between the three modes of conflict and Freud's Id–Ego–Superego trichotomy may have been noted. Aside from the specific interpretations of these components in Freud's framework of thought, the trichotomy may be a useful conception in a variety of contexts. Certainly, there are processes that go on in all living organisms, including human beings, of which the organism is totally unaware —the constant delicate adjustments that keep certain internal states of the organism in a dynamic equilibrium. These can be said to constitute the Id. In human beings at least, there are, in addition, other behavior-governing processes—goal-directed and "rational"— such as mentation, problem-solving, imagination, planning. These can be said to constitute the Ego. Besides these there are still others, probably present only in human beings: the imperatives of duty, conscience, solidarity, identification with groups—in short, the dictates of ideology. These latter processes, entirely the results of socialization, correspond to Freud's Superego.

Can these categories be applied to "living organisms" larger than an individual? In other words, can aggregates such as tribes, cities, states, or nations be viewed as organisms with "psychologies"? An affirmative answer is suggested when we turn our attention to the aggregates of social insects. The beehive, the ant hill, the termite nest certainly have many attributes of an organism. Individual insects resemble "cells" even to the extent of functional specialization (production and procreation in the case of some ants; also defense). As with the cells of ordinary organisms, their activities are strictly coordinated and directed toward the survival of the "superorganism" rather than toward the survival of individuals. Because of the incomparably greater plasticity of human behavior and because of individual ego-awareness (probably not present in social insects), human aggregates are not nearly so completely integrated into organic wholes. Still, they do possess organic features in the sense of being more than simply aggregates of individuals.

Assume, then, that a nation state—say, a major power—is a "superorganism." What is its psychology like? It has a "superego" (an ideology). An "ego" is ascribed to it by political scientists of the "realist" persuasion. Indeed, the strategic calculations that are said to determine the relations of states to each other serve the goals ascribed to the state rather than necessarily to the individuals comprising it. (The fact that individuals identify with the state and adopt its goals as their own simply attests to the presence of a superego in the individuals.)

The nation state also has an "id." It is this "id" that is at the center of attention in a systemic theory of international conflict. Embodied in immediate reactions to mutual stimulation, this "id" drives the conflicting states, regardless of the goals that may be posed for it by rational, calculating individual minds. Indeed, the whole thrust of the arguments advanced by the "realists" with regard to foreign policy can be interpreted as appeals to substitute the "ego" for the "id" at the controls. Policy, the realists insist, as Clausewitz did, should be optimal with the view of maximizing success in the pursuit of well-defined national interests.

But how is this "national interest" determined? If it is itself determined by pressures emanating from the "id," then rationality will not effectively emancipate the policy-maker from the tyranny of "unconscious drives." (I am referring, of course, to the unconscious drives of the State, not the unconscious drives posited by Freudian theory.) The presumably rational goals will be only rationalizations of these drives. An examination of the origin and locus of these drives suggests itself as the analog of psychoanalysis extended to the "psychology" of the species *status bellagerens*. Such an analysis can be undertaken with the view of uncoupling the actions of men from the blind forces that may propel them to self-destruction.

"Systemic" peace research can be conceived as a step in that direction. In fact, the proponents of peace research of this sort often provide it with just such a rationale. They seek indices of international weather. (This is what Richardson, himself a meteorologist, did when he took armament budgets as a crude measure of the "amount of hostility" between rival blocs, and trade volumes as a measure of the "amount of cooperation.") The search goes on for more reliable indices composed of many factors. The assumption is that, if such indices are found, they can be watched, and controls can be devised to prevent the "system" parameters from deviating beyond specified safety limits, somewhat in the way proper measures can be taken when the bacterial count in the water supply or the pollution index in the atmosphere exceeds certain limits.

There is one crucial flaw in this analogy. Agencies entrusted with the task of, say, controlling the bacterial count in the water supply exist; agencies empowered to take proper measures when the pollution index exceeds prescribed limits can be conceivably created. But no agencies exist that can perform analogous services when a crisis threatens to erupt into war, nor can they be created as long as the present international system persists. Such an agency must, by the nature of the problem, be supranational. While supranational agencies promoting cooperation between states in certain areas do exist, an agency *effectively* dealing with war-threatening crises cannot be created as long as national sovereignty embodies the right to make war. For that right is invariably identified (at least, in our day) with self-defense. *All* wars are now waged in "self-defense," and this claim cannot be refuted as long as each sovereign nation defines its own national interest.

To some, the way out of this impasse seems obvious—national sovereignty must be given up and replaced by a world government. But this "solution" does not get to the root of the matter, because the insuperable obstacle to world government is precisely the obsession with national interest, which embodies, first and foremost, sovereignty and the "right of self-defense."

The "right of self-defense" is an abstraction. To impart concrete meaning to the phrase, one must examine the available means of self-defense. For instance, self-defense is recognized as the right of every individual in most societies. Yet, in most societies the individual's right to carry a deadly weapon is severely limited. Thereby the incidence of fatal encounters is greatly reduced. At one time, a person of noble birth, say, in Renaissance Italy or Spain, never ventured forth without a sword. When the right of self-defense was guaranteed to armed men, murder was a common occurrence. The important lesson to be drawn is that it was not because the Italian and Spanish noblemen were more ready to kill their fellow men that they carried swords; it was because they carried swords that they were ready to kill their fellow men.

The destructive potential of war is today manyfold greater than it was even one generation ago. Consequently, if total war breaks out between nuclear powers, we can expect a slaughter many times more severe than in former wars. But it would be wrong to say that weapons of mass destruction were acquired because people had become so much more bloodthirsty in just one generation. It is because weapons of mass destruction are on hand that some people (those entrusted with the task of planning the next war) envisage the slaughter at best as a regrettable necessity and at times with equanimity. (At least this is the impression one gets from the terminology of modern military science: "city exchanges," "exemplary attacks," "acceptable civil casualities," etc.)

In failing to grasp the autonomous role of the giant war machines in directing and controlling men's thinking about international relations, the "realists" *fixate* this thinking so that the most obvious questions cannot be asked.

Consider the following naive but sensible question: Of what use is the defense establishment to the United States? This question evokes an apparently sensible answer: to protect the United States from attack, especially an attack by the Soviet Union (which throughout the Cold War was considered practically the only serious "enemy" of the United States). If the same question is directed to almost anyone in the Soviet Union, one is sure to get a perfectly symmetrical answer. Thereby both questions are answered and the necessity of both war machines has been justified. The obvious question to ask is: Of what use are *both* war machines —not each separately, but both? This question has no reasonable answer because a possible answer, "to protect both against both," does not make sense, unless one ascribes suicidal tendencies to the *combined* system. Such a tendency may well exist (because of the internal dynamics of systemic conflict), but, certainly, reasonable men will not regard this state of affairs with equanimity or identify it with "security," as is done in justifying each war machine separately.

To take another example, consider again the two men in the warehouse filled with explosives, fighting a duel with blow torches (the picturesque example offered by Herman Kahn as an illustration of the difficulties and complexities of arms control). All kinds of intricate questions occur to people genuinely interested in arms control and aware of the dangers inherent in the "system." The one question that is never asked in those circles is what are those two imbeciles doing in that warehouse in the first place? Why does not someone take them by the scruffs of their necks, knock their heads together, and put them away someplace where they cannot get access to blow torches and explosives.

SUMMARY

In summary, it seems that prospects for a détente between the United States and the Soviet Union should be examined in three contexts: the ideological, the strategic, and the systemic.

An ideological détente is already in the making—not, to be sure, in the sense of a resolution of the ideological war by insights emerging from an ethical debate, but in the sense that the ritualistic character of the ideological conflict is becoming increasingly apparent in both societies. The reasons for this development are different in the United States and in the Soviet Union. In the United

States, the principal contributing factor seems to have been a massive repugnance against the Vietnam War, particularly among the young and the enlightened. In the Soviet Union, hostility against the power elite seems to be confined to only a small sector of the intelligentsia, and even among them it does not take the form of a categorical rejection of Communist ideology itself. For instance, Roy Medvedev, in his book *Let History Judge,* condemns Stalinism as a disease that has pervaded Soviet society and traces it to a perversion of Leninist principles. This sort of critique is coupled with an appeal for a return to a socialist ethos and for the implementation of its ideals rather than for a radical examination of the ideology itself or for its outright rejection. In contrast, American social critics do not usually call for a return to the pristine tenets of free enterprise or to an isolationist foreign policy, the historical underpinnings of American ideology.

In the Soviet Union, the erosion of ideological fervor seems to be simply a consequence of "bourgeoisification" of Soviet society. At last the tremendous sacrifices of forced industrialization are beginning to bear some fruits. These fruits are eagerly seized. The greater availability of consumer goods, apartments, etc., coupled with the large differentials of wage and salary levels, stimulate competition for well-paying jobs and for educational opportunities which make the acquisition of goods and comforts possible. It is these trends that provide some justification for the notion of the "convergence of the two systems," often advanced as an optimistic prognosis in American liberal circles, a prognosis that is promptly and energetically denounced by the Soviet power elite. On closer examination, the convergence amounts to little more than the growth in the Soviet Union of consumer orientation, of preoccupation with personal careers, of white-collar mentality, and similar values characteristic of Western middle-class societies. They are, perhaps, inevitable consequences of incipient affluence.

Still, the importance of these changes should not be minimized. They do portend an ideological détente, if only because it becomes more difficult to justify the continuation of the Cold War on the grounds of "incompatible ideologies." Similarities between the aspirations of Soviet and American citizens become too obvious.

When policy-makers and their military, political, and academic entourage speak of a détente between the United States and the Soviet Union, they usually conceive it on the strategic level. The détente is pictured in terms of the classical notion of a "balance of power," a realization by both sides that neither can extend its power beyond certain limits without evoking determined resistance by the other side. The dangers of such confrontations being now generally recognized, it seems desirable to define those limits clearly and to have them recognized by both sides.

The problem is not an easy one, because the limits cannot be obviously defined, for instance, in terms of state borders, as was traditionally done by European states between wars. Neither the United States nor the Soviet Union has designs on the national territory of the other. The problem is essentially that of dividing the *rest* of the world into spheres of influence. It cannot be solved in the way it once was when the Pope drew a line through South America, allotting all the territory east of the line to Portuguese plunderers, and west of it to the Spanish. For one thing, there is no one to act as Pope. Second, the modern "heathen," that is, the inhabitants of the Third World, are not quite as helpless as were the Indians of the New World. Finally, the meaning of "influence" in the phrase "spheres of influence" is not the same for both sides. Throughout the ideological phase of the Cold War, the United States insisted, as a matter of course, that all impending social changes in the Third World not to its liking were results of Soviet "influence." The Soviet Union, on its part, views all forms of aid from the United States, not to speak of capital investments, as an extension of "influence" by the United States or its allies. A case in point is the intervention in Czechoslovakia. In one interpretation, the intervention was undertaken on ideological grounds to prevent a subversion of political orthodoxy in a satellite state. In another interpretation, the grave fear dominating the Soviet ruling group was the prospect of the loosening of economic bonds between the Soviet Union and Eastern Europe which would have resulted from an extension of trade with the West, particularly with West Germany.

Whatever be the difficulties in interpreting "spheres of influence," some sort of tacit understanding seems to be developing between the Soviet Union and the United States about inviolable limits. To what extent this form of collusion can persist—for example, in the situation developing in the Middle East—remains to be seen.

Examining the relation between the United States and the Soviet Union from the systemic point of view, we see no encouraging sign of a détente. To be sure, attempts to stabilize the arms race continue. But the success of these attempts hinges on the ability of decision-makers to control the process, and this is precisely the assumption that appears highly questionable from the systemic point of view. The whole concept of stabilizing the arms race reveals the impotence of decision-makers to cope with the megawar machine. "Stabilization," in their way of thinking, means confining the function of the machine to that of deterrence. In plain language, this means that the continued existence of the two megawar machines is assured by the necessity of protecting both against both. The absurdity of this conception is camouflaged by the metaphysics of the "realistic" model of international relations. The decision-makers remain prisoners of that metaphysics not only because their roles constrain them to think and to act within its framework, but also because they could not have been cast in their roles without having internalized the metaphysics requisite for those roles.

From the systemic point of view, the power of decision is not linked with a freedom of choice. Only decisions within a certain range can be made within a given system, namely those in harmony with the resultants of all the forces operating in the system. Therefore, from the systemic point of view, the warnings by the critics of U.S. foreign policy against the dangerous influence of the military-industrial complex are only partially justified. That complex came into being through the coincidence of the interests—at least, of perceived short-range interests—of many groups, encompassing all levels of the society. Some critics implicitly acknowledge this when they extend the scope of the war-oriented sector of society and call it the military-industrial-labor-academic complex. In fact, it is difficult to see what sectors of the society are *not* included in it. Each group is concerned with its own "interests." Labor unions are concerned with high employment. Industrial enterprises are concerned with viability, profit, and growth. The military, being also organized on the pattern of the giant corporations, is also concerned with growth, because growth in the corporate mentality is associated with robustness and progress. Besides, the professional military man is not different from any other professional. He welcomes technological progress in his field just as the physician welcomes advances of medical science.

No one of these concerns is decisive, but all of them together add up to a mighty momentum, which no deliberate decisions, even at the pinnacles of power, can reverse.

The dynamics of this process are probably different in the Soviet Union. I suspect that a conversion to peace, once decided upon, could be carried out, possibly in the wake of purges of the sort that have often attended major policy decisions in that country. However, the decisions of the Soviet leaders are also constrained by the supersystem that comprises both war-oriented states. Thus is the parasitic growth of the megawar machine insured.

The success of a parasite typically depends on its ability to mask its "foreign" nature and so to escape the immunological defenses of its host. Perhaps this is why malignant growths succeed while transplants often fail, in spite of the fact that transplants might save the host's life, while a malignant growth eventually destroys it. Ironically, the transplant cells are rejected as foreign in the organisms, while the malignant cells are recognized as the organism's own. The megawar machine successfully simulates a beneficent function—that of "protecting" the society in which it is embedded. If the analogy between the megawar machine and a malignant growth is valid, the machine must eventually destroy its host. From the perspective of history, there are good reasons to take the analogy seriously.

Therefore, from the systemic point of view, a détente between the United States and the Soviet Union is meaningless unless the system dynamics that nurture the megawar machine are understood and means for dismantling the machine are undertaken. The understanding, when and if it comes, must be pervasive, not confined to an enlightened but powerless minority. Is this too much to expect? I do not know. The experiences of recent history have radically changed the thinking of Europeans on matters of war and peace. Europe is no longer a Clausewitzian system. True, European states still have military establishments, but these are mere adjuncts to the establishments of the Big Two. The thought of a classical nation-state war between Sweden and Denmark or even between France and Germany now seems bizarre. But in our memory the military establishments of France and Germany were zealously preparing for war which was expected with near certainty, and not so long ago in history the same was true of the military establishments of Sweden and Denmark, of England and Spain, and even of the city republics of Renaissance Italy.

We have witnessed the integration of Europe. The integration did not give birth to a cooperative commonwealth, nor to sentiments of affectionate brotherhood. National rivalries, perhaps even hatreds, still exist. What is gone, maybe forever, is *institutionalized* nation-state war, conceived as a *normal* phase in the relations between states and internalized as a realization of national glory.

One might, of course, point out that this institutional change was a consequence of severe blood letting, in the course of which the erstwhile power elites lost the allegiance of populations: at first, the hereditary aristocracies with their warrior castes; then their successors, the strutting demagogues, instigators of war hysteria. If power elites can lose their legitimacy only in consequence of cataclysms, then there is, indeed, not much consolation in looking forward to the demise of the present power elites under similar circumstances. It is not likely that civilization, as we know it, can survive another total war, and speculation about what will emerge in its place is vacuous for lack of relevant historical experience.

One can only hope, therefore, that the present ruling elites, for whom the height of wisdom in international relations is a stand-off based on a balance of power, will lose their legitimacy before the inevitable cataclysm occurs. By legitimacy I mean the power to elicit *voluntary* compliance. Under present conditions, this power constitutes a power of life and death over practically the entire population of the planet. This power is embodied in the tendency of comfortably situated people to do what is expected of them in the network of obligations that govern their everyday activities. The worker does his job, turning out miniscule parts that eventually fit into the megawar machine. The plant manager faithfully fulfills the terms of the contract. Getting the next contract is an indication of his competence. The politician procures contracts for his region and so gains the political loyalty of his constituency. The research scientist mobilizes his ingenuity to "improve" the effectiveness of a weapon of mass destruction. The bureaucrat insures the transmission and the implementation of directives. The policy-adviser analyzes alternative options, always within the prescribed framework of "national interest." The top decision-makers make their decisions, again in the same prescribed framework of the "thinkable." *All* of these jobs well done, responsibilities discharged, loyalties sustained, add up to the autonomous dynamics of the system. No participant can drop out without suffering more or less severe consequences, be it the loss of job, loss of satisfactions derived from technical or professional competence, political death, or literal death. Moreover, every participant from the lowliest worker to the President knows that he is replaceable. According to Robert Kennedy, his brother John was convinced that if he did not threaten war unless the Soviet missiles were removed from Cuba, he would have been impeached.

However, it is not primarily these dramatic instances of compulsion that point up the autonomy of the system process, but the routine character of the ordinary activities of ordinary people. The hope, if there is hope, is that the acceptance of "business as usual" will be gradually eroded, that the voices of protest and the voices of reason emancipated from ancient constraints will become louder, thereby making it more difficult for the system to function smoothly. Perhaps, eventually, the recurrent internal crises will produce radical changes in the collective mind that have been formerly produced only by convulsions and mass violence. This may happen if people will begin to see the systemic conflict along a different interface, as it were: not between "ways of life" represented by shopworn clichés of officially blessed ideologies, not between two superpowers contending for supremacy or "spheres of influence," but along the interface between entrenched power and humanity. A stand-off détente between the Big Two may bring that interface into focus. For the "détente" may reveal itself as a collusion between the centers of entrenched power to keep the system that sustains their power going, a collusion to defend it against the challenge of the powerless.

There have been historical precedents of such collusions; for example, the "Holy Alliance" of the powerful monarchs of Europe after the revolutionary convulsions of the French Revolution. If the powerless perceive this meaning of the détente and what it portends for the future of world politics, the lines of allegiance may be redrawn, and the erosion of entrenched power may begin in earnest.

NOTES

1 *Arms and Insecurity: A Mathematical Study of the Causes and Origins of War* (Pittsburgh: Boxwood Press, 1960).

2 R. W. Van Alstyne, *The Rising American Empire* (Oxford: Basil Blackwell, 1960), p. 187, quoting R. J. Bartlett, *The Record of American Diplomacy*, 3rd ed. (New York: Alfred A. Knopf, 1956), 385-88.

8

The United States and China in the Seventies

JAMES C. THOMSON, JR.

The spring of 1972 marked the end of one watershed year and the beginning of a new one. Not only did Mr. Nixon, who some years ago was deeply incensed about the loss of China (and tried to find out who lost it), actually rediscover China for us all; China also acknowledged our existence by receiving him. The President and his retinue came and went without incident—and seem generally to have concluded that it was a great place to visit though one probably wouldn't want to live there. Nixon gained much "face" at home for going to China—moonwalk acclaim; and China gained much "face" by his coming—from Peking's viewpoint, a belated exercise in homage and even ritual apology.

So, as I say, we have witnessed the end of one era, the beginning of another. And regardless of what happens next, nothing will ever be quite the same again in American-East Asian relations.

For whatever the consequences, Mr. Nixon with a Zen-like stroke cut through the Gordian knot of Sino-American deadlock (in Washington parlance, he bit the bullet, but to bite the Gordian knot seems somehow inelegant). He made a clean break with the creeping incrementalism—the bit-by-bit-ism—of his Democratic predecessors, a process to which some of us contributed and which laid a useful foundation, but was clearly much too slow. And whatever his motives, which were undoubtedly mixed, like most, he deserves much credit and hearty applause.

When Henry Kissinger shook hands with Chou En-lai in July 1971, and when Nixon did so the following February—as John Foster Dulles had pointedly refused to do at Geneva in 1954— those handshakes symbolically bridged a 22-year chasm of tragic and unnecessary hostility. The by-products of that bridging will assuredly force the region away from the stagnant, outdated, and dangerous bipolarity of the past: the U.S. and Japan versus the U.S.S.R. and China, with all others forced to choose sides. And they will move the region toward the geopolitical rationality and reality of a fluid but far less dangerous four-power configuration that can lead to a new balance of power in Asia.

In the wider world beyond Asia, the Nixon-Kissinger initiatives hastened Peking's long-overdue seating in the United Nations as the legitimate representative of "China." Rather than weakening the U.N., this has made that organization more potentially relevant, more pertinent to a host of issues, more reflective of reality. Indeed, it can at least begin to put the U.N. back on the map. Meanwhile, those who predicted that the Chinese would enter as shrill obstructionists—hair-pullers, shouters, and shoe-bangers—have been proved dead wrong; never was a new U.N. delegation more careful, studious, even punctilious.

At home, the Nixon-Kissinger moves have at long last de-fused a most poisonous issue in the American political bloodstream: the old debate over the so-called loss of China. And the de-fusing was accomplished as it could probably only be done—by a Republican President of impeccable anti-Communist credentials, immune to charges of "appeasement" from the opposition party, and safe from his own rightwingers who had nowhere to turn.

The President may still mismanage or misbehave, in Chinese eyes—in Indochina or Taiwan, for instance. The opponents of Chou En-lai and Mao Tse-tung may still temporarily gain the upper hand. And there may still therefore come a temporary slowdown or even halt to the process of détente.

But the unnaturally frozen power relationships of the East Asian and West Pacific region will never again be the same. As Cold War begat Cold War, so thaw begets thaw. As the ice breaks between Peking and Washington, so it breaks between Peking and Tokyo, and so it breaks between the two Koreas. This is the complex and potentially promising new reality of our curious new era.

Why has all this happened? What, specifically, has motivated Chinese and American statesmen over the past two years of groping toward détente?

My own answer is quite simple. The one paramount reason for the actions of both parties is *the existence and behavior of the Soviet Union:*

—For China, a traditional enemy, a dangerous neighbor (sharing a 4500-mile frontier), and an heretical rival in the fierce struggle over Marxist orthodoxy; thus, a source of real fear, given a million Soviet troops on China's borders and sabre-rattlers in the Kremlin well armed with nuclear weapons.

—For the United States, an uneasy sharer of world nuclear

power, one we face in an endless series of bargaining situations in efforts to avoid nuclear war. The question for Washington has been how to increase its leverage vis-à-vis the U.S.S.R. And one answer has been to develop relations with China, thereby persuading Moscow to be more forthcoming lest we move too close to Russia's Chinese enemy. This strategy has already produced results on such important Soviet-American issues as the SALT talks, a Berlin settlement, and trade agreements.

But there have been other reasons, as well, for the Sino-American breakthrough.

For China, there are what one might call cartographic imperatives: the map viewed from Peking. Closest at hand in Northeast Asia is China's most memorable and persistent enemy, Japan, a U.S. ally now revived as a spectacular economic force and potential military threat. Also in the northeast is that breeding ground of conflict, Korea, divided between an American client state and a rigid Communist regime. To the south lies the central piece of un-"liberated" China, the province of Taiwan, still under U.S. protection—and the only other claimant to the Peking throne. Farther to the south is Indochina, torn by an apparently endless war between American-supported states and their Communist adversaries.

In each case the answer to China's fears and hopes must lie in some sort of accommodation with Washington. But most central to the dynamics of détente, beyond the Soviet ingredient, are Peking's fairly recent convictions that America "wants out" of Indochina, and Peking's hope that Washington can act as a brake on the resurgent Japan.

Similarly, other considerations beyond the Russian factor took Mr. Nixon to Peking. By the mid-1960's, as a private citizen and traveler through Asia, he had begun to show a realization that a viable Asian balance of power required China's participation; and by 1969 that realization was certainly reinforced by the views of his chief foreign policy adviser, Henry Kissinger, a persuasive advocate of global stability through the creation of a balance among the great powers. In office, Nixon also succumbed, quite understandably, to the presidential itch for success in global statecraft: for epoch-making "deals" among the world's great leaders. And like his predecessor, who failed to bring it off, he further hoped to engulf a Vietnam settlement in some larger act of trans-Pacific diplomacy. China as one key to a Vietnam solution has certainly been a factor in presidential thinking. And so, needless to say, was China as an element in Nixon's quest for re-election in 1972.

In short, what we have seen are multiple motivations on both sides of the Pacific. And they meshed, belatedly, to produce the extraordinary watershed of 1971–72.

One might note, in passing, one significant side-effect of the watershed: the impact of China's reopening on China specialists inside the U.S. government, that corps of well-trained officers many of whom had long pressed for a change in China policy.

For the executive branch in general, the thaw since late 1970 and the flirtation since ping-pong were initially a somewhat mixed blessing for the simple reason that they seemed to force to the forefront the thorny issue of Taiwan. But for governmental China-watchers, the blessing's mixed quality was undoubtedly an asset. For it made China *a problem,* and therefore something worthy of high-level attention.

In years past, executive inattention was very much the norm. In the absence of diplomatic ties—no ambassador in Peking bombarding the State Department with cables on his clients' behalf—China specialists in Washington and Hong Kong were considered purveyors of exotica at best, sheer tedium at worst. Data on fertilizer production in Szechwan or on schisms within factions in the Cultural Revolution caused executive eyes to glaze over. Except on the intermittent question of Peking's possible intervention in Vietnam, China was a "room-emptier": its existence was uninteresting, if true.

Not so since the Great Sudden Thaw. For the first time in 20 years, China policy became a focus of prolonged Washington attention. A full-scale China policy review ensued.

That policy review initially held high hopes for State's gifted China specialists, and those hopes may yet be realized when service on the China mainland, so long closed, becomes available to a generation of younger diplomats who have pined away at listening posts on China's periphery, in Hong Kong, Taiwan, Singapore, and Tokyo.

Yet one intermediate irony of the Nixon policy shift is that China, long regarded as the esoteric domain of specialists (hence hardly worthy of White House attention), suddenly became so "center-stage" that the White House barely let the State Department in on the action at all. China, for the time being, has been regarded as too important for the professionals; it is, in the local lingo, "White House turf."

How can one best understand the significance of these recent stirring events, the Sino-American breakthrough and the Nixon trip? By putting them, I would suggest, in the wider perspective of a three-fold legacy of Sino-American relations. For it is important to keep in mind the historical context of these developments as we prepare for a new page or chapter in the 1970's, and as we attempt to project the shape of that new installment.

A first important ingredient in the Sino-American relationship is the historical legacy of American perceptions—juxtaposed against Chinese perceptions. If one reviews the record of America's participation in East Asia from the 1780's onward, when our ships first entered the China trade, and particularly from the turn of this century, one detects a persistent and paramount fascination with China as an object: as a potential source of wealth for our traders, from earliest times; as a potential source of Christian converts for our thousands of missionaries (mostly Protestant); as a potential source of customers for our manufacturers; as a potential source of Jeffersonian democrats and tutees, once the Confucian Empire collapsed in 1911; and, throughout, as a focus for our national itch to do good and as a receptacle for our alleged altruism. "To change China"—a missionary impulse in both the secular and religious realms—was the aim of significant numbers of Americans in the century and a half prior to 1949. And in the course of pursuing that aim, largely under the umbrella of British naval power, we developed a sense of our specially clean hands, our special benevolence, vis-à-vis the Chinese—concepts enshrined in our much revered "Open Door" policy of 1899–1900. The Europeans did most of the fighting against the obstinate Chinese throughout the nineteenth century, though our consuls cheered them onward, and then rushed in to demand our share of the results. And we regularly assured ourselves that, unlike the others, *we* were not imperialists.

To the Chinese, however, things seem to have usually looked quite different. To Chinese historians, Chinese statesmen, and Chinese observers—on both sides of the Taiwan Straits, on both sides of the bifurcated Chinese Revolution—there has been little distinction to be made or found among the Western intruders. We were *all* participants in more than a century of China's semicolonial bondage under the imposed unequal treaties, extraterritoriality, and gunboat diplomacy. Little matter that many Americans, like many Britons, Europeans, and others, had benevolent intentions. The Western intrusion was not divisible, and good intentions meant little in the overall context of Chinese humiliation and Chinese impotence. To be sure, there were times when one foreign power was preferred over another, usually in order to use one "barbarian" to restrain or impede the others. But a central continuity was the desire to get rid of *all* the barbarian intruders—to remove the semi-colonial shackles, to assert China's independence and greatness, at very long last. This China did in 1949, when, as Mao put it, China "stood up." (The last of the intruders were the Russians; but in due course they too were sent packing.)

I am surprised at how firm a hold the legacy of American perceptions still has on the best of us despite the glaring reality of the Chinese counterview. One of our greatest dangers today still seems to me a mix of sentimentalism, euphoria, and overexpectation as we face a reopened China. Such dangers, I might add, are hardly new to us. Consider, out of a turbulent history, one notable example: Washington's first Minister to China, and later China's Ambassador-at-Large to the world, Anson Burlingame, a bighearted and silver-tongued former Massachusetts congressman, who told his enraptured New York audience on a world tour in 1867:

> China, seeing another civilization approaching on every side, has her eyes open. . . . She finds that by not being in a position to compete with other nations for so long a time she has lost ground. She finds that she must come into relations with this civilization that is pressing up around her, and feeling that, she does not wait but comes out to you and extends to you her hand. She tells you she is ready to take upon her ancient civilization the graft of your civilization. She tells you she is ready to take back her own inventions, with all their developments. . . . She tells you that she is willing to trade with you, to buy of you, to sell to you, to help you strike off the shackles from trade. She invites your merchants, she invites your missionaries. She tells the latter to plant the shining cross on every hill and in every valley. For she is hospitable to fair argument. . . . The imagination kindles at the future which may be, and which will be, if you will be fair and just to China.

Not long after Burlingame's high-flown rhetoric came the Tientsin Massacre of foreign missionaries, followed by a quarter-century of antiforeign riots that culminated in the Boxer Rebellion. Sadly, nonetheless, the Burlingame syndrome has persisted—and persists to this day in our American intellectual bloodstream.

A second ingredient in the Sino-American relationship is the fact and the legacy of American intervention in the Chinese Civil War. To put the matter simply, in December 1941 the Japanese attack on Pearl Harbor threw the United States into a formal alliance with the embattled Chinese Nationalist Government at a time when that government had lost its vital sources of support and had become essentially one faction among several. By 1941, ten years of intermittent rebellion at home and aggression from abroad had gravely weakened the Chiang Kai-shek regime and had intensified its worst features: corruption, repression, resistance to social change.

Despite the clear warnings of our official observers on the scene, we proceeded nonetheless to tie our fortunes to the Nationalists in their doomed postwar struggle with their Communist opponents. We rejected early overtures from the Chinese Communist leadership in 1945. And once Chiang fled to the island of Taiwan, we chose to retain our diplomatic ties to his government and to reinforce those ties with military aid and a defense treaty. In short, by 1954 we had permanently re-intervened to freeze the unfinished Chinese Civil War.

We did this in part as a reaction to the outbreak of the Korean War, misperceiving this Stalin-sponsored adventure as a sign of Mao's aggressive aims. More fundamentally, we did this because of our ignorant assumption that the Chinese revolution was a Russian creation and that the People's Republic was merely a Soviet satellite, a "Slavic Manchukuo," as Assistant Secretary of State Dean Rusk called it in 1951. What we failed to understand was the far more powerful tide of nationalism that fueled the Chinese Revolution—as all others—and would eventually prevail in shaping China's future.

A third and final ingredient in the Sino-American relationship has been the more recent legacy of post-1949 deadlock between Washington and Peking: twenty years of hostility, ranging from the bitter fighting of the Korean War to constant American harassment of the China coast and the sterile exchanges of polemics at the ambassadorial-level meetings in Geneva and later in Warsaw from 1955 onward.

Despite the surface appearance of enmity and rigidity on both sides, it has not actually been a deadlock devoid of dynamics. Indeed, a careful reading of the record tends to indicate—and here I am indebted to the analysis of Michel Oksenberg of Columbia University in *Foreign Affairs*, October 1971—a pattern of policy "oscillations" between phases of militancy and moderation on both sides. In the post-Korean War 1950's, for instance, when Secretary Dulles attempted to impose close containment and isolation on Peking, China was in a phase of relative moderation characterized by the "Bandung spirit" and the Geneva Conference on Indochina. By the 1960's, however, when both the Kennedy and Johnson Administrations attempted small initial overtures toward the People's Republic, Peking was in a phase of relative militancy after the failure of the Great Leap Forward and during the turmoil of the Cultural Revolution. What is striking about the past two decades is how out-of-phase each power has been with the other, how little their oscillations have meshed. And what is most striking about the period in which we have found ourselves today is the evolving reality of relative moderation on both sides—a "meshing" to be used while it lasts.

It should be added that the process of oscillation has not meant a periodic return to precisely where one was before. There is, on the contrary, linear progress as well, so that each side moves forward, and breaks some new ground, in its effort to deal with the other.

So much for the difficult three-fold legacy of the past, not to mention the bad habits on both sides that derive from that past.

The question now is whether we can learn from this very troubled record that has produced five American wars in the Far East in 75 years (if you count our suppression of the Philippine Insurrection), most of them relating in one way or another to our deep-rooted China obsession.

My own answer is yes, if we understand the present watershed for what it is: not a magical moment that will somehow vaporize the legacies of the past and the problems that divide us, but rather as a second chance, an opportunity specifically to pick up where we left off a quarter-century ago when we ceased our promising talks with the Chinese Communist leaders and chose instead continued alliance with the Chinese Nationalist faction.

Against this historical backdrop and the dramatic moves of 1971–72, how might we now project the seizing of this opportunity, and the actual development of Sino-American relations in the 1970's?

First, it seems safe to predict that there will be no massive increase in travel and trade between the two countries. Americans will continue to be admitted to China in batches—groups for specific purposes and larger numbers of Chinese-Americans; and smaller and less frequent batches of Chinese may come to the United States—scientists, performers, and the like. But an open faucet for tourism is most improbable. As for trade, it is likely to grow slowly but not significantly (despite Washington's unprecedented license for the sale of Boeing jets), perhaps reaching a $500-million ceiling by the decade's end. This is primarily because China can get much of what it wants cheaper elsewhere, because China is determined to remain self-reliant, and because there is nothing we really need from China. Our imports of the past are instructive: hog bristles, dried eggs, human hair for wigs, straw, ceramics, and, of course, materials for Chinese cookery.

Second, there will be no establishment of formal diplomatic relations—despite the new "liaison offices" in both capitals—until our government expels the Chinese Nationalist Embassy from Washington, a highly unlikely action under Mr. Nixon. In the meantime, however, talks through these liaison offices, and in Paris, New York, Ottawa, and elsewhere, plus direct communications facilities and occasional high-level travel between Washington and Peking, should be enough to develop a healthy dialogue. Within these channels of dialogue it is reasonable to expect some progress toward cooperation on arms control, weather and pollution control, and scientific, medical, and technological sharing.

Third, as for the process of détente itself, it will surely go through ups and downs but will probably continue—barring major U.S. military re-escalation on China's periphery—because both sides have a stake in it. Mao's and Chou's successors may try new tacks; but a sharp break is unlikely now that Maoism's founder himself has given his public, personal blessing to the new relationship. One assumes here Maoism's survival after Mao, as a civic religion, a social cement, and a replacement for Confucianism, despite on-going struggles within this civic religion as to who is the purest heir and interpreter of doctrine. As for the U.S. side, there is little sign that any conceivable Nixon successor would take action to renounce the détente.

Fourth, leaving Indochina aside again, the possible sources of Sino-American friction within détente include Taiwan, Japan, and the complex of isues that engage Peking, Tokyo, and Washington.

On the matter of Taiwan, it had seemed likely that the island might become more of a problem for Japan than for the United States prior to the late 1972 Sino-Japanese agreement under Premier Tanaka. The Chou-Nixon communiqué had embodied mutual acceptance of a short-term stand-off within the longer-term probability of reunion between Taiwan and the mainland. (Indeed, the only real losers seem to have been proponents of Taiwanese independence.) But the ensuing Tanaka initiative has put Tokyo ahead of Washington in terms of a Taiwan solution, i.e., de-recognition of Taiwan but continued economic relations. The island's future will now surely be resolved through the corroding power of time and mortality; and the probable outcome over the next generation will be slow-motion reunion through mutual accommodation—without the use of force and with the acquiescence of both Washington and Tokyo. This is a solution far better for all parties concerned than its alternative: the creation of a poisonous irredentist issue in the West Pacific through permanent separation.

One central question nonetheless for both Peking and Washington in the years ahead is: whither Japan? Here is a nation endowed with extraordinary energy, with dazzling economic power, and with potential military power. Japan remains our best trading partner, after Canada. But Japan collided with China, and then with us over China and Southeast Asia, not very long ago in a very bitter war. Today, the Japanese are a volatile force in search of a national role-definition and national purpose.

In dealing with Japan, what is required of Americans is the closest possible consultation, though not collusion, with the Japanese—a willingess to walk together, but not in locked-step. Such an approach was not taken by Washington in 1971 when the "Nixon shocks" on China policy and economic relations were administered by intention, not inadvertence. Nor is it an easy approach to attempt, for Japanese policy-makers and planners are traditionally reluctant to speak their minds directly, and therefore sometimes breed impatience and suspicion among Americans. But both China and America share a stake in the muting of Japanese anxieties, and here Washington's obligation and opportunity are great.

Finally, what of the tone of our relationship with China in the seventies?

If one surveys the record of American relations with China— the American approach to China—since the beginning, one finds that the process has been something of a roller-coaster. One veteran China observer, M.I.T. political scientist Harold Isaacs, has identified at least six separate phases:

1. The Age of Respect (eighteenth century). Europeans and Americans shared an admiration for Confucian methods of governance, Chinese philosophy, the exotic goods of the China trade, Chinese art and ceramics.

2. The Age of Contempt (1840–1905). The Chinese Empire semed hostile, decayed, and corrupt, the Chinese people sinister and obdurate, the Chinese nation unwilling to accept the alleged blessings of Western religion, learning, and trade.

3. The Age of Benevolence (1905–37). In the last days of the Empire and the chaotic years of the Republic, China seemed hungry for Western technology, learning, goods, ideology, and even religion.

4. The Age of Admiration (1937–44). "Heroic" and "democratic" China struggled bravely for survival against the Imperial Japanese aggressors.

5. The Age of Disenchantment (1944–49). Americans suddenly discovered the deep flaws in the demoralized Chinese Nationalist Government, and the former heroes lost their charm.

6. The Age of Hostility (1949–71). China, now Communist, seemed a dangerous new threat, a latter-day Golden Horde or Yellow Peril.

As one reflects on this roller-coaster of fluctuating American attitudes toward China and the Chinese, one wonders how the new age that began with ping-pong and Kissinger will be described by historians of the future. If it is an "Age of Euphoria," it will be short-lived and its sequel unpleasant, for euphoria is flimsy stuff indeed for the bridging of the very wide gulf between Chinese and Americans. But if, instead, it develops into an "Age of Live, Let-Live, and Learn," the Nixon chapter could help produce new qualities of realism and understanding among both Americans and Chinese that previous chapters have lacked.

"Live, let-live, and learn" can only evolve from an utterly new American approach, alien to those of the past—both our patronizing and self-assumed benevolence of the pre-Communist period and our inflated fear and hostility of the past two decades. It will require of us, instead, a willingness to treat China as an equal, as an adult, as a great power, and as a great people; and it will require of us a sensitivity to China's legitimate national security interests in the region and the world.

If we move to adopt such an approach, there is no guarantee that a peace-producing four-power balance will evolve with great ease in East Asia. But at least we will be responding, at long last, to our obligation as a great power to try to help achieve such a balance—and also to help secure the long-term benefits that it can bring to all the peoples of the Asian and Pacific region, including our own afflicted nation.

9

Nuclear Policy in the Post-Vietnam Period

GEORGE W. RATHJENS

1

Since the use of atomic weapons against Japan, and more particularly since the demonstration of thermonuclear fusion twenty years ago, the utility of nuclear weapons as instruments of policy has been a matter of debate in political-military circles and in the intellectual community that has concerned itself with such matters. Often the debate has seemed to be focused on rather sharply defined issues: e.g., the necessity for on-site inspections as a means of verifying compliance with a nuclear test ban treaty; the wisdom of the NATO multilateral nuclear force (MLF) proposal; the significance of Chinese nuclear tests; and, in the recent past, the questions of whether the United States should build an anti-ballistic missile (ABM) defense system, and if so, of what kind; whether we should continue the development and deployment of multiple independently targetable reentry vehicles (MIRVs) for our missiles; and what kind of an outcome from the strategic arms limitation talks (SALT) would be acceptable to us.

In fact the different positions taken with respect to these and a host of other issues reflect fundamental differences in perception about the political and military utility of nuclear strength—differences which are often not articulated, and are sometimes even denied, by those most intimately engaged in debate on the more specific issues.

At one end of the spectrum there have been, and are, those who see the differences between conventional and nuclear weapons more as one of degree than of kind. To this group, American nuclear strength is seen to some degree as a possible substitute for conventional forces, and, as with conventional forces, qualitative and quantitative differences between the American and adversary nuclear stockpiles and delivery systems are important. The concept of strategic nuclear superiority is meaningful because of its political utility, because it could make a significant difference if a nuclear war were to occur, or both. Typically, those holding these views have argued that the Cuban missile crisis was resolved in a way generally satisfactory to the United States because of superior American strategic strength.

At the other extreme are those who see nuclear weapons, particularly thermonuclear weapons, as fundamentally different from conventional arms—different because small numbers seem sufficient to destroy whole societies. Nuclear superiority is felt to be a meaningless concept: once certain minimum capabilities are obtained, further acquisition provides nothing but "overkill" capability. Nuclear weapons may be totally useless as instruments of policy because of the peril of self-destruction when confrontation involves another nuclear power; and even when the other power has no nuclear strength, they may well be useless because of moral revulsion or the fear of escalation involving other nuclear states. It is believed that the gravest threat from nuclear weapons is not that they will be used based on a deliberate high-level decision by an adversary superpower, but rather that their use may be triggered through accident or miscalculation and that uncontrolled escalation might follow. In the view of this group, the Cuban missile crisis was resolved as it was because of U.S. local superiority in conventional strength; and Soviet unwillingness to expand the confrontation by moving on Berlin or elsewhere was perhaps more out of fear of escalation that could destroy both superpowers than out of explicit concern about U.S. nuclear superiority.

There are, of course, "intermediate" views. For example, many who would subscribe to most of the statements of the last paragraph will argue that U.S. nuclear superiority has been important in the past because, whether reasonably or not, it has sustained the confidence of U.S. allies in American resolve to stand with them if they are attacked or threatened.

However, notwithstanding such qualified views, substantial polarization of attitudes about the utility of nuclear strength exists. Despite occasional protestations to the contrary, some people simply cannot accept the idea that nuclear weapons do not fit into the same kinds of models that have seemed appropriate for political-military behavior in the past. Others believe, as McGeorge Bundy has said, that "the American people know in their bones that nuclear weapons are different." [1]

While there will be many exceptions, people from the right part of the political spectrum and those with a backgruond in the military-industrial complex seem more likely to see nuclear weapons as useful instruments of force or diplomacy, while those from the left and intellectuals, particularly scientists, will more often see the weapons as different in kind from conventional arms —useless politically and militarily, but nevertheless dangerous.

The general question of whether nuclear weapons can, or should, have a role as instruments of policy is in the broadest sense a philosophical one, the resolution of which would seem to depend on differing views regarding psychology and morality—views on the way individuals and societies interact with one another, particularly in confrontation and crisis circumstances. It is almost a doctrinal matter conditioned to only a limited degree by the details of technology, military planning, and force levels.

However, as one moves down in the hierarchy of issues to such questions as the meaningfulness of nuclear superiority and the stability of the strategic balance, and then to still more specific ones, e.g., weapons development and acquisition decisions and the terms of arms control agreements, discussion becomes increasingly dependent on details of the political-military environment. Before attempting to go further, then, in speculating about future nuclear policy directions, it seems useful to try to identify some of the factors that will characterize that environment during the 1970's, particularly focusing on points of contrast with the previous two decades, and then to try to answer the question, "what will be the effect of those changes on nuclear policy for the 1970's?"

2

From the perspective of international relations, the major changes of the post-World War II period have been the renaissance of Western Europe and Japan as major centers of power and the splintering of the communist world.

Because of the former, and even aside from questions of internal change on which I shall comment in a moment, the United States finds its position as leader of the western world much eroded. This has come about simply because of the dramatic increase in strength, particularly economic, of Japan and Western Europe relative to the United States; because dependence on the United States in the economic sphere has come to an end; and because it has become increasingly clear to people of these countries that American interests and theirs are different, if not in conflict, in a growing number of respects. It is perhaps worth noting that the recognition of Japan and Western Europe as important centers of power has been much enhanced as the perceived importance of economic strength in international affairs, at least in the West, has increased, while that of military strength has declined. The latter development no doubt is in part a consequence of the obvious inability of the United States to use its military strength to achieve political objectives.

The changes in the communist world are in many respects more dramatic: China has become both a competitor with the Soviet Union for leadership, and its most worrisome adversary militarily. Curiously, the emergence of China as a world power has occurred despite its economic weakness, and at the same time economic strength has seemed to be of increasing importance in the West.

Despite prodding from others, notably General de Gaulle, American recognition of changes in relationships among the major powers has come about with disappointing slowness, particularly in the American establishment and particularly regarding the changes in the communist world. While one rarely hears these days of a monolithic Sino-Soviet bloc, there still appear to be men of importance, or at least there were until the President's trip to Peking, who were defending U.S. involvement in Vietnam primarily as a bulwark against Chinese expansionism in Southeast Asia, not recognizing that just as Chinese policy is not determined in Moscow so neither is North Vietnamese policy determined in Peking (nor, for that matter, in Moscow).

However, notwithstanding both bureaucratic inertia and the commitment of individuals to the past, we do seem at long last to be recognizing that the post-World War II era of bipolar international politics has come to an end. The attractiveness of a "balance of power" view of the world to the Nixon Administration is a reflection of this (as well as, no doubt, Henry Kissinger's prior interest in early nineteenth-century European politics).

Important as the structural relationships among the major world powers are as determinants of American nuclear policy, they seem (at least from the admittedly unrepresentative perspective of academic Cambridge) to be of less fundamental importance than the changes that have taken place in the last few years, and which are still taking place, within the United States itself.

One cannot but associate the change largely with the Vietnam experience, although the extent to which there is causality and the extent to which the war has served simply to make latent problems visible is unclear. In any case, though, the nation is bitterly disillusioned and this is reflected in a number of ways: in greatly diminished confidence in executive leadership, and in neo-isolationism, fed from the right by frustration and xenophobia, and from the left by guilt and a sense that it is beyond the capability and right of the United States to decide on values to be defended in, or foisted on, the rest of the world. Polarization developed as a result of the war seems also to have spilled over or exacerbated that which exists with respect to domestic issues: questions of economic growth, allocation of resources within the domestic economy, environmental issues, and civil rights. It is not too much to say that there is a crisis of legitimacy, with the Nixon Administration seen by its supporters as the conservator of past values—American greatness and leadership, property values, the work ethic, and an economy where growth is king—values increasingly questioned or rejected particularly by the young, the blacks, and the intellectuals. Moreover, each move by the Administration with respect to one issue that is seen by the alienated and disenchanted as an affront serves to diminish its legitimacy of action with respect to all others. Thus, the nation is split. There is much turning inward; and presidential calls to greatness notwithstanding, a large segment of the population rejects an imperial role as arrogant and unwise.

The rejection of a world role acquires a growing constituency as external threats seem less real. The Soviet Union is seen as more of a status quo power, less adventurous and under less personal leadership. The fear of its great superiority in conventional strength has diminished as China is viewed as a major Soviet problem, and as better intelligence information and analysis have demonstrated that Soviet conventional strength was exaggerated in the past. China too is considered less of a threat, particularly since the President's trip. This has come about both because of recognition that fears about its expansionist ambitions may have been much exaggerated, and because of a growing belief that even such tendencies as may exist are not a threat to the United States.

But while Soviet and Chinese *intentions* to use military force against the United States, its allies, or other states are increasingly discounted, the nuclear *capability* of the two communist powers grows, with China developing both thermonuclear weapons and means for their delivery, and with the Soviet Union finally achieving parity with the United States in strategic strength. This growth in nuclear strength is, along with the demise of the bipolar world, the other major change in state relationships between the great powers. Its importance will be perceived very differently depending, as I have noted earlier, on how one feels about the political and military utility of nuclear weapons. But except for those extremists who would argue that nuclear weapons do not have, and have not for some time had, *any* significant political-military utility, the changes of the last few years will have some importance. Certainly, the credibility of American action in response to Soviet moves in, for example, Europe or the Near East that might result in nuclear weapons being used is less than it would have been some years ago. While many would argue that the peril to the United States has not changed as a result of the attainment by the Soviet Union of strategic parity—that even a decade ago a nuclear exchange could have been an unmitigated disaster for us —others would argue that our proclivity for taking risks was probably greater then or at least perceived to be so by others, including both the Soviet Union and U.S. client states.

Time also makes a difference. With each passing year of non-use of nuclear weapons, the credibility of use diminishes. This is true not only in regard to direct confrontation between nuclear powers but also the possible use of such weapons against non-nuclear states. It is unlikely that use in Vietnam was as seriously considered during the last few years, when we were directly involved, as at the time of Dien Bien Phu, when we were not.

In summary, then, I see changes of four major kinds that bear on the question of nuclear policy for the 1970's.

First, there has been the splintering of the communist world, and the development of Japan and Western Europe as centers of increasingly independent and influential strength—the end of the bipolar world.

Second, there has been the polarization in American society, substantially related to the Vietnam experience, with a large fraction of the country and the Congress disillusioned with executive leadership, the defense establishment, and America's imperial role.

Third, if everyone does not agree that the cold war is over, there is nevertheless substantially less concern about military threats from abroad (and more about economic competition) than a decade ago.

Fourth, the credibility of the use of nuclear weapons has diminished. The fraction of those believing they have little or no political-military utility has doubtlessly increased and continues to do so.

3

The effect of these developments on U.S. defense policy is clear in a general sense. It is discredited and cannot command the kind of support it did during the 1950's and 1960's. For the next few years neither having been a war hero—in fact, there appear to have been none—nor a key official in the Defense Department is likely to be an asset in aspiring to high elective office. While the military budget may remain fairly high it is unlikely that any administration in the next few years would ask for, or that the Congress would provide, well-equipped military forces, particularly Army divisions at the levels of the late 1960's.

Yet, some discrimination is in order. While the Army and the tactical air forces have been tarnished by Vietnam, this is less true of the nonflying part of the Navy and of the strategic forces. While Army divisons are being reduced, the budget for strategic weapons systems is increasing. Because they have not been used, and until they are, the strategic nuclear forces and policy regarding their use are likely to command only a fraction of the public criticism that has been focused on Vietnam. Deterrence of massive attack will be less questioned as a reasonable and necessary policy objective than U.S. intervention in the third world with conventional forces. Thus, the President is likely to be able to command support for a "position of strength" and to act with more flexibility on strategic nuclear issues than on the structuring and use of conventional forces.

Consider the implications of all this in a Nixon Administration. The President has repeatedly taken pains, e.g., in his definition of the "Nixon Doctrine," to argue that he is committed to a role of leadership and involvement on a world scale.[2] Yet, he recognizes, "approaching strategic parity with the Soviet Union and the developing Chinese nuclear capability may have reduced the range of conflicts deterred by strategic forces alone."[3]

Over a decade ago President Kennedy reached a similar conclusion, and, rejecting the reliance on nuclear strength that had characterized the Eisenhower Administration, went ahead with a substantial strengthening of American conventional forces, coupled with military assistance to the developing world and an effort to induce our NATO allies to strengthen their conventional forces.

Now, however, similar options are not available to the White House. For the reasons given earlier, Europeans are likely to be far less responsive to American leadership, and the American public and Congress will be far less responsive to calls to continue with generous military assistance programs, to build conventional strength, or to commit American forces abroad. Witness the support for the Mansfield amendment and opposition to "home porting" American naval vessels in Greece. And with each passing day of involvement in Indochina the constituency on which the President can count for support for these programs will diminish. Thus, while from the President's perspective the need for conventional strength may be, if anything, greater than in the past (he has said: "General purpose forces, therefore, now play a larger role in deterring attacks than at any time since the nuclear era began." [4]) he, or his immediate successor, will do well if he can obtain support for forces, commitments, and military assistance programs at even pre-Vietnam levels. (Some of his would-be successors would, of course, presumably not try to do so.)

The President has clearly recognized the problem. Almost certainly predisposed to see nuclear weapons as useful instruments of policy anyway, he has an added incentive to do what he can to make others see them in a similar light, despite the attainment by the Soviet Union of strategic parity with the United States. To the extent he succeeds he can expect to prolong the utility of American nuclear strength as a deterrent where U..S and allied conventional strength may be inadequate. If he fails, the whole NATO edifice may well collapse (some would argue it is an anachronism anyway), and one of the cornerstones of the Nixon doctrine—the commitment to serve as a guarantor for American allies against nuclear threats—will be shown to have been made of clay.

The attitudes of others will necessarily be strongly affected by their perceptions of the attitude of the United States. If they can be convinced that an American president may initiate the use of such weapons in some crisis, then those weapons may have political utility, even if their use would in fact be absolutely disastrous to the United States. And even aside from initiating the use of nuclear weapons, if one can convey the impression to others that one believes that nuclear strength is psychologically advantageous and that one is prepared to conduct foreign policy in a more aggressive way as a result of that belief, then very likely such strength can be exploited to some degree simply because others will prefer not to test the sincerity of one's convictions.

Thus, we have the first of several approaches that have historically been useful in making nuclear weapons useful, and which may continue to be so. I would point out here that President Nixon's cultivation of an image of machismo and his demonstration of unpredictability and a capacity for dramatically changing his position would appear to place him in an unusually strong position to capitalize on nuclear capability in this way.

By a variety of other approaches one can also make escalation more likely and therefore something less likely to be risked or provoked. Increasing the numbers of nuclear weapons, deploying them where they are more likely to be overrun, delegating to lower command eschelons authority or capability to use them, and developing additional centers of political control (nuclear proliferation) are examples of such measures.

The remaining alternative for enhancing the political and military utility of nuclear weapons is the development of defensive or, more broadly speaking, damage-limiting capabilities, which would permit defense against adversary nuclear weapons so that one could use one's own, or take actions which might lead to their use, with less risk.

Thus, the President, or the political leadership of any other nuclear power, has at his disposal several mechanisms for exploiting nuclear strength as an instrument of policy. The last, however, is a realistic one, if at all, only where there is a great disparity in strength, as, for example, between one of the superpowers and emerging nuclear powers. In what follows I should like to discuss the extent to which the present administration appears to be moving to maintain or enhance the credibility of these mechanisms and some of the consequences of its doing so. I hasten to point out that I believe that the primary motivation for much of what is being done is probably not so much a well-thought-out desire to exploit nuclear strength as it is simply a deep-seated belief that in the nuclear case, as with conventional weapons, "more is better" and a genuine, albeit in my view exaggerated, concern about the stability of the strategic balance. The important thing is not so much what motivates both the rhetoric and actions as the consequences.

Let me turn again then to the question of whether the same framework is appropriate for thinking about both conventional and nuclear strength, and then to the issue of the stability of the nuclear balance.

4

While military force has been used throughout recorded history to interdict commerce, to destroy civil populations, and to lay siege to cities and destroy them, until the early part of this century such forces were largely designed to engage other military forces and were used for that purpose. By the 1920's Douhet and other air power extremists were advancing the thesis that it might be possible to destroy nations directly and quickly through strategic bombing. The destruction of Hamburg, Dresden, Tokyo, and

Hiroshima demonstrated that at least whole cities, if not whole nations, could be so destroyed by using conventional or atomic weapons, but it was not until the development of thermonuclear weapons that it became clear that the whole fabric of society in such large powers as the United States and the Soviet Union could be destroyed by relatively small offensive forces.

With the development of thermonuclear weapons it also became clear that the historical rationale for strategic bombing no longer has validity. In World War II, deterrence was hardly the game. Rather, the bombing was justified on the grounds that destruction of an industrial base would reduce an adversary's ability or will to continue the war. With thermonuclear weapons and their delivery systems available to one's adversary, this is irrelevant: destruction of a nation's population and industry need in no way interfere with its ability to visit almost limitless destruction on others. We now find ourselves in a situation where the population which deterrence holds hostage, although perhaps having been responsible for creation of a "strategic" nuclear force and the elevation to office of those who might commit it to use, may not be able to influence its use at any given time. Thus, the efficacy of strategic attack as a mechanism of deterrence depends on a few leaders' solicitude for the welfare of the societies for which they have responsibility. This is in sharp contrast to the World War II situation when the rationale for strategic bombing was in its impact on the minds and capabilities of a society collectively.

Notwithstanding these differences, the two cases are similar in terms of the characteristics required of the weapons systems employed; and in both cases there are important points of difference as compared with the use of weaponry for the engagement of other military forces.

First, in regard to destruction of urban-industrial complexes, there is the possibility of saturation effects; once one has assurance of being able to deliver a heavy enough attack to destroy, say, all an adversary's major cities, more destructive capability might not be very useful. As long as the major role of military forces was to destroy like forces, arms races were a more or less natural concomitant of conflict. One side could hope, by increasing its forces, to be able to destroy an adversary's force more completely, and it could hope to ensure that a larger fraction of its own would survive. But when targets are cities, there is a limit to the force required to destroy them, and it is a fairly fixed limit since one nation can hardly build more cities quickly to offset the development of strategic offensive forces by another. In this difference is the basis for the concept of "sufficiency."

Closely related is the fact that with the development of thermonuclear weapons the supremacy of the offense over the defense has occurred. The best defense in World War II was capable of inflicting perhaps 15 percent attrition on an incoming bomber raid. However, in the 1950's, with the possibility of an attack by several hundred bombers, each armed with perhaps several thermonuclear weapons and with cross targeting so that each major city would be attacked by perhaps several aircraft, defense at the level of 15 percent or even 50 percent effectiveness became uninteresting. If one bomber were shot down but another got to the same target, it would be almost as thoroughly destroyed as if both got there. Defense seemed particularly fruitless if one believed that one's adversary could, and would, compensate for any defenses by simply building more bombers, or later more missiles, at a cost far less than that incurred in building the defense. If, during the bomber period, there were lingering doubts that the offense had the advantage over the defense in an attack against population and industry, they disappeared with the advent of the ballistic missile. Defense against such delivery vehicles seemed even more difficult than against bombers; moreover, with the advent of the missile, the prospects for bomber defense also diminished because of the possibility that the radar and computer centers that were supposed to direct interceptor aircraft to bombers would be destroyed by missiles at the beginning of any nuclear exchange.

The third change implicit in the development of strategic offensive forces is the decline in criticality of tactics and timing. Tactics and timing may of course be important, and perhaps critically so, to the extent that strategic forces themselves may be subject to destruction by adversary attack, a point that will come up when I turn to the question of stability of the strategic balance. However, when cities are the targets, the situation will be less dynamic for the reasons pointed out earlier than when the primary purpose of each of two contesting forces is the destruction of the other. Cities can hardly change much on a short time scale—or move.

These characteristics of the strategic balance—particularly the first two, the possibility of saturation effects and the superiority of the offense—were clearly recognized during the 1960's in the United States, at least at the political level, if not always among the military.

Although the concept of sufficiency and the futility of attempt-

ing to limit damage that adversary strategic forces might inflict
had been advanced in the 1950's, it was during the Kennedy Administration that the implications of these arguments were most
clearly reflected in force posture decisions.

After a brief flirtation with the idea of a "spare the cities"
strategic doctrine, Secretary McNamara developed the view that
U.S. strategic offensive forces should be structured primarily so that
we, and more importantly the Soviet Union, would know that were
they to be used there would be high assurance that a very substantial fraction of Soviet industry and population would be destroyed in retaliation. Thus was born the "assured destruction"
doctrine for strategic offensive forces, a concept which the Secretary
used to resist service pressures to enlarge force levels so that an ever
expanding list of military installations could be targeted. How
much was needed to deter was of course an unresolvable question,
but McNamara advanced the thesis that a capability of destroying
one fourth to one third of the Soviet population was surely sufficient. Although the figures were almost surely excessive to accomplish the deterrence of the Soviet Union, and moreover were
underestimates because they failed to take into account uncalculable
and synergistic effects of a nuclear attack, predictably they became
enshrined in Pentagon planning not as a ceiling but rather as a
floor for what was required.

At least as important for the 1960's as acceptance of the idea
of "assured destruction" or "sufficiency" was the rejection of efforts
to limit damage to the United States from adversary attack. Thus,
U.S. air defenses were allowed to atrophy, civil defenses were
neglected, and the Kennedy and Johnson Administrations, like
Eisenhower's, rejected efforts by the Army to build a large scale
anti-ballistic missile defense—all, at least in part, because of feeling that any defensive efforts would simply be offset by improvement or enlargement of Soviet offensive forces. Not only was
defense rejected as futile, but, as remarked above, pressure from
the Air Force to build forces that could, by attacking Soviet
military targets, limit damage to the United States were also resisted. It was held that if we built more missiles as the Air Force
wanted, the Soviet Union would do the same so that its ability to
inflict damage on us would not be diminished. Only against a
much weaker nuclear power, such as China, was damage limitation
held to be a realistic objective.

In his first year in office President Nixon's thinking about
nuclear strength seemed consistent with that of the previous few
years. In facing up to a decision on the ABM question, he, like his

predecessors, rejected a defense designed to cope with a massive Soviet attack, reiterated the feasibility and possible desirability of a defense against Chinese missiles, and seemed to accept the concept of "sufficiency" in regard to strategic strength.

On the last point one finds in his first "state of the world" message these words: "Formerly, any additional strength was strategically significant; today, available power threatens to outstrip rational objectives." [5] We all thought we understood what he meant at the time: the possession of further strength by either superpower in excess of that required to inflict a high, albeit ill-defined, level of damage on its adversary was meaningless and not worth pursuing.

We have subsequently had a clarification, some would say a redefinition, of what the President means by "sufficiency." Thus, in the 1971 and 1972 "state of the world" messages he rejected McNamara's "assured destruction" criterion and a narrow definition of "sufficiency" as suggested above, and made it clear that "sufficiency" as he saw it implied forces not only to deter attack against the United States but to permit him and his successors to act with some ill-defined flexibility in response to Soviet actions. I quote him to make the point. "A simple 'assured destruction' doctrine does not meet our present requirements for a flexible range of strategic options. No President should be left with only one strategic course of action, particularly that of ordering the mass destruction of enemy civilians and facilities." [6] "Sufficiency has two meanings. In its narrow military sense, it means enough force to inflict a level of damage on a potential aggressor sufficient to deter him from attacking. . . . In its broader political sense, sufficiency means the maintenance of forces adequate to prevent us and our allies from being coerced. Thus the relationship between our strategic forces and those of the Soviet Union must be such that our ability and resolve to protect our vital security interests will not be underestimated. I must not be—and my successors must not be—limited to the indiscriminate mass destruction of enemy civilians as the sole possible response to challenges. This is especially so when that response involves the likelihood of triggering nuclear attacks on our own population. It would be inconsistent with the political meaning of sufficiency to base our force planning solely on some finite—and theoretical—capacity to inflict casualties presumed to be unacceptable to the other side." [7]

Other evidence also suggests that the Administration has in fact hardly accepted the idea of sufficiency in "the narrow military sense" as a basis for force planning, but has rather continued to view nuclear "superiority" as important. Thus, one reads in the second state-of-the-world message: "Our strategic forces must be numerous enough, efficient enough, and deployed in such a way that an aggressor will always know that the sure result of a nuclear attack against us is unacceptable damage from our retaliation. That makes it imperative that our strategic power not be inferior to that of any other state." [8] The second sentence is clearly a *non sequitur,* and can be explained only by relating the need expressed in it to a broader range of objectives than that spelled out in the first. We have also had the Deputy Secretary of Defense characterize "sufficiency" as a good word to use in a speech but otherwise one that "doesn't mean a God-damned thing." [9]

In addition, there have been numerous expressions of concern about the growth of Soviet strategic forces, some related to the possible impact on stability, a point I shall discuss further, but others seemingly based on a more general feeling that "more is better" (if the forces are American) or "worse" if, as in the case in point, Soviet superiority is the prospect.

The Administration statements to the effect that one cannot uncouple the problem of strategic forces from other military and political problems also makes it clear that it sees nuclear weaponry as having a range of uses consistent with the President's broader interpretation of "sufficiency" rather than with the narrower one.

Finally, there has been great emphasis on negotiation as a means of establishing strategic force levels and of the importance of negotiating from strength. Note in this last connection that if one regarded strategic forces as truly "sufficient," in a narrow sense, modest quantitative increments or qualitative changes would seem meaningless, and one would be much more likely to base strategic force levels on unilateral decisions and restraint rather than on hard bargaining. While the President has acknowledged that small changes in force levels are unimportant, in other respects the negotiating process, as evidenced in the strategic arms limitation talks, hardly reflects an acceptance of the concept of "sufficiency," narrowly defined. Instead, we see something of a game-theory approach, and a two-person, zero-sum game theory at that: an approach where one side's gains are seen very much as the other's losses, something totally incompatible with the conventional or narrow concept of "sufficiency." Directly related is the "bargaining from strength" philosophy, the idea that one needs bargaining chips—in the case of the recent SALT negotiations, an ABM system.

But there are contradictions in what appears to be the Administration's policy. Two particularly come to mind.

First, there is the question of the balance of power view of the world which the Administration seems to favor. With the emergence of Western Europe, Japan, and China as centers of power, the first two largely because of economic strength and the latter perhaps more by virtue of numbers and political growth, a balance with five centers makes some sense if nuclear strength is heavily discounted. But if it is not, are not we still in very much a world of two superpowers?

Second, there is a seemingly irreconcilable conflict between the desire, noted earlier, to make nuclear weapons usable in a limited way and the desire to make escalation credible so that it can serve to expand the utility of nuclear strength as a deterrent. The first will be best achieved through precise control and a minimum of ambiguity about use; the second requires just the opposite qualities.

Notwithstanding these conflicts and some early statements which seemed to suggest otherwise, it is perhaps fair to say that the President seems largely to have rejected the common view of nuclear sufficiency, believing and acting as if, or at least attempting to convey the impression that, nuclear strength is exploitable and can be made relevant for deterrence of a wide range of threats.

The Administration seems also to have taken a more relaxed view, and I believe a more realistic one, than did its predecessors about another possibility of making nuclear weapons credible instruments of policy: nuclear proliferation. Thus, we have a recognition of the utility of the nuclear forces of our allies as a component of deterrence [11] whereas spokesmen for the last two administrations denigrated, in my view unjustly, the utility of such forces.[12]

5

The other major respect in which the President's views of strategic weapons seem at variance with those of many critics concerns the stability (or delicacy) of the Soviet-American bilateral balance.

In discussing that stability it is convenient to differentiate between what we have come to call crisis stability and arms race stability.

The first relates to likelihood that one nation, in a crisis situation, might initiate an attack against another. It has been commonly held that insofar as one is concerned about the Soviet-American strategic balance the situation has been stable for some years. At no time since the early 1950's could either nation have attacked the other with the expectation that the damage it would sustain in retaliation would be commensurate with any war aims. Even in the event an attack by the adversary seemed almost certain, prudence would have dictated restraint in the use, or even the deployment of one's own forces, in the hope that the anticipated attack could somehow be avoided.

Yet, during much of the period there have been those, often men of great influence, who feared that the situation might change for the worse with time. Thus, we have seen periods of what we call arms race instability as one side feverishly developed and built new arms in order to forestall a period of crisis instability. One can read today in Secretary Laird's annual report that one of our strategic objectives is

> Maintaining an adequate second-strike capability to deter an all-out surprise attack on our strategic forces. Providing no incentive for the Soviet Union to strike the United States first in a crisis.[13]

The fear of disabling surprise attack is an old one. In the nuclear era it perhaps reached a high point in the missile-gap period —during the late 50's when, having seen some Soviet ICBM tests but otherwise lacking good intelligence on what was going on in the Soviet Union, this country developed a fear that within a few years we might be confronted with an adversary who could by preemptive attack destroy virtually all our bombers and the few missiles we would have. And it was feared that in a crisis exactly that might happen. We would have no effective deterrent.

The most influential spokesman for this view was perhaps Albert Wohlstetter who directed a famous study at RAND relating to the basing of our bombers and who then wrote an article based on it which appeared in January 1959 entitled, "The Delicate Balance of Terror." Wohlstetter examined the many possibilities of degradation of capability of our retaliatory forces, hypothesized a very effective Soviet civil defense and a highly effective attack against us, and then pronounced that "strategic deterrence, while feasible, will be extremely difficult to achieve, and at critical junctures in the 1960's we may not have the power to deter attack." [14] He particularly dismissed those who cited the fact that, while there might be uncertainties in the performance of our retaliatory force, there would also be uncertainties in the effectiveness of a Soviet attack, and that in the light of such uncertainties, the Soviet Union would be ill-advised to attack on the assumption that it could escape devastating retaliation.

The range of uncertainties and the importance of the delicacy theory to the arms race would be hard to exaggerate. P. M. S. Blackett, perhaps Wohlstetter's best known critic, noted in a paper written in 1961 that "the truth or falsehood of the delicacy thesis will remain for many years of vital importance." [15] He could not have been more right, for it has been a critical factor in planning with respect to strategic weaponry since then, and it will very likely continue to be for some years in the future. Indeed, the debate over the ABM, the present controversy about military research and development, and current debates about new strategic systems are all reflections of differing views on the delicacy of the balance. One might also characterize them as surrogates for a debate on the broader issue of how to treat uncertainty when considering nuclear strategy.

That the uncertainties are large is not surprising considering our very limited experience in the use of nuclear weapons and the systems that may be required to deliver them under combat conditions; and considering that different men will hold dramatically different views on how much is enough for deterrence. I can illustrate the last point by a few citations. Much Defense Department planning has been based on McNamara's aforementioned "assured destruction" criterion: on the assumption that an ability to destroy 25 to 30 percent of the Soviet population would be adequate for deterrence. This equates to delivery of 200 to 400 one-megaton warheads according to some sources. [16] However, the number of warheads required to inflict this level of damage could be substantially less considering that the figures are based on only the easily calculated damaging effects of nuclear weapons and do not consider such effects as fall-out and fire storms and the interdependence of modern societies. On the other hand, the force requirements would be much higher if one accepted other estimates such as, for example, those of Albert Wohlstetter and Eugene Wigner about the vulnerability of Soviet population. Some years ago the former suggested:

> . . . five half-megaton weapons with an average inaccuracy of two miles might be expected to destroy half the population of a city of 900,000 spread over 40 square miles, provided the inhabitants are without shelters. But if they are provided with shelters capable of resisting over-pressures of 100 pounds per square inch, approximately 60 such weapons would be required; and deep rock shelters might force the total up to over a thousand. [17]

More recently Wigner has suggested that Soviet cities might be evacuated, in which case ". . . our present missile power . . . could cause a fatality level of [only] about 9½ million," a figure he claims is probably on the high side since it is based on some extreme assumptions: to wit, that all our missiles are used against population, none against military targets; that the ballistic missile defenses of the U.S.S.R. are completely ineffective; that we suffer no losses whatever from a first strike; and that all our submarines are on station.[18]

At the other extreme, Bundy has this to say,

> Think-tank analysts can set levels of "acceptable" damage well up in the tens of millions of lives. They can assume that the loss of dozens of great cities is somehow a real choice for sane men. They are in an unreal world. In the real world of political leaders—whether here or in the Soviet Union—a decision that would bring even one hydrogen bomb on one city of one's own country would be recognized in advance as a catastrophic blunder; ten bombs on ten cities would be a disaster beyond history; and a hundred bombs on a hundred cities are unthinkable.[19]

Ought one to be surprised that with such different views on the requirements for deterrence there are radically different views as to whether the deterrent might indeed be in jeopardy at some ill-defined time in the future?

There are other uncertainties relating to weapons performance that are at least as great. They are perhaps well illustrated by the debate that has gone on in American defense circles for over a decade about Soviet anti-ballistic missile defenses. I shall comment only on the recent part of it.

The Soviet Union has deployed an ABM system using some 64 interceptor missiles around Moscow, and to this one could have envisaged quite a range of reactions by the United States, all in the context of somehow preserving an adequate deterrent. At the one extreme one could have simply disregarded it, if one believed, with Bundy, that holding a few other large cities hostage would suffice for deterrence. Alternatively, if one insisted that Moscow be among the hostages, one could plan on delivering, just prior to a missile warhead on the city, other warheads to be detonated at high altitude. These, it is widely believed, would render the ABM system temporarily inoperative because the radars would not function in such an environment. More conservatively, one could have targeted several warheads against the city anticipating that one would leak through the defenses. Still more conservatively, one could have targeted 65 or more warheads on the city, assuming that at most the defenses could intercept 64. Or finally, anticipating that the observed deployment might be just a precursor of more to come, we might have greatly increased the number of warheads we could deliver against the whole country. We are doing the latter, increasing the number of warheads in our missile force not by 64 but by about 5000—from less than 3000 to about 7500.

It is an example of what we have come to call "worst case analysis"—analysis that gives the adversary the benefit of every doubt while giving ourselves none. It is the kind of analysis that can lead one to conclude, as Albert Wohlstetter did, that the balance may indeed be delicate.

Our own ABM debate provides a perhaps even more dramatic example of worst case analysis run wild. In this case the decision to defend our Minuteman missiles against a hypothetical Soviet attack was justified by the Administration's assuming that all of the following were plausible developments:

1. that the Soviet ICBM force would grow substantially;

2. that the Soviet Union would develop a technology, not demonstrated by it so far, for delivering multiple warheads with high accuracy using a single booster;

3. that the U.S.S.R. would discount the possibility that our missiles might be launched based on radar warning of attack before any Soviet warheads could be delivered;

4. that it would be possible for the Russians to prevent the launch of our ICBMs during the period between attack against our bomber bases and the arrival of their ICBMs over our missile bases by detonating over the latter very many nuclear warheads launched from submarines;

5. that the Soviet command and control system for its missiles would be such that it could compensate for failures of individual missiles by immediately launching new missiles aimed at the same targets;

6. that the nuclear strike forces we have in Europe would either be destroyed or not counted by the Soviet Union as having a significant retaliatory capability;

7. that we would not put our bombers in the air armed with weapons prior to the hypothesized attack, or that such fraction as might be airborne could be destroyed by Soviet air defenses;

8. that in some undefined way the Soviet Union would be able suddenly to destroy virtually all of our Polaris missile force.

One cannot prove that any of these assumptions are wrong,

but in assuming *all* are possible one imputes to the Soviet Union a combination of risk-taking proclivity and technical proficiency which has no basis in experience.

Actually, it is doubtful that many in the Administration believed in the reasonableness of the line of argument advanced or in the utility of the Safeguard defense, the real reason for pushing it being much more political. Yet, the frequency with which the President and his principal spokesmen have remarked about the delicacy of the strategic balance suggests that the belief is there and is deep seated. Quotations from the three state-of-the-world messages make the point: ". . . continuing Soviet deployments and improvements—in particular, the large SS-9 missile with accurate independently targetable multiple warheads—could threaten the survivability of the land-based portion of our forces. That would not, of course, be an acceptable situation." [20] "We are approaching a crucial turning point in our strategic arms programs. If the Soviet Union continues to expand strategic forces, compensating U.S. programs will be mandatory." [21] "Modern technology makes any balance precarious and prompts new efforts at even higher levels of complexity." [22] The last statement, incidentally, stands in interesting contrast to a conclusion reached by a number of technical people, including some from both the United States and the Soviet Union, at a symposium in 1970 on the impact of technology on the arms race: "From a technological and scientific point of view, nothing is coming in the next ten or so years which would completely change the strategic balance." [23]

The implications of the delicacy theory are compounded by what we sometimes refer to as "the parallax problem"—the propensity to place an interpretation on adversary actions that is quite different from that which one applies to one's own quite similar actions. This special application of worst case analysis is perhaps nowhere better illustrated in public statements than in the President's discussion of the development of multiple warhead technology. Referring to the Soviet construction of SS-9's, the President's second state-of-the-world message has this to say: "Deployed in sufficient numbers and armed with multiple independently targetable warheads (MIRVs) of sufficient accuracy, this missile could threaten our land-based ICBM forces. Our MIRV systems, by contrast, do not have the combination of numbers, accuracy, and warhead yield to pose a threat to the Soviet land-based ICBM force." [24] One might with equal logic have argued that U.S. MIRV's pose a potential threat to Soviet ICBMs—all that would be required to make them effective counterforce weapons would be further accuracy improvement; but that Soviet multiple warheads pose no near-term threat to the U.S. retaliatory capability since they do not incorporate individual guidance and since the SS-9 force which might carry them is small and not growing rapidly. The truth is that at the time of the President's statement neither side had a very effective counterforce capability against the other's missiles, none was in the immediate offing, and there was no objective reason for believing the Soviet Union could have an effective counterforce capability on a shorter time scale than could the United States.

6

The consequences of a belief in both the delicacy of the strategic balance and the political-military utility of nuclear strength can be pernicious in the extreme. The true believer will see in all kinds of adversary moves a basis for concern and response: fear that the moves may presage the development of an adversary "first strike" capability, or an increase in strategic strength that might be exploitable politically, or, very often, both. To the extent that potential adversaries also hold the two beliefs, they may be alarmed by one's responses to their actions, and so may react in turn. Thus, in the acceptance of such beliefs one has the seeds of a vicious action-reaction spiral. Regrettably, the beliefs are contagious: the more one power's policies appear to be based on them the more so will be those of others.

A simple arms race is perhaps the most benign consequence. More troublesome is the prospect that one nation may actually make political or military moves based on the belief that it can safely exploit its superior nuclear strength or reputation for a greater willingness to risk nuclear war. It may well succeed, but it may also fail, with that kind of war as the result. Herein are both the strengths and the weaknesses of a belief in the exploitability of nuclear power, in the linkage of a broad range of political-military issues to the question of nuclear strategy and capabilities. A nation can hope to play a larger role in the world and further its interests by basing policy on these beliefs, but it will do so at great economic cost and at great risk both to itself and to all mankind.

Alternatively, if one accepts the concept of sufficiency as conventionally defined and, rejecting the delicacy theory, believes that the strategic balance is and will remain stable in the crisis sense, one reaches some very different and important conclusions about strategic weapons policy:

    a. There is no particular reason for matching an adversary weapon for weapon as he builds his forces or develops new ones.
    b. There may well be no merit in even reacting at all to much of what he does.

Were the United States to base its policy on these latter beliefs we could not cut as wide a swath on a world scale—many would think that would be just as well—and the risks of incinerating ourselves would be diminished. We would also be able to devote substantial economic and intellectual resources that would otherwise be devoted to reacting to, and even to anticipating Soviet moves with respect to strategic weaponry, to other more constructive endeavors.
    One can imagine going even further, rejecting deterrence and nuclear "sufficiency," no matter how defined—broadly or narrowly—as sterile concepts which must ultimately fail with catastrophic consequences. Surely this rejection will come as diminishing numbers of people are willing to see their existence and that of all society mortgaged to the possibly mercurial behavior of a limited number of political leaders on whom, in a time of crisis, they can have no influence and in whose stability and sense of humanity they would have to trust blindly. In such rejection is the strongest hope for real disarmament and for nuclear nonproliferation. But this is a fairly distant prospect, at least for the United States (and the Soviet Union).
    Far from seeing movement in this direction, I see us moving, if at all, in a backward direction with a continuation of the Nixon Presidency—toward emphasizing the delicacy of the strategic balance and the significance of nuclear weaponry; and I say this even taking account of the possibility of an early agreement to limit strategic arms.
    As regards SALT, the Administration has placed so much emphasis on bargaining from strength, using the Safeguard ABM as a bargaining chip, and treating the whole process, as mentioned earlier, as something approaching a zero-sum game, as to give credence to the view that nuclear superiority is meaningful and exploitable. Indeed, when one couples with this the unlikelihood that many qualitative constraints on strategic weaponry will be imposed by SALT and the repeated statements from the Defense

Department that the United States must maintain a technological lead in these areas, one is diven to wonder if SALT will have been worthwhile. Quantitative restraints on, say, ABM and ICBM systems will be of value in codifying the acceptance by both sides of numerical parity in these areas, and, with the limitations on ABM systems, in reducing concerns about the delicacy of the strategic balance. But these gains may mean little if, because of beliefs in the delicacy theory and the exploitability of nuclear strength, the arms race is simply channeled into new dimensions. And it is at least possible that the net effect of SALT may even be negative if one or both sides persist in building new systems for bargaining purposes, if not for use in SALT I then for SALT II.[25]

Aside from SALT, the President has seen fit to use the flexibility and the leadership potential inherent in his office to otherwise give weight to the role that nuclear weapons will play in world affairs. In this respect the Administration's decisions, e.g., to go ahead with a new bomber, a new submarine-based missile system (ULMS), and a continuation of unneeded multiple warhead programs, speak more persuasively than do its words.

Of course, no matter what the Administration's position, there would be those who would argue the importance of such weaponry, that nuclear superiority is meaningful, that the strategic balance is delicate, that policy must be based on worst case analysis, and that lesser conflict can be deterred by the threat of deliberate use of nuclear weapons by the United States, by the creation of new centers of nuclear control, or by the creation of ambiguity which might mean escalation to nuclear war in time of crisis. But given a different presidential lead, their numbers and influence would be smaller.

As it is, we appear to be confronted, numerous protestations to the contrary notwithstanding, with a combination of deep-seated beliefs that nuclear weapons are not really different in kind from conventional arms and a desire to have the United States play a world leadership role in which military strength will be a prominent feature—a role greater than that which publically and congressionally supported conventional forces and commitments abroad will permit. With these considerations in mind, I see for the years immediately ahead continuing, and possibly increasing, emphasis on nuclear strength.

I say this despite my belief that time is on the side of those who would argue that such strength is an asset of diminishing utility and credibility. My fear is that in a futile effort to stay the tides of change, we may destroy ourselves.

NOTES

1 McGeorge Bundy, "To Cap the Volcano," *Foreign Affairs,* XLVIII (October, 1969), 20.

2 *U.S. Foreign Policy for the 1970's, Building for Peace,* A Report to the Congress by President Richard Nixon, February 25, 1971 (Government Printing Office, 1971), pp. 10ff.; *U.S. Foreign Policy for the 1970's, The Emerging Structure of Peace,* A Report to the Congress by President Richard Nixon, February 9, 1972 (Government Printing Office, 1972), pp. 3ff.

3 *The Emerging Structure of Peace,* p. 163.

4 *Building for Peace,* p. 178.

5 *U.S. Foreign Policy for the 1970's, A New Strategy for Peace,* A Report to the Congress by President Richard Nixon, February 18, 1970 (Government Printing Office, 1970), p. 111.

6 *The Emerging Structure of Peace,* p. 158.

7 *Building for Peace,* p. 170.

8 *Ibid.*

9 *The Washington Post,* June 16, 1969.

10 *A New Strategy for Peace,* p. 135; *Building for Peace,* p. 161.

11 *The Emerging Structure of Peace,* p. 43.

12 Robert McNamara, *The Essence of Security* (New York: Harper & Row, 1968), p. 154; Bundy, p. 12.

13 *National Strategy of Realistic Deterrence,* Annual Defense Department Report (FY 1973) by Secretary of Defense Melvin R. Laird (Government Printing Office, 1972), p. 65.

14 *Foreign Affairs,* XXXVII (January, 1959), 211.

15 "Critique of Some Contemporary Defense Thinking," *Encounter,* XVI (April, 1961), 17.

16 Alain Enthoven and K. Wayne Smith, *How Much is Enough?* (New York: Harper & Row, 1971), p. 207.

17 *Op. Cit.*

18 Strategic and Foreign Policy Implications of ABM Systems, Hearings Before the Subcommittee on International Organization and Disarmament Affairs of the Committee on Foreign Relations, U.S. Senate, Part II, May 14 and 21, 1969.

19 *Op. Cit.,* p. 10.

20 *Building for Peace,* p. 173.

21 *The Emerging Structure of Peace,* p. 160.

22 *A New Strategy for Peace,* p. 142.

23 B. T. Feld, T. Greenwood, G. W. Rathjens, and S. Weinberg, eds., *Impact of New Technology on the Arms Race* (Boston: M.I.T. Press, 1971), p. 230.

24 *Building for Peace,* p. 190.

25 Since the preparation of this paper, SALT agreements have been announced. They are consistent with my expectations except that ceilings on the deployment of submarine-launched ballistic missiles and undertakings not to interfere with national means of verification are also included.

Consistent with the worst fear suggested here, the Administration has stated that it intends to continue, and indeed accelerate, the B-1 bomber and the ULMS (renamed Trident) programs, one of its rationales being the need for a strong bargaining position for SALT II.

10

Disarmament: The Domestic and Global Context

J. DAVID SINGER

It is never easy to tell whether governments are "serious" in their negotiations on disarmament, or any other issue, but if the amount of energy devoted is any indication, there is a major difference between the post-World War I and post-World War II periods. In that earlier epoch, between the two great wars, the powers were not particularly successful in arriving at agreements for the prohibition, reduction, or elimination of weapons, but it was not for lack of effort. In the decades following World War II, despite the radically increased destructiveness of the available weapons, very little effort went into negotiations for disarmament. Admittedly, there were hundreds of meetings, in and out of the United Nations, and a variety of international committees and commissions was created. But—in the name of realism and sophistication—the focus was not on *dis*armament, but on the much more modest problem of arms *control.*

While the Soviet bloc nations talked of the need for "general and complete disarmament," it is fairly clear that those governments were no more serious about it than the Western governments, who steadily resisted anything more drastic than the control of existing weapons. In recent months, however, one gets the impression that both of the superpowers may be edging toward a set of arrangements which might embrace both arms control and arms elimination. While I cannot go here into the possible explanations for this particular development, it is useful to look at the more general factors which seem to move governments toward and away from the acquisition—and elimination—of national armaments. In so doing, we may not only shed some light on the intimate relationship between a nation's military strategy and its disarmament policies, but also better understand why it is not easy for major powers to be serious about disarmament.

THE INCENTIVES FOR ARMING AND DISARMING

Perhaps the most fruitful way of trying to account for the general disinterest in the arms reduction problem is to summarize some of the reasons that appear to lie behind the decisions of governments to increase—and to decrease—their military preparedness levels. On the side of incentives *toward* armament, the first point to observe is that, given the culture of the international system, armed forces are the most tangible evidence of a nation's independence and sovereignty. Second, armed forces at the disposal of the governing elites can be, and often are used to impose and maintain domestic order. Third, their establishment provides jobs (and training) for otherwise underemployed people, and legitimate economic activity for the nation's industry and technology.[1]

In addition to these symbolic and domestic considerations, political elites may arm their nations in order to secure and enhance the nation's position in the still ungoverned international community. Legal norms, moral restraints, and political institutions at the international level may all impinge on such efforts, but a nation's power remains the most effective basis for pursuing its self-defined interests. And though there is increasing evidence that other components are beginning to replace military capability in a nation's power equation, arms are still the primary component. Thus, national leaders will seek to develop and maintain military capability not only in order to use it, but to *threaten* to use it. The actual employment of such capability could be for the purpose of weakening or destroying another nation, or of defending or counterattacking if such action were undertaken in the first place. More often, however, military capability exists in order to be brandished or alluded to in the normal processes of diplomatic confrontation and bargaining; the objective is to back up demands or requests, or to resist those made by others. Paradoxically, they may even be used as possible bargaining counters in negotiations for *dis*-armament. Finally, armed forces may be used or kept in readiness for such disparate purposes as carrying out enforcement obligations under international organizations, such as the League of Nations or the United Nations, or for occupying the territory of a defeated nation.

In considering the incentives *away* from arming and towards arms reduction, it is worth recalling that there is a sharp discrepancy between the number of weapons and men that nations retain in peacetime and the numbers deployed in wartime. Since the diplomatic and military effectiveness of a country's armed forces is partly a function of the size and quality of one's allies and one's adversaries, there is little incentive for a nation that supports the status quo to arm up to full capacity unless the potential adversaries are doing so or are expected to do so. This tendency toward modest levels of military preparedness is reinforced by two essentially domestic considerations. First, voluntary enlistments in most societies are relatively low, and conscription is usually unpopular in peacetime. Second, the designing, testing, building, and maintaining of military hardware can be quite costly, and unless it is acquired from outside, under a military aid program, the money must be raised by some form of public or corporate taxation. Lower taxes are always preferable to the public; if taxation is relatively high, the general preference is for its application to services of a more socially useful nature. Finally, in many societies there is a deep suspicion of, and hostility to, the military establishment on ideological or historical grounds.

Given this combination of incentives and disincentives, it becomes clear that the size and quality of a nation's armed forces represent a compromise between the two sets of pressures. Only within the context of these two types of pressure can a nation's tendency to arm or disarm be understood. Even in periods of extreme diplomatic tranquillity, there will be serious pressures toward an increase in capability even in nations having no aggressive designs; likewise, pressures for arms reduction often exist even in nations at, or over, the brink of war. It is in response to these contrasting external and internal forces that nations get caught up in both armament and disarmament "races."

The cost and danger of an arms race, or the actual consequences of one, usually produce the incentives for disarmament. If we bear in mind the contrasting economic, political, and military considerations at work, it becomes evident that an arms race is a highly reciprocal social process, involving interaction not only between the governments of the nations involved, but also among conflicting factions within and across the national boundaries. In the absence of effective international government, nations have no real source of security other than their own power. In seeking to maximize such power vis-à-vis others that might threaten their security, nations compete with one another for prestige, markets, raw materials, waterways, territory, allies, and spheres of influence. The pursuit of such goals by one nation is often detrimental to the interests of another, which can resist by using various diplomatic, economic, and psychological techniques.

Most often, these clashes of interest are temporarily resolved by tacit or negotiated compromise, but occasionally both parties commit themselves to goals that are clearly incompatible and not susceptible to such settlement. Arms races are often an integral part—both cause and consequence—of that process, which will be examined more fully in the next section.

PREPAREDNESS AND POSITIVE FEEDBACK

The above is, of course, a superficial summary of the pressures which move governments and their citizens toward or away from increasing arms levels. Moreover, it is a very static summary. To understand the *process* by which nations get into armament "races" or into disarmament "races," we must tie many of these factors together. Let me try to do so, by using the simple but powerful notion of "feedback." [2]

A credible—if not familiar—scenario should make the concept clear. We find Tom and Mary (happily married, of course) sharing not only a king-sized bed, but a king-sized, dual control, electric blanket as well. Under normal conditions, either of them can raise or lower the heat on his/her side without affecting the temperature on the other's side. If Mary feels too cool, she reaches for *her* control knob and sets her thermostat for a higher temperature; and if Tom feels too hot, he sets *his* thermostat for a lower temperature. This electric blanket is characterized by what we call *negative*—or self-*correcting*—feedback; the mechanism is designed to keep each half of the blanket within a small temperature range, with no human intervention once the desired range has been reached.

Suppose, however, that the factory which turns out these blankets has the kind of quality control we all too often expect from modern industry, and someone "gets the wires crossed" in manufacture. During its first night of use, Tom feels too warm, and reaches for his knob to turn his thermostat down. But the trouble is that even though it's on his side, the control isn't his, but *hers*. Pretty soon, Mary begins to feel too cool, so she turns her control up; but again, it isn't hers, but *his*. Poor Tom, instead of feeling cooler, gets even warmer. So he turns "his" down further, leading Mary to turn "hers" up further. And so on. That is *positive* —or self-aggravating—feedback. Instead of the mechanism serving to keep some sort of fairly stable equilibrium, the crossed wires produce a pair of runaway temperature spirals; the hot one keeps getting hotter, and the cold one keeps getting colder.

Many social systems manifest these two kinds of feedback process, sometimes simultaneously and sometimes sequentially. In

international conflict, I would suggest, we often see such simul-
taneity, but with the positive and self-aggravating mechanism soon
getting the upper hand, and ultimately dominating the negative,
self-correcting feedback mechanisms. Let me begin by expanding
on some of my earlier comments regarding the structure and culture
of the modern international system, and how they make for *some*
continuing minimum levels of conflict between and among *some*
nations at any time.

What makes a certain level of such conflict almost inevitable?
As noted earlier, given the absence of legitimate supranational
authority in the global system, national elites have relied on the
ultimate threat of military power as a means of defending "national
interests" against possible interference by other nations. This traditional reliance on force as the final arbiter has, in turn, inhibited
the growth of an alternative basis for internation harmony: a
widely accepted normative code which provides for peaceful settlement of the inescapable conflicts and clashes of interest. In the
absence of both coercive authority and normative consensus, and
in the presence of many material and psychic scarcities, the only
remaining basis for cooperative behavior is a utilitarian one—a
payoff matrix which rewards short-run restraint and accommoda-
tive strategies.

And there is the rub. If two nations become involved in a
conflict, the general options are two. The most natural, and probably the most frequent, response is to stand firm on the original
conflict-inducing position, or perhaps even to increase the original
demands. Within most well-integrated national societies, this response tends to be applauded, and the limited opinion survey data
suggest that it generally enhances the popularity of the regime.
Moreover, this behavioral response tends to reinforce the existing
norms of world politics ("this is the way things are done") and
hence the probability that other nations will handle subsequent
conflicts in the same general manner.[3] But this is a fairly standard
and stylized opening round routine, and not particularly pregnant
with danger. The critical question is whether the protagonists now
succeed in "backing off" sufficiently so that routine diplomatic
procedures can be brought into play, or whether one or both
parties will continue to press their claims in a more vigorous
fashion.

The other general option is to recognize the opening moves
for what they are and to then initiate and reciprocate moves of
a more conciliatory nature. But the probabilities are all too high
that the competence, courage, or patriotism of one or both sets of

elites will then be challenged by a "hard-line" domestic opposition, be it a legitimate political party in a democratic system or a less institutionalized faction in a more autocratic system.[4] Moreover, the efficacy of that challenge from the "outs" will generally be high, due largely to the prior actions of the "ins." That is, political elites cannot man an army and finance a military machine without some sort of psychological mobilization.[5] In persuading an appreciable sector of their society that preparedness is necessary, they inevitably create a climate which must be relatively responsive to jingoistic appeals from the opposition.[6] As a matter of fact, had some minimum psychic and material preparedness not existed prior to the conflict, there might well have been no conflict; had the nation been militarily weak or psychologically unprepared, the competitor would probably have had its way *without* any diplomatic conflict.

Having suggested the general linkages between the national and the international systems, creating largely incompatible sets of demands on the national elites, let me now describe the feedback processes in greater detail. My purpose here is to indicate more precisely where the self-aggravation tendencies are greatest, and to indicate how they inhibit most efforts toward arms reduction.

The first point is found at the apex of the foreign policy hierarchy within the nations themselves.[7] The political elites, often unwittingly, "paint themselves into a corner" in order to accomplish two short-run objectives when engaged in diplomatic conflict. One objective is to demonstrate to the foreign adversary that they have both the intent and the capability to stand firm; the other is to head off any potential domestic attack based on the inadequacy of that intent and capability. In order to satisfy both these objectives, however, the elites will ordinarily resort to the kind of rhetoric that does little more than "raise the ante" all around. The intended message to the adversary may be merely one of firm determination, but since it will be heard at home as well, it cannot be too conciliatory; as a matter of fact, by making a commitment audible to the domestic audience, the decision-makers may hope to make their foreign policy threats more credible, given the domestic costs, real or apparent, of capitulation.

Assuming for the moment that the early verbal behavior has demonstrated the appropriate degree of firmness abroad and at home, what are the likely consequences? The adversary's regime, of course, "will not be intimidated," and so responds in public messages to the several relevant audiences. At this point in the scenario, if we are fortunate, the interactions shift toward quiet diplomacy, both domestic oppositions turn their attention to other matters, and the publics forget the episode in short order. Suppose, however, that the prior episodes had been so handled by the regime, the opposition, and the media that there was sufficient public hostility toward this particular adversary, and, further, that the opposition prefers not to let the issue drop out of sight. Quite clearly, the regime takes a fairly serious domestic risk if it ignores the cries for justice, revenge, national honor, and so forth; but it takes a different (and also far from negligible) risk of escalating the conflict if it tries to satisfy the domestic critics.

In order to examine the second point at which positive feedback can get us into serious trouble, we can focus on another set of factors. Let us assume, reasonably enough, that both nations in the conflict are moderately well armed by contemporary (but non-nuclear) standards, but that one enjoys a discernible superiority over the other in the relevant military categories, and that neither can turn to close allies for diplomatic or military support. The regime of the disadvantaged protagonist, having permitted the conflict to pick up some momentum, now has the choice of (1) bluffing, (2) retreating, or (3) delaying while improving its military position. The first can lead to a sharpening of the conflict and a more humiliating retreat later (or even a stumbling into war); the second makes it vulnerable to political attack at home. Thus there is always some temptation to try to close the manpower and weapons gap in order to bargain from a position of parity or even of greater strength. If this route is taken, the regime will first need to launch a program of psychological mobilization, without which neither the volunteers and conscripts nor the funds for weapon acquisitions might be forthcoming.[8] In the process of mobilizing public and sub-elite support for these preparedness activities, however, two new conditions are generally created. First, the adversary is not likely to sit idly by, watching its superiority disappear; its regime therefore embarks on a similar set of programs. Second, both publics must become more persuaded of the need to resist the menace to their nation's security, and as a consequence, offer a more fertile ground for any militant domestic opposition. Given the almost irresistible temptation to exploit this state of affairs, the net effect is to raise hostility levels in both nations, and therefore to raise the expectations as to what would constitute a satisfactory settlement, negotiated or otherwise. Since these rising expectations tend to be fairly symmetrical, neither regime is in as good a position to compromise as it was during the first round of the conflict. The probability of further escalation, diplomatic rupture, or war itself is now appreciably greater.

Let me now turn to a third source of danger in the cyclical conflict processes that seem to characterize so much of international politics. To this point, the role of the media has had little attention, yet mass communications would seem to play a particularly central role in helping along the self-aggravating process. Again, the differences between a highly autocratic and a relatively democratic nation are seldom as profound as contemporary elites—communist, anticommunist, and other—profess to believe. At almost any point along the autocratic-democratic continuum, the political elites need the media, and the media need the political elites, be they regime or opposition. The regime relies on the media to help mobilize the population, to bargain with and ridicule part of the domestic opposition, and even to communicate with other nations.

While "managing the news" may be simpler to arrange when the party in power exercises *formal* control over its media, any effective and stable regime has little difficulty in doing so. First, the words and actions of the elite are, by definition, newsworthy, and therefore widely transmitted. Second, members of the regime have information available which can be of great help to the reporter or commentator to whom it is made available. Thus, by judicious release or righteous restraint, government officials can all too readily help or hinder the careers of many journalists. Third, as regimes become more conscious of the need—and possibilities—of domestic propaganda, they begin to recruit media people into their very ranks as "public information" officers. Many newsmen are thereby involved in competition for these often attractive bureaucratic positions, and one way to stay in the running is to describe the appropriate agency's activities in a generally favorable fashion. While access to, and control over, the media may not be quite as simple for the "outs" as for the "ins," factions or parties in legal opposition are not without the sorts of media amplifiers they need to berate the regime for being "soft on. . . ," devoid of courage, or incapable of defending the nation's honor. In some nations, each political party has its own newspaper, magazine, or radio station; in others, the possibility of the opposition coming to power can make the media somewhat more responsive than might be expected.

I am not, in this section, arraigning the media of most nations on charges of "selling out," although the charge would be far from groundless. Rather, despite the existence of a vigorous and independent sector in the media services of many nations, the general impression is that the incentives work to make these institutions a major factor in amplifying internation conflicts and contributing to the positive feedback, escalation process.[9]

The fourth and final factor to be considered in this analysis is the effect which a nation's participation in an escalating conflict can have upon the distribution of social, economic, and political power within the society. Without accepting those conspiratorial models that see generals and "munitions makers" actively fomenting rivalry, conflict, and war, one must be extraordinarily naive to expect no systematic biases in the foreign policy preferences of those who comprise the military-industrial-labor-academic complex.[10] Even more than with newsmen, questions of ambiguity will regularly tend to be resolved in the hard-line direction by many military officers, corporate executives, labor leaders, government bureaucrats, defense intellectuals, and technical consultants, as well as the standard phalanx of patriotic organizations. Given the state of our knowledge about international politics, most foreign policy problems are indeed matters of opinion, rather than of knowledge or fact; and *in* matters of opinion, the point of view which gets the benefit of the doubt can be expected to win out most of the time.

The problem here of course is that in most nations the major positions of power—as well as the public plaudits—go to those who are in the ideological mainstream; this seems to hold even if the mainstream of the moment is allegedly pragmatic and nonideological, as in the United States of today and (probably) the Soviet Union of tomorrow. Having acquired power, prestige, and credibility by advocating, or acquiescing in, the modal foreign policy positions, these middle elites are seldom likely to shift too far in their views. And they are particularly reluctant to shift toward a position which could be interpreted (or misinterpreted) as giving aid and comfort to the enemy, whoever the enemy of the moment may be.[11]

Furthermore, as the intensity of the internation conflict increases, the higher becomes the value of the professional and extracurricular services of these middle elites. On top of this, as their individual influence and status increases, the *size* of their sector also increases. When the armed forces expand, officer promotions accelerate, and when more weaponry is being designed and produced, more engineers and technicians are promoted and recruited. Even academics in the social and physical sciences find that foreign policy conflicts lead to increased opportunities for money, status, and influence in the modern world. The high energy physicist or the professor of biology has his role to play in the preparedness program, just as the political scientist or anthropologist finds himself consulting on military strategy or counterinsurgency. If for no other purpose than to give intellectual legitimacy to the conventional wisdom, academics are almost as likely to be co-opted into the foreign policy mainstream as are the more obvious members of the military-industrial complex.

My point here is that it does not take a so-called totalitarian regime to mobilize key sectors of the society. The basic properties of the sovereign national state in the industrial age are such that this mobilization occurs with little effort. No secret police, no dictatorial government, not even any veiled threats are required to generate the joint "conspiracies" of silent acquiescence and noisy affirmation, once a nation becomes embroiled in a conflict of any magnitude. For the past century or so, the self-correcting mechanisms have gradually withered, despite the assumptions of economic liberalism and classical democratic theory. In the absence of vigorous countervailing forces within the nations or in the larger global community, the self-correcting mechanisms of international politics are feeble indeed, with the consequence that all too many of the inevitable conflicts among nations are free to grow into costly rivalries and, occasionally, into tragic wars. In the next section of this paper, I will try to suggest certain arms control and disarmament procedures whereby these four basic self-aggravating mechanisms might be partially weakened or controlled.

FROM DETERRENCE TO ARMS CONTROL

It is customary to think of deterrence and disarmament as two distinctly different and antithetical policies; a nation follows *either* a deterrence policy or a disarmament policy. This tendency to dichotomize is quite unfortunate, since there turns out to be a very strong interdependence between the two sets of policies. To put it another way, one may think of deterrence policies as designed to help a somewhat insecure nation (such as the U.S. and the U.S.S.R. in the post-World War II period) survive in the short run, and disarmament policies as designed to make the global system into a safer environment over the long run. Moreover, the design of one's deterrence policies will often affect not only the probability of short-run survival, but also the probability of ever making the transition to disarmament. Most such policies fall under the rubric of arms *control,* as they are designed to enhance our capacity to live with and exercise control over major weapon systems, rather than to eliminate them from the nations' arsenals.

The key question in any such transition—on both sides—is whether or not to risk the implications of a strategy based on uncertainty as to the other's intentions. While the weapons themselves almost compel the assumption of implacable hostility and inevitable military showdown, it is nevertheless possible for the decision-makers to recognize a modicum of reciprocity and symmetry in the basic relationship, and to appreciate that one of the major factors in the adversary's decision to arm heavily is the fact that you are also doing so. If this recognition occurs, and the strategists on each side come to appreciate that the other's pursuit of power *may* be for purely deterrent and retaliatory purposes only, they may then seek to adopt postures which reflect such a suspended judgment. In so doing, they might very well encourage a stance on the other side which turns out to coincide with such ambivalent expectations.

More specifically, if either opts for weapon systems and doctrines which reflect a high expectation of war, the other will almost invariably do likewise. On the other hand, if either selects those postures which suggest uncertainty as to the other's intent, and allows for the possibility (or, better, probability) that he arms primarily out of *fear*, the other may possibly attribute the same motives to the first, and likewise opt for less provocative policies. Though it is generally correct to assume that today's technology almost precludes a defensive-type stance and that the advantages of the offense have corrupted the traditional notions of military defense, there are nevertheless certain alternatives that might be either negotiated or undertaken unilaterally. What are some of these?

While admitting that defense has largely given way to retribution, and that punitive capabilities play the dominant role in all major power strategic doctrines, there is still the important distinction between a strike-first and a strike-back posture, and there are several areas in which one may indicate which is the basic strategy adopted. The first point at which such a choice becomes apparent is in the *nature of one's offensive delivery systems and launch sites.* If one's strategy is primarily retaliatory,[12] then he does not go in for weapons which are better for strike-first than strike-back missions. For example, he does not put his air bases or missile sites in highly vulnerable positions, where they are obviously incapable of carrying out the retaliatory mission. More specifically, the NATO powers should not have (despite the time and cost in-

centives) constructed their Thor and Jupiter IRBM sites so close
to Soviet boundaries that they could easily be destroyed by a first
strike, and hence be almost useless for a strike-back operation.
Such acts encouraged the belief in the Kremlin that these were
aggressive, surprise-attack weapons and probably strengthened
those Rusian strategists (including Khrushchev) who favored in-
stalling their missiles in Cuba in 1962. One consequence of that
dangerous confrontation was a recognition of this principle, and
the "soft" NATO sites in Western Europe were dismantled at
about the same time as those in Cuba.

Likewise, both sides must avoid the construction of vulnerable
launch sites even on their home territory. The more they are made
capable of withstanding an opening attack, the more they will look
like strike-back weapons only. Thus, in a rough sense, the mode
of deployment, dispersal, hardening, and concealing of these sites
should help persuade the adversary of your own fear of a surprise
attack and that your posture is primarily for retaliation.

A second step which each side can take to build a bit more
stability into the contemporary stand-off is to *make no effort to
discover the location* of the other's retaliatory bases and launch
pads. If one is not interested in getting in the first blow, there is
no point in knowing these locations, as most of them will already
have been vacated in the event of the need to retaliate against
their possessor. In a finite or minimum (and hence, less provocative)
strategy, it is enough to know where the cities, rail terminals, and
harbors are, in order to mete out "adequate" retribution. Thus,
the United States may have erred greatly in sending the U-2's over
Soviet territory in search of, *inter alia,* their missile sites. On the
other hand, it was an understandable move inasmuch as the Soviets
already knew the location of most American silos, through press
reports and normal intelligence operations; parity of knowledge
is pursued as eagerly as parity of weapons.

Much can (and should) be done in this particular sector of
arms control possibilities. For example, each power could slow
down, if not terminate, their satellite surveillance of the other's
ICBM sites. This could be handled by a ban on the augmentation
or replacement of those orbiting space vehicles which have such
a high-resolution detection and identification capability. Similarly,
but more difficult to inspect, each could cut back on its efforts to
track the other's missile-launching submarines. Unfortunately, such
stabilization measures seem to have received little attention in recent arms control conversations.

A third step—though of greater ambiguity—is the *rejection of any civil defense program.* With warning times and defenses as limited as they are, a civil defense program could not be terribly effective against surprise attack, but could be reasonably useful against an expected retaliatory attack. Thus, as I urged a good many years ago [13], the decision to go in for serious civil defense would almost inevitably compel the other side to increase its suspicions and fear of the first's intentions.

Fourth, and just as important as these *passive* defense measures, are those of an *active* variety, of which the ABM is the prime example. Enough is known about the current generation of such anti-missile weapons to conclude that they would make hardly a dent in the waves of offensive missiles coming in on a massive and coordinated first strike. But against an attack launched by a badly damaged and disorganized missile force—that is, one which had already been hit by a coordinated missile and bomber assault by the enemy—the ABM interceptors could make quite a difference. Hence, any kind of ABM system, especially if associated with one's ICBM force, can turn out to look like part of a counter*force* (as opposed to counter*city*) capability, and thus be highly provocative and destabilizing. On the other hand, a modest or "thin" anti-ballistic missile system *does* have certain virtues. Because it could be effective against not only an originally powerful force which has been partially destroyed, but also against one which is small to begin with, a thin defense system might: (1) reduce the damage done by a small accidental or unauthorized attack from another nuclear power; and (2) reduce the incentive for non-nuclear nations to begin acquiring a nuclear missile capability.[14]

An awareness of the dangers—as well as monetary costs—inherent in an ABM race gradually dawned on Soviet and American decision-makers in the late 1960's, and efforts to halt that competition were made in seven successive rounds of the SALT (strategic arms limitation talks) negotiations. Finally, in May of 1972, with President Nixon in Moscow, an important agreement was reached. Each side would be limited to only two ABM sites, one of which would defend the capital cities and the other of which would be near a major ICBM installation.

Returning to offensive forces again, a fifth measure is to *build and deploy only enough* missiles, warheads, and strategic bombers to carry out a devastating retaliatory strike. That number is surrounded by controversy, but we do know that a good *retaliatory* force needs to have many fewer deliverable warheads than a good *first strike* force. Because the "kill ratio" in a first strike is still quite low, the deterring side can threaten a successful second strike with litle more than half as many warheads as the attacker has. An oversupply of missiles or an increase in warheads per missile via MIRV (multiple independently targeted re-entry vehicles) can be expected to make the other side increasingly nervous. Of course, the size of an "adequate" offensive force depends on the size of the adversary's defensive force, and in the ABM negotiations mentioned above, relative missile and bomber capabilities were under constant discussion. Thus, students of arms control were not surprised to find that the Moscow agreements of May 1972 also included an upper limit on each side's land-based and sea-based offensive missiles. Covering the period through 1977, it stabilizes—without on-site inspection—the Soviet and American missile forces at a level of approximate parity, with the former enjoying an edge of 1618 to 1054 launchers and the latter having about a 3 to 1 edge in warheads, largely due to the U.S. lead in the design and deployment of its MIRV system.

Finally, each side must be careful to avoid a *strategic doctrine* which suggests either preventive or pre-emptive strike by bombers or missiles. In other words, by opting for maximum invulnerability of retaliatory forces, neither would be indicating plans for getting in a first blow in moments of crisis. Each could afford to sit out the crisis, knowing that it could still get the punitive blow in, even after accepting an opening blow. This stance can be communicated not only by the nature of one's strike-back facilities and one's articulated target selection, but by the command and communication system. If these latter arrangements are of a hair-trigger variety or so constituted as to go off on the basis of very limited and inconclusive information, they may not only trigger an "accidental" war, but reflect less concern for stability than is really needed to reassure the adversary.

These, then, are a few of the measures which can be undertaken by the individual governments—either as a result of negotiation or by unilateral decision—as steps toward stabilizing the military stand-off. But it would be quite naive to expect important results from them. For example, one may decrease vulnerability by maintaining an airborne alert of some portion of one's bombers, designed to indicate a retaliatory strategy only. But this measure, because it makes surprise attack easier for the aggressor and more difficult for the apparent victim to forecast, also can be rather provocative and destabilizing. We must not lose sight, in our fascination with the game of tacit communication, of the fact that no weapon system or strategy can be purely retaliatory. In the eyes of the beholder, all suggest *some* measure of hostile intent, though some are less likely to do so than others.[15]

Shifting now to measures which would require not only negotiated agreement but also continuing collaboration in order to be effective, another arms control arrangement is the creation of a United Nations agency which would have the equipment, personnel, and authority to supervise and regulate *all* rocket and missile and satellite launchings. Such an arrangement would be easily inspectable and could provide several benefits to a nervous world. First, it would virtually assure that no test or experimental launch could be mistaken for a surprise attack, since all such launches would be pre-announced, with time, location, direction, payload, and so forth all well known by both sides. And second, if this arrangement were coupled with a total ban on the testing of purely military vehicles, it would greatly inhibit the development of more destabilizing weapons. The point here is that neither side has quite approached perfection in missile guidance, and if tests were inhibited or prevented, neither could fully develop the sort of weapons which are ideal for counterforce strategies, aimed at enemy launch sites. At the same time, each has guidance and mapping techniques which are fully adequate for hitting larger targets such as cities and ports.

The establishment of such a monitoring system might well lead to another and equally auspicious arrangement—the negotiation and establishment of a system for mutual early warning against surprise attack. The crucial element in such warning systems, after adequate detection ranges and accuracy, is that of data interpretation, and a highly reliable third-party supervision could be most effective in providing the assurance that the system is working and at the same time inhibit the tendency toward overresponsiveness and premature retaliation.[16] Moreover, it would not only give warning if and when an attack were being launched, but would provide continuous negative intelligence, i.e., that *no* attack is being prepared or launched. Both these monitoring systems could play a crucial stabilizing role as well as offer the nucleus for the sort of inspection system which the actual reduction and elimination of armaments would require later on in the transition from deterrence to disarmament.[17]

Other reciprocal steps might include an extension of the ban on nuclear tests to the underground environment, and a ban on the dissemination of either nuclear warheads or missile delivery systems to Nth powers. As to the underground test ban, one of the major arguments against it is that Western (and presumably Soviet) development of tactical nuclear weapons would be dangerously retarded and the United States and its allies would be less capable, therefore, of fighting a limited war. The consequence of this retardation, it is argued, makes it more likely that they would have to fight a larger-scale war and use high-yield warheads. This argument, however, overlooks the fact that the development of small, or tactical, nuclear weapons would obliterate the profound and clear difference between conventional and nuclear warfare which now obtains, and create a continuum along which escalation could go by minor increments until the limited wars that we anticipate gradually evolve into wars in which multikiloton and megaton weapons would be used. The best way to keep limited wars limited (if we must have even these conflagrations) is to preserve a dramatic and self-evident line of demarcation between the nuclear and non-nuclear. Tactical nuclears would demolish that line.

SOME FIRST STEPS TO DISARMAMENT

So far, we have concentrated primarily on ways in which we might survive in a world in which the arms race continues. And despite the attractiveness and potential value of some of these and similar ideas, they still make no fundamental change in the politico-military relationship between the hostile coalitions. One step which could help in moving out of the armaments spiral and its concomitant tensions is that of *banning the production* of new weapons; the recent SALT agreement carries us, finally, over this first threshold.

Given the extreme difficulty of detecting the presence of existing weapons, and the relative importance of *existing* vis-à-vis *potential* weapons to a nation's security, the possibility of certain production bans looks rather promising. Whether it be nuclear warheads, missiles, and bombers, or even conventional weapons or BCR (bacteriological-chemical-radiological) types, the detection and monitoring of future production is relatively manageable.[18] One of the emerging assets of the age of industrialization and bureaucratization is the development of complex but fairly reliable techniques for monitoring everything from matériel flows to personnel utilization. Employing "operations research" and similar approaches, the nations could readily devise and construct an arrangement of checks and inspections which could be reliable enough to deter even the most ingenious and motivated would-be violator.[19]

I emphasize the ban on production for reasons that should be obvious, but which have been fully appreciated only in the past year or two. As suggested above, inspection for existing weapons is most difficult, and even with an onerous and elaborate system, clandestine stockpiles could be preserved with a low risk of discovery. As to the *testing* of weapons, a test ban is often thought of as the most logical step toward disarmament, and I would generally agree. But it must be remembered that policing a *test* ban—let us say on nuclear weapons—would be more difficult than policing a *production* ban on the same weapons. This is, of course, especially true in regard to underground tests of lower-yield weapons, whose detectability is still a matter of some debate and diplomatic impasse.

Another juncture at which the production of weapons might be slowed or halted is at the pre-test stages, where most of the effort is concentrated in the laboratories and shops, and on writing pads and blackboards. Though the possibilities of such a research ban are fairly attractive at first blush, I would tend to discount them. It must be remembered that the dividing line between pure and applied research, and between nonmilitary and military research, is extraordinarily indistinct. Consequently, it would pose great problems of adequate inspection and would either inhibit nonmilitary research (to which I would be opposed) or lead to widespread and often undetected evasion, with a consequent degradation in the overall disarmament inspection system. The important thing in inhibiting weapons production is to find that point in the research-test-production sequence at which the process becomes clearly military, and apply the restrictions there. Any other juncture would be too early and onerous, or too late and dangerous.

Finally, one way to prevent the acquisition of new weapons is to prohibit their transfer from the nations which already *do* have them to those who do *not*. This is the antiproliferation strategy which is often attractive to the "haves," if not to the "have-nots." While the argument of inequity as well as the more dubious argument of multiple deterrence may be leveled against such a strategy, the case for restricting modern strategic weapons to a small number of powers seems very persuasive. And, after years of tough debate and negotiation, three of the major nuclear powers (United States, U.S.S.R., and United Kingdom) finally agreed in 1968 to ban the transfer of nuclear weapons or fissionable material to non-nuclear nations. And while France and China have remained aloof, the agreement (which entered into force in 1970) looks as if it will indeed slow down the spread of nuclear warheads.

Not until we direct our attention to the actual *reduction and elimination* of weapons, however, do we really begin to make substantial changes in the military, and hence the political, environment of the cold war. As I have already suggested, all prior steps, no matter how ameliorative they may be, still leave that environment substantially untouched. Mutually invulnerable second-strike capabilities, even if accompanied by a highly expensive and still unreliable monitoring and early warning arrangement, still leave the capabilities more or less intact and hence make only a slight dent in reciprocally perceived threat. Likewise, bans on testing, pre-production, and production processes, though they slow the flow of new and more weapons, fail to get at the nub of the problem.[20] Thus, we must ultimately (and the sooner, the better) face the really difficult problem of eliminating existing stockpiles, or more specifically, a large enough portion of them to make aggressive war almost impossible. In many places and from many sources (on both sides), the general principles which must guide any actual disarmament program have been heard, and for the most part there is no need to quarrel with them. Elimination of weapons must be gradual and phased, completion of each phase must be verified before going on to the next, and no phase must offer a significant offensive advantage to either side.

The issues that divide governments and students of the problem flow from these general requirements. One concern which has received considerable attention is the degree of inspection necessary at each stage, and the timing of its commencement. Though there is much ambiguity on both sides, one might say that the U.S.S.R. has come to a position favoring verification at the *end* of each phase but prior to going on to the next, while the United States and its allies insist on the establishment of an inspection system *prior* to each (especially the initial) stage, on two grounds. First, there is the fear that once the phase is completed, the Soviets will not accept adequate inspection of it, and that there may be less than complete compliance. Second, there is the belief that the quantitative and qualitative reductions negotiated can only be a function of an adequate *pre*-reduction census, which in itself requires a comprehensive surveillance program.

My own analysis of the negotiations (up through the current SALT sessions) indicates that the inspection issue, and others related to it, may well be somewhat more soluble now that the Soviets have accepted the principle of inspection and have even negotiated at length over its application to such items as the nuclear test ban.[21] But such a resolution seems unlikely until a new element is injected into the plans and schedules under debate. That element must deal with the following kinds of questions seldom articulated but always implicit in the negotiations, in or out of the United Nations. First, no inspection system can be fool-proof or 100 percent effective; therefore, what is there to protect the side which *does* comply against the one which may *not?* Second, if the program progresses to a midway point, and there is then disagreement as to the conditions of its continuation, what agency is to adjudicate and enforce a solution? Third, once the nations have disarmed all the way, or nearly all the way, to levels designed for domestic "security" only, who is to adjudicate political disputes, enforce these decisions, and protect the nations from any who might attempt to re-arm or who may have managed to secrete enough weapons to pose a significant threat?

ONE APPROACH TO THE PROBLEM

The answer to all these questions seems to lie in an altered United Nations Organization with markedly increased political and legal powers. But it is perfectly evident that in a world which is (and would be then) still far from a community in the literal sense, an international organization must have more than purely "paper" powers. In the absence of impressive *psychological* power (i.e., strong tendency of nations to comply with directives) it must be endowed with adequate *physical* power; compliance usually requires some mixture of consensus and coercion. Thus, I would contend that if we are to get started on the road to disarmament of the nations, we will have to make the difficult decision to give the United Nations a degree of political and military power markedly superior to that which it now enjoys. I say it is a difficult decision because it means, in effect, that we would be taking a large step toward federal government, a step which would mark the abrogation of the nations' traditional "right" to use or threaten force in their relations with one another.

Assuming such a decision, we are still faced with a bewildering complex of technical and political and strategic problems, but we are then at least on the right path. The first step in the disarmament program would be to ascertain what types and quantities of weapons each of the signatories possesses at a given date and to then project those figures to a number of somewhat later dates at which the first cessation of production might be expected to commence. To establish these two sets of figures, a survey team (precursor and nucleus of the subsequent inspection agency) with certain powers of access and interrogation would have to be recruited and organized and its powers clearly defined. Once these data were in, and more or less accepted by the powers involved, the process of negotiating the specific reductions and cutbacks would commence, and four specific problems would have to be dealt with. First, how much of what class of existing weapons would be given up during each stage? Second, what extent of what class of weapons production would be halted at each stage? Third, what types of inspection would be required (and acceptable) virtually to assure compliance at and during each stage? Fourth, what dispensation would be made of the existing weapons that are to be removed from the national stockpiles and the materials (especially nuclear) which are to be diverted from military production?

Though the first three are perhaps the most technical and complicated, they all seem to be susceptible to the application of expertise and sincerity, providing the fourth—and most crucial—is solved. Here I return to the notion mentioned above, that of endowing the United Nations with physical as well as symbolic power. What I would propose is that, for each stage of the reduction and cutback program, a specified quantity of particular weapons and material be sold to the United Nations.[22] The *conventional* weapons so transferred would be assigned to paramilitary United Nations units which have been recruited, specially trained, and deployed, prior to that stage. Located on bases (and subsequently naval vessels) sold to the Organization, these personnel would receive, account for, maintain, and operate an increasingly ample supply of non-nuclear weapons. Inasmuch as the first stage (of perhaps ten semi-annual stages) would see the reduction of only a small quantity (approximately 1 percent) of conventional weapons and their purchase by the United Nations,[23] it would not pose an appreciably difficult administrative or logistic problem at the outset. Nor would the first several stages see either a major deterioration of the nations' individual military capabilities or a dramatic upsurge in that of the Organization. The first few stages would be primarily of a confidence-building, training, and acclimatization nature, marking the beginning of a more impressive transition in the distribution of world power.

So far, I have been discussing the transfer of weapons other than the nuclear-missile types, and a word regarding this lethal combination is now in order. I would propose that a ban on the production of both missiles and warheads be instituted as early in the disarmament program as possible, and preferably at the very outset. But any transfer of existing stocks in these two categories would be delayed until perhaps the fourth stage (two years after initiating the schedule). At that time, given the growth of some limited confidence in one another and in the burgeoning Organization, the nations might be ready to begin dealing with existing stockpiles, in the following manner. A small but specified number of missiles—without warheads—of various thrust (governing as it does payload and range) would be placed at several well-dispersed United Nations depots, where they would be accounted for and maintained in a condition of semi-readiness. These depots would be close enough to the nation from whence the missiles came, but separate enough to require very identifiable efforts if repossession were to be attempted. And though the depots and the missiles would be under control of the world Organization, the former owner would be permitted to station a small number of its own specialists therein, to ensure that the acceptable level of readiness was maintained. The objective here (as in purchase rather than confiscation) is to ease the parting between nation and delivery system and to permit repossession if the whole disarmament program happened to collapse, but not otherwise. Obviously, any effort at repossession would be readily discernible and would, in effect, spell the near-demise of the entire plan.

As to the nuclear warheads, a portion would—at each stage, and very few at the beginning—be placed in United Nations depots other than those where the missiles are kept, but equally available/unavailable. Another portion of the warheads transferred at each stage would, however, actually be dismantled by the Organization with the fissionable material transferred—in turn—to the International Atomic Energy Agency for application to peaceful uses. Thus would several purposes be fulfilled: reduction of war-making potential, confidence-building, growth of United Nations competence, and expansion of the Agency's peaceful uses program.

As the separate stages of the conventional and nuclear-missile disarmament program progress, a very important tangible change in the international system might begin to take place.[24] National economies begin to re-divert resources to nonmilitary productivity,[25] national governments begin to lose existing and future weapon capabilities, and the United Nations begins to acquire a measure of conventional military power by which it may deter aggressive behavior. About half-way through such a process we reach, in a sense, a point of no return. At such a point, we find that the world Organization has acquired a capability in terms of manpower and conventional weapons such that it may no longer be defied with impunity. A significant new deterrent to aggressive behavior has emerged, especially since the national capabilities to fight non-nuclear wars have diminished appreciably and resort to nuclear war has become much less attractive.[26] This latter seems to be true because each no longer has a sufficiency to wipe out the other's remaining retaliatory weapons (which should, by then, be highly invulnerable) without either trying to forcefully repossess those sold to the United Nations or obviously violating the production ban and re-creating new stockpiles.

At such a no-return juncture, it would then be safe for the nations to give their approval to the Organization to begin dismantling the remaining warheads and converting the missiles to such nonmilitary uses as space probes, communication satellite launching, and the like. Similarly, the United Nations would have little use for further accretion to its conventional weapons levels, and these, too, could then be put into reserve maintenance, converted, or scrapped. From there on out, the United Nations could begin to reduce its own manpower and weapon levels, eventually becoming a small, highly mobile gendarmerie, equipped with adequate naval and air craft to serve as an effective symbol of the world community wherever internation conflict becomes acute and where small arms violence might tend to erupt and overflow national boundaries. (This latter comment is made to indicate that small arms could not possibly be eliminated, and that the United Nations must not, for a long time to come, be permitted to interfere with the right of dissident groups to revolt against established governments; there is still a great absence of social justice and violent rebellion will often be seen as the only alternative to despotism.)

CONCLUSION

What I have tried to do in this paper is: (1) outline the domestic and global context within which deterrence and disarmanent policies are formulated, suggesting at the same time that the weapons acquistion process itself exacerbates that context; and (2) suggest a range of steps by which the nations might safely rid themselves of the nuclear-missile monstrosities which they have created, without too many of the risks of unilateral disarmament. Having said all of this, however, I must confess to a strong sense of pessimism—a sense of pessimism arising out of the history of disarmament and arms control negotiations in particular and diplomacy in general.

Almost certain that a continued reliance on strategic deterrence will produce the ultimate detonation, having little more confidence in unilateral or multilateral efforts to stabilize the military environment, and unwilling to take the risks of unilateral disarmament, one is compelled to argue for multilateral and comprehensive disarmament. And yet, one can not be particularly sanguine when he looks at the past, and at the problems which such an approach implies. The major question seems to be: can we *by diplomacy* cast off the shackles of that very sort of diplomacy which makes war a recurrent phenomenon in relations among nations, and move into an era in which the diplomats will have to rely, not upon military force, but upon skill, imagination, the righteousness of their policies, and the less destructive elements of national power? What we are asking for, in seeking disarmament and international government, is that diplomacy actually *abolish itself* as it has been known, to be replaced with a far more subtle and difficult process by which competition and cooperation among nations will be continued, but without the constant menace of nuclear holocaust.

If this transformation is to occur, and to occur in time, it will probably have to be as the result of a sharp revision in the Western and Soviet approaches to military policy. We cannot, for example, afford to regard deterrence as relevant only to an implacable enemy, or arms control and disarmament applicable only to a reformed—and acquiescent—friend. The fact is that the United States, the Soviet Union, and China are engaged in an epic struggle, which each side hopes to win even while averting total war. But even if a military showdown is avoided, and the strategic stand-off is preserved, we will still be confronted with adversaries which have lost little of their revisionist dynamism. What is needed is a military philosophy which permits us to survive the present while shaping the future. Thus, in pursuing a strategy of deterrence we must not embrace postures that preclude escape from this mutual homicide pact. Nor must we demand more from deterrence than it can provide. All that we can ask of our weaponry is that it help persuade the adversary of the dangers of military adventurism. And this requires that it not jeopardize his capacity for intelligent calculation; we must add to his fears and frustrations no more than is minimally necessary. Apprehension may generate caution, but panic can result in violence.

And as rapidly as the situation permits, we must try to build greater stability into the stand-off, imaginatively employing non-reciprocal as well as multilateral arrangements. There is much we can do alone, but more that we and the others can do together. Unintended war is to no one's advantage, and each has some powerful incentives for collaborative measures. Thus, deterrence must blend into and merge with arms control, and arms control must, in turn, be designed so that it may flow into arms reduction and arms elimination.

Finally, in order to construct a strategy that integrates all major aspects of weapons policy, we will have to begin applying the same general criteria to each of them. The nuclear stand-off generates, on each side, an almost irresistible pressure to destroy the other's capacity to destroy one's self, and we cannot, for example, accept the tremendous day-by-day risks of this relationship and at the same time shrink from the less familiar—but certainly no greater—risks of arms control and disarmament. We cannot ask 100 percent reliability from an inspection arrangement while accepting perhaps a 50 percent reliability from our posture of threatened retribution. Each has its risks, as each has its opportunities, and our task is to balance both the risks and the opportunities as we seek to navigate the challenging road from deterrence to disarmament. The modest progress of the past decade, bringing the "hot line" agreements, the partial nuclear test ban, the Antarctic, Latin American, and outer space weapon bans, the BCR convention, and the recent SALT arrangements all suggest that the hard realities of the arms race are beginning to be recognized. We have, thus, some momentum now, and it is essential not to lose it.

NOTES

[1] See Emile Benoit and Kenneth E. Boulding, eds., *Disarmament and the Economy* (New York: Harper & Row, 1963).

[2] See Lewis F. Richardson, *Arms and Insecurity: A Mathematical Study of the Causes and Origins of War* (Pittsburgh: Boxwood Press, 1960); Thomas L. Saaty, *Mathematical Models of Arms Control and Disarmament* (New York: John Wiley & Sons, 1968); and Peter Busch, "Mathematical Models of Arms Races," in *What Price Vigilance?*, by Bruce Russett (New Haven, Conn.: Yale University Press, 1970), 193-233.

[3] The analysis suggested here does not of course apply to every conceivable internation conflict. While most such conflicts are, in my judgment, matters of routine incompatibilities between and among traditionally defined national interests, some do indeed raise legitimate issues of justice and morality. Unfortunately, we have not yet developed any generally accepted criteria for distinguishing between the two types of cases, and even if we could, nationalistic appeals would often overwhelm them.

[4] Among the studies which deal with public response to foreign policy moves, at least in the United States, are those by Karl W. Deutsch and Richard Merritt, "Effects of Events upon National and International Images," in *International Behavior: A Socio-Psychological Analysis*, ed. by Herbert C. Kelman (New York: Holt, Rinehart & Winston, 1965), 132-87; James N. Rosenau, *National Leadership and Foreign Policy* (Princeton, N.J.: Princeton University Press, 1963); and also James N. Rosenau, *Domestic Sources of Foreign Policy* (New York: Free Press, 1967).

[5] See Karl W. Deutsch, *Nationalism and Social Communication* (Cambridge, Mass.: M.I.T. Press, 1953).

[6] An important (and hopeful) exception to this generalization would be

those cases in which the psychic mobilization has been too hysterical, has gone on too long, or has otherwise rested on a less than credible base; in such cases, the domestic opposition, or some sector of it, might possibly push the "ins" toward a *less* bellicose position.

7 For the sake of simplicity here, I not only assume that there is a viable opposition in most nations but that the political spectrum is largely based on a two-faction, quasi-pluralistic division, with one or the other in power at a given time. These are, of course, drastic simplifications, but they do not affect the argument at hand.

8 A similar interpretation is offered by Thorstein Veblen in looking at the extent to which the Spanish-American and other wars were forced upon the respective governments: "The more that comes to light of the intimate history of that episode, the more evident does it become that the popular war sentiment to which the administration yielded had been somewhat sedulously 'mobilized' with a view to such yielding. . . . So also in the case of the Boer War. . . . And so again in the current European war . . . here again it is a matter of notoriety that the popular sentiment had long been sedulously nursed and mobilized to that effect, so that the populace was assiduously kept in spiritual readiness for such an event." *The Nature of Peace* (New York: B. W. Huebsch, 1919), p. 3.

9 For a cross-national range of interpretations of the media's role in foreign policy, see Bernard C. Cohen, *The Press and Foreign Policy* (Princeton, New Jersey: Princeton University Press, 1963); Theodore E. Kruglak, *The Two Faces of Tass* (New York: McGraw-Hill, 1963); James Reston, *The Artillery of the Press* (New York: Harper & Row, 1966); Dan Nimmo, *Newsgathering in Washington* (New York: Atherton Press, 1964); and O. J. Hale, *The Captive Press in the Third Reich* (Princeton, N.J.: Princeton University Press, 1964).

10 The Vietnam War has led to a number of excellent studies which illustrate the naturalness of the process by which those who stand to gain from the escalation or continuation of the conflict drift into behavior which contributes to such escalation. See, for example, Richard J. Barnet, *The Economy of Death* (New York: Atheneum, 1970); Leonard Lewin *et al.*, *Report from Iron Mountain* (New York: Dial Press, 1967); and Eliot Janeway, *The Economics of Crisis* (New York: Weybright & Talley, 1968).

11 The fact that some members of the middle elite (including political officeholders) do eventually get off the bandwagon in no way contradicts the model. They seldom do so until the conflict has reached its apogee and shows little tendency to decline; recent examples might be Germany in 1944, France in 1957, and the United States in 1970.

12 It must be understood, of course, that there is no such thing as a purely retaliatory or strike-back weapon system. Every system has certain strike-first characteristics, but some have more than others.

13 J. David Singer, "Deterrence and Shelters," *Bulletin of the Atomic Scientists*, XVII (April, 1961), 11-13.

14 Further implications of active defense systems were explored in the public and private debates of 1969 and are summarized in the Holst and Schneider (pro-ABM) and Chayes and Wiesner (anti-ABM) anthologies of that year. See Johan Holst and William Schneider, eds., *Why ABM?* (New York: Pergamon Press, 1969), and Abram Chayes and Jerome Wiesner, eds., *ABM* (New York: New American Library, 1969).

15 This question is more fully discussed in J. David Singer, "Stable Deterrence and Its Limits," *Western Political Quarterly*, XV (September, 1962), 449-64.

16 For an early and thoughtful proposal, see Thomas Schelling, "Arms Con-

trol: Proposal for a Special Surveillance Force," *World Politics*, XIII (October, 1960), 1-18.

[17] Here is, however, another illustration of the paradox of inspection. The inspection system for surprise attack would have to be considerably more complex and responsive than one dealing with some aspect of real arms limitation such as a ban on nuclear production. The same would be true of a nuclear *test* ban vis-à-vis the *production* ban. This inverse correlation between degree of disarmament and inspection requirements has been noted in Jerome B. Wiesner, "Comprehensive Arms Limitation Systems," *Daedalus*, LXXXIX, No. 4 (1960), 915-50.

[18] On this matter, Hans Bethe told a Senate hearing as far back as 1958 that "for *current* production [of nuclear weapons] I think there is not much difficulty. For *past* production, I think it is impossible or nearly impossible." Subcommittee on Disarmament, *Hearings . . .* , 17 April 1958, p. 1542.

[19] On the requirements and feasibility of various forms of inspection, see Seymour Melman, ed., *Inspection and Disarmament* (New York: Columbia University Press, 1958); Louis Henkin, *Arms Control and Inspection in American Law* (New York: Columbia University Press, 1958); and Bernard T. Feld, *et al.*, *Technical Problems of Arms Control* (New York: Institute for International Order, 1960).

[20] It has been suggested by some that the production and test bans would really accomplish the arms elimination objective, albeit more slowly, because existing weapons would gradually deteriorate and obsolesce. But this seems both too slow and too speculative, and also fails to provide for another key element, discussed below.

[21] For a detailed treatment of the inspection issue as seen by successive U.S. administrations, see the reports of the Senate subcommittee on Disarmament and those of the Arms Control and Disarmament Agency. The most comprehensive study of the entire test ban problem is found in Harold K. Jacobson and Eric Stein, *Diplomats, Scientists, and Politicians* (Ann Arbor, Michigan: University of Michigan Press, 1966).

[22] The plan developed here is quite similar to that outlined in Grenville Clark and Louis Sohn, *World Peace through World Law* (2nd rev. ed.; Cambridge, Mass.: Harvard University Press, 1960). This comprehensive book is mandatory reading for the serious student of the deterrence-to-disarmament problem. See also, J. David Singer, *Deterrence, Arms Control and Disarmament: Toward a Synthesis in National Security Policy* (Columbus, Ohio: Ohio State University Press, 1962).

[23] Though reference is to an existing organization, the United Nations, this does not preclude the possibility that a semi-autonomous, or completely new agency might be necessary or desirable.

[24] As to BCR weapons, President Nixon ordered the destruction of a very large fraction and perhaps all of them in 1971, and it is assumed that several other nations are doing likewise.

[25] Regarding some of the necessary domestic prerequisites and problems, see Emile Benoit *et al.*, *Economic Adjustments to Disarmament*, Part II of *Economic Factors Bearing upon the Maintenance of Peace* (New York: Institute for International Order, 1960).

[26] Some will argue that we still have military deterrence, that deterrence is bad, and that all we have done is put the means of mayhem in other hands. Perhaps, but who can object to the threat of force in political relations? To some extent, every local, provincial, and national government depends upon it, and it does matter very much *who* wields that force.

11

American Foreign Policy in the 1970's: The Role of the United Nations

INIS L. CLAUDE, JR.

Since my topic refers both to American foreign policy and to the role of the United Nations, my task is to consider the relationship between the two. How might and should the foreign policy of the United States be affected in the years that lie ahead by the existence and the operation of the United Nations? To what degree and in what ways will the role that the United Nations can be expected to play in world affairs influence the nature of the role that the United States will find necessary, possible, and proper for itself? What effect will American foreign policy have upon the character of the United Nations and its capacity for effective performance? What goals pertaining to the United Nations should the United States undertake to promote, and how can American foreign policy in general, and American policy in and toward the United Nations in particular, be most effectively geared to the promotion of those goals? This essay is intended to contribute to thinking about such questions as these.

I should like to examine several conceptions, all of them in more or less general circulation, concerning what the United Nations is, or might be, or should be, in the context of its relationship with the United States.

The first of these is the conception of the United Nations as a tool of the United States, an instrument readily and reliably available to our government for carrying out, or mobilizing support for, American foreign policy. This view of the organization served for some years as the major theme of the case presented to the public, by both governmental and nongovernmental spokesmen, for American membership in and support of the United Nations. To stimulate enthusiasm for that involvement and more especially to defend it against those who would "take the U.S. out of the UN and the UN out of the U.S.," it was often proclaimed that the United Nations was our kind of organization and, indeed, *our* organization, a valuable adjunct to our diplomacy and a useful supplement to the other means at our disposal for pursuing our international objectives. This American boast was made more plausible by foreign complaints; the Soviet Union, in particular, followed by Communist China and others, buttressed the claim by railing against American domination of the United Nations and condemning the organization as little more than an arm of the State Department. This was not sheer propaganda on either side. The United States sometimes acted as if it owned the United Nations, and it frequently undertook, sometimes success-fully, to use the organization as an instrument of policy. Antagon-ists of the United States often acted as well as spoke on the premise that the organization was an American tool. The basic Soviet-American agreement concerning the facts of the situation was re-flected in the divergent attitudes of the two powers toward the veto rule in the Security Council; the Soviet view that the veto was indispensable and the American view that it was intolerable indicated the conviction on both sides that the United Nations was an institution serving the interests of the United States.

This conviction was largely, but not wholly, justified. There was always an element of exaggeration in the allegation that the United Nations was simply owned and operated by the United States—an element stemming from wishful thinking on the Ameri-can side and from fearful thinking on the Soviet side. The "auto-matic majority" attributed to the United States was never auto-matic, as numerous American representatives who had to work long and hard at building support for American positions could testify, nor was the United States consistently and uniformly suc-cessful in imposing its will upon the organization. Nonetheless, the record of the United Nations in its early years—roughly, the first decade—lent considerable support to the view that it was, above all, an instrument at the disposal of the United States.

Whatever truth there once was in this proposition has for some time been steadily draining away. The dike was broken by the open membership policy and the decolonization process. Be-tween late 1955 and late 1960, the character of the United Nations was fundamentally changed by the growth of its membership from 60 to 99. As the United Nations has moved through increasing size to different shape, American control over the organization has inexorably diminished. The contrast between the old and the new situations can be dramatically illustrated by reference to the Chinese representation issue. For some twenty years, the disposi-tion of this issue was a striking indication of the capacity of the

United States to call the tune in the United Nations. The will
of the United States was decisive in blocking a decision to acknowledge the Peking regime as the rightful occupant of the Chinese
seat; the State Department was clearly correct when it intimated,
in 1958, that Peking was kept out of the United Nations only
because of American insistence, and that a reversal of the position
of the United States would inevitably lead to the seating of
Peking.[1]

Turning to the events of 1971, we find that the United States
recognized the bankruptcy of its position and switched to advocacy
of the seating of the Communist government of China, coupled
with the retention of a place in the organization for the Nationalist
regime. The outcome proved, however, that the erosion of American influence over the United Nations had gone even farther than
the government of the United States had realized; the United
States had lost not only the capacity to exclude representatives of
the People's Republic of China, which it conceded, but also the
capacity to prevent the expulsion of representatives of the Nationalist regime, which it sought unsuccessfully to exercise. The con-
spicuous gloating in which many members of the General Assembly
indulged after the Chinese issue was settled, unseemly as it may
have been, was a reaction to the symbolic significance of the occasion; the issue that had served to dramatize the firmness of the
American grip upon the United Nations had now come to symbolize
the shaking off of the controlling American hand. The United
States had acknowledged the necessity of relaxing its grip; it had
discovered the impossibility of keeping its hand in place. This
incident revealed, for all to see, the collapse of American control
over the United Nations.

There is as much danger of exaggerating the new impotence
of the United States in the United Nations as of exaggerating the
degree of control previously exercised. The end of domination is
not equivalent to the elimination of influence. The United States
could not, even if it tried, fail to make a substantial impact upon
the world organization, and it certainly can, if it tries with intelligence and sensitivity, have a major effect upon the shape and
the direction of the organization. Nonetheless, it is clear that the
United Nations is no longer a tool of American foreign policy to
any considerable degree, and it is virtually impossible to imagine
that it will again become so.

In my opinion, this is a healthy development for all concerned, including the United States. There was always a self-defeat-

ing aspect of American control; when we confronted the need for the United Nations to do for us and for the world the things that it was uniquely capable, in principle, of doing, we always found it essential to pretend that we were less dominant than we actually were—and the difficulty of persuading others on particular occasions that the organization was more independent of our will than we customarily claimed that it was, and insisted that it should be, was a severe handicap to the exploitation of the organization's most valuable possibilities. Whatever a state gains from hegemony over a general international organization tends to be overshadowed by the loss that results from the spoiling of the organization's international character. A United Nations that can no longer be plausibly represented as a tool of the United States has more valuable, not less valuable, potentialities for serving our basic interests.

The second conception of the United Nations that I wish to consider is one in which the organization figures as a substitute for the United States—a "George" whom we can "let do it." To invoke this image is to call attention to the basic difference in the thinking about America's proper role in world affairs that prevailed in the 1940's and the thinking on that matter that has emerged since the mid-1960's. In the earlier period, attention was concentrated upon the disastrous tendency of the United States to be lazy, indifferent, indecisive, unreliable, and ill-prepared for involvement and action in international affairs. If we were not guilty of doing too little, we did it too late and too unpredictably —and therefore ended up by having to do too much. We convicted ourselves, and were indicted by others, as having been persistently irresponsible in our refusal to accept commitments and our failure to act in timely and decisive fashion to forestall challenges to global order and security. Most of the world shared our conviction that the fatal flaw in the international system was the lack of assurance that the United States would be willing and able to do whatever might be necessary to cope with threats to the stability of the system. Intent upon mending our ways, we resolved to adopt a new and vastly more active and responsible role in world affairs and to give clear and firm notice of that resolution. Our joining the United Nations was the first and in many ways the most basic expression of that decision; it symbolized an unprecedented American commitment to responsible leadership in international relations, a commitment that had been urgently requested by most other states and was in 1945 solemnly accepted and proclaimed by the United States. American membership in the United Nations

was originally conceived and interpreted as a promise concerning
what this country would be prepared to do, and could be counted
upon to do, for the maintenance of world peace.

Today's mood, in the United States and abroad, is obviously
very different. Americans are weary and disillusioned; many of us
feel guilty. We are tired of bearing the burdens, running the risks,
paying the taxes, and fighting the battles that our new international role has entailed. Dissension over our proper role has torn
our society apart and shattered whatever tradition of civility we
had managed to develop. We tend to blame our concentration on
foreign problems for our neglect of, or our failure to achieve great
progress in solving, pressing domestic problems. We resent the
taxation of the poor in this rich country for the benefit of the rich
in poor countries (if I may paraphrase a slogan coined, to the best
of my knowldege, by Peter Bauer). We see ourselves as unassisted
and unappreciated, exploited and imposed upon—or as wicked
imperialists and militarists, ruthlessly and recklessly attempting to
impose our reactionary will upon the world. We are sorry for ourselves or ashamed of ourselves; take your choice. We are exerting
ourselves to combat a threat that no longer exists or never did
exist, thus convicting ourselves of being either foolish or dishonest;
in any case, we are either wasting our substance on matters that
are of no real concern to us or we are masquerading as our brothers'
keepers while actually sticking our nose unconscionably into other
people's business. Whether our role has actually turned out to be
that of a world policeman or a global busybody or a vicious im-
perialist, we reject it. The problem posed by the United States for
the world now tends to be described as irresponsible activity, not
irresponsible passivity—as trigger-happiness, not gun-shyness. We
are overburdened, not undercommitted. We do too much, not too
little, and our most urgent task is to erect safeguards against our
undertaking to do what is unnecessary and improper, rather than
to remove impediments to our doing what is necessary and proper.
Inhibiting wicked and foolish policy, not promoting its opposite,
is the order of the day.

I confess to a certain inaccuracy in the foregoing description
of the current American mood. It would have been more nearly
correct to use "they" rather than "we," for I do not share that
mood; indeed, I am discouraged and disturbed by it. There is
hyperbole in the description, for many Americans in addition to
myself are excluded from the "they" group. The "they" under consideration, however, is a large, growing, and influential group,
and "they" are part of "us"; all of us are involved in America—

and the world—together, and the international performance of our country in the years ahead will certainly be affected by the prevalence of the mood that I have sketched.

A significant manifestation of this mood is the tendency to regard the United Nations as a substitute for the United States in world affairs. In one of its versions, this notion represents an appeal for a more equitable sharing of the burdens and the costs of international responsibility. If the world needs a policeman, why should it not be a multilateral agency, rather than the United States? We have played Atlas long enough; neither our power, nor our wealth, nor our patience is infinite, and we deserve relief! In another version, emphasis falls upon the multilateral purification of the role. The United States is invited not so much to lay down its burdens as to drop its unilateral pretensions; we deserve not to be relieved, on the ground that we have become weary in well-doing, but to be fired for misconduct in an office that we usurped in the first place. Let the arrogant unilateral pretender give way to the legitimate multilateral authority, the irresponsible vigilante to the responsible agency of the community! In either version, the basic logic is that a vacancy must be filled. The United States, for whatever reasons, is intent upon reducing its international load, and it is therefore incumbent upon the United Nations to pick up whatever the United States drops off.

I suspect that to some extent this talk of transferring functions to the world organization is merely a device for countering the charge of "neo-isolationism." One does not wish to be, or to appear to be, guilty of advocating the irresponsible withdrawal of the United States from its global responsibilities, though one insists upon withdrawal; shifting the burdens to the United Nations has the semblance of more, not less, responsible behavior. Unfortunately, however, those who offer this solution seldom appear to have engaged in serious consideration of the capacity and will of the United Nations to compensate for the diminution of the role of the United States in world affairs. Really responsible buck-passing requires that one take the precaution of ascertaining that one has a willing and able buck-receiver.

How realistic is the proposition that the United Nations is, or how meaningful is the possibility that it can become, an adequate substitute for the United States in the bearing of burdens that the latter has carried throughout the postwar period and now seems determined to relinquish? By and large, my answer must be a skeptical one. There are, indeed, certain things that the United Nations can do without the active involvement and support of the

United States—or, to put it more accurately, other states can use the machinery of the organization and act through its channels for certain purposes, even though the United States may adopt a stand-offish attitude. These possibilities are chiefly in the declaratory realm, the realm that I have previously characterized as that of "collective legitimization." [2] The United Nations can be used, without or against the United States, to proclaim, to recommend, to insist, to condemn, to deplore—in short, to pass judgment upon and to stake out positions concerning all sorts of international issues.

What the organization can *do,* however, in contradistinction to what it can *say,* without the interested and dedicated participation of the United States, is another matter. Theoretically, of course, the United Nations need not be dependent upon American support; it has 131 other members capable, in varying degrees, of supplying the wherewithal for its projects. In fact, however, the record suggests that the activeness of the United Nations is closely correlated with the willingness of the United States to provide the political leadership and the largest single contribution to the resources required for the activities of the organization. It might be suggested that the fielding of United Nations peace-keeping forces should be excepted from this generalization, for this is a function designed to be carried out by personnel from smaller states and thus explicitly to exclude the involvement of such superpowers as the United States. I must point out, however, that the financial, logistical, and political support of the United States has so far proved the critical ingredient in the recipe for effective United Nations performance of the peace-keeping function.

On the whole, I find it hard to imagine the world organization's moving into whatever voids the United States may create by its national program of retrenchment. The established formula is that United Nations activity tends to increase when the United States is willing to engage more actively in multilateral programs and projects, and to decrease when the American commitment diminishes. I see no reason to expect the reversal of this relationship. If we decide to do less internationally, I think we shall be foolish to suppose that the United Nations will do more. The real issue is not what contributions to a decent and stable world order will be made by the United Nations instead of the United States, but what the United States will leave undone, will do on its own, and will do in and through and with the United Nations, to promote that end. American by-passing of the United Nations is a more meaningful issue than American buck-passing to the organization. It may be that the United Nations can and should develop a more vigorous role in international relations, but let us not delude ourselves; that will happen not in response to a retraction of American involvement in world affairs but in consequence of a reaffirmation and redirection of that involvement by the United States, and, far from permitting the United States to shift its attention toward domestic affairs, it will require American acceptance of more weighty international responsibilities. If we are determined to adopt the position that what happens in far-off places is of little concern to us and that what the world needs most is for the United States to mind its own narrowly conceived business, we are free to do so. It would be unrealistic to expect and dishonest to suggest, however, that such an attitude on our part would trigger the development of a compensatory role in world affairs by the United Nations. What the United States is prepared to do remains the key question in determining what can and will be done by and through the United Nations for the peace and order of the world.

The third conception of the United Nations that deserves our attention pictures that organization as the potential master-controller of the international system—a superstate, a government over governments. One conceives the United Nations of the future as a mighty and authoritative multilateral nay-sayer, with the responsibility and the capacity for prohibiting, regulating, restraining, preventing, and suppressing antisocial behavior by states. In the current American perspective, this conception of how the organization might and should develop emphasizes the issue of the willingness of the United States to subject itself to the controlling will, the disciplining authority, of the United Nations. All states, the United States no less than any other, must accept subordination to the community's central organ. Respect, obedience, and deference to the collective will are the marks of loyal adherence to the United Nations; if the organization cannot yet, as a practical matter, enforce its decisions, it can nonetheless legitimately demand observance of them—and the latter will help to build the possibilities of the former. In the manner of a self-fulfilling prophecy, acting as if the United Nations is competent to impose a beneficent order upon the world of states will contribute to the realization of that ideal.

What is the United States willing to stop doing, and not to undertake again? What aspects of sovereignty is it willing to relinquish? What restraints and inhibitions is it prepared to accept? What pretensions and ambitions will it forswear, and to what degree will it renounce the claim of right to make unilateral judgments and decisions and to take unilateral actions? These are the primary concerns of those who read the postwar record of American foreign policy—and especially the latter part of it—as a chronicle of arrogant and abusive misdoing, of ruthless and reckless violation of the norms that should guide international behavior. Just as those who feel that the United States is overburdened tend to suggest a transfer of responsibilities to the United Nations, those who regard our behavior as overweening envisage the United Nations as the custodian of the law—the principles, rules, and procedures—that should discipline American foreign policy. Admittedly, the world organization does not now have, nor can it be expected soon to acquire, the capacity to enforce its will upon the United States, but the acid test of America's international morality and its commitment to responsible international behavior is, from this point of view, its willingness to respect the limitations defined and applied by the United Nations. Can the United Nations become the authoritative and respected arbiter of the foreign policy of all states, including the most powerful ones?

To consider this question in its fullest sense would be to speculate about very long-range possibilities, not to discuss prospects for the 70s, and therefore to exceed my terms of reference. The short run is the beginning of the long run, however, and it is entirely legitimate to consider the extent to which states can and should be expected in the present era to be restrained by the Charter and the collective opinions and decisions of members of the United Nations.

This question applies to the United States as much as, but no more than, to any other member, and it cannot be answered with respect to any state considered alone, outside the context of its relations with other states. The element of reciprocity is crucial; realistically, no state can afford to commit itself unconditionally to respect inhibitions laid upon it by the United Nations without assurance that other states will do the same, without confidence that the organization will be evenhanded in its judgments and decisions, and without evidence that the organization can and will provide effective protection against the perils to which the state may expose itself by following a policy of restraint. To state these conditions is to admit the improbability that states will allow themselves to be governed in any meaningful sense by the United Nations in the foreseeable future. Some idealists may conjecture that if states would only act as if the United Nations were what it is not yet, and as if it could do what it cannot yet do, they would help the organization become what it should be and develop the capacity to do what it should be able to do. Most statesmen, however, must be expected to regard this "act as if" doctrine as a call for disastrous unrealism rather than for creative idealism. Their disposition is to base national policy on their best under-standing of the present nature and capacity of the United Nations, not on their highest hope as to what kind of organization it might someday become.

There is a great deal to be said for the cautious position of the statesman in this matter. The demand for deference and obedi-ence to the United Nations is most clearly justified if one postulates an "ideal" United Nations; the more cognizant one becomes of the reality of world organization in our time, the less compelling that demand becomes. The fact that the United Nations is no longer a tool of the United States to the degree that it once was does not mean that it is not a tool of states. It is, as it should be, a multi-lateral instrument. But multilateralism works no moral alchemy; there is no cosmic guarantee that collective decisions and resolu-tions will be suffused with wisdom or decency, or will lead to justice and order. The United Nations is an earthbound institu-tion, and its spirit is compounded of the political biases and am-bitions of its members, not infallibly purified by their being shaken together in the multilateral process. It is not invariably respectful of its own constitutional principles and norms, or fair, judicious, and consistent in applying its rules and asserting its judgment regarding particular cases. Even less is it disposed or competent to offer security to its members in compensation for the restraints that it may press them to accept.

To say all of this is not to build a case for ignoring judgments and resolutions of the United Nations, or for treating them with contempt. Both normative and practical considerations dictate that the will institutionally expressed as that of the United Nations be taken seriously and weighted heavily by makers of national foreign policy. There is substantial evidence that this takes place. The fact that states frequently defy the United Nations should not be allowed to obscure the fact that they regularly exert themselves to secure collective judgments favorable to their cause and to de-feat the adoption of unfavorable judgments, or of resolutions with which they feel unable or unwilling to comply. When states violate United Nations decisions or recommendations, they often seek to deny or to justify such violation. Such behavior indicates the con-viction that there is significant profit in obedience and loss in disobedience to the proclaimed will of the organization. The calculus of decision typically includes far more than this, and this factor seldom appears decisive, but it is, as it should be, influential. To assert the incapacity of the United Nations to govern states is not to deny its capacity to influence them. That capacity will grow or shrink, according to whether the organization comes to be regarded as more or less fair and dispassionate in its political judgments, just as respect for law varies with perceptions of the respectability of the law.

The most basic objection to the conception of the United Nations as a potential regulator and controller of the behavior of states is to be found in the fact that, for better or for worse, this is not the end toward which the development of the organization has been directed. One may wish that the organization were dedicated to the subordination of states to its will, the diminution of their effective capacity to challenge its authority, and the development of its own global supremacy, but wishing does not make it so. It should not surprise us, though it may disappoint some of us, that the United Nations has not become a competitor of states, intent upon reducing their competence and significance —for, let us not forget, the organization is a collection of states, a creature of states, an instrument of states, and a property of states. Hence, the United Nations is responsive to the will, the needs, and the purposes of states; its role in relation to states is that of servant, not that of master.

Realistically, the question to ask about the United Nations is not what it can do to states, but what it can do for them—not how much power it has over them, but how useful it is to them. How have states undertaken to use the organization? Looking at the record from this angle, I think the outstanding fact is that the United Nations has become, above all, a state-serving, state-assisting, state-supplementing, and state-building agency. It has been turned toward the problems that stem from the weakness of its constituent states more than toward the problems deriving from their power. Its business has been defined as that of strengthening weak states, rather than that of weakening strong ones. It has been used to help states deal with the causes and the effects of their various incapacities. Perhaps the most striking illustration of this dominant trend is to be found in the economic activities of the organization, which have been focused with ever increasing intensity upon the promotion of the economic development of member states. The intent of this multifaceted program is clearly to enhance, not to reduce, the capacity of states to function effectively—to undergird, not to undermine, their statehood. The organization has been used in other ways as well, but I submit that it has been devoted fundamentally to the service and support of states. It follows that the appropriate criterion for the evaluation of the United Nations is the quality of the service that it has rendered, not the degree of the mastery that it has acquired; it ought to be judged in terms of the primary purpose for which it has been used.

It follows also that the most significant consideration pertaining to the evaluation of the past and the determination of the future behavior of the United States in and toward the United Nations is not American submissiveness to the will and control of the organization. I am convinced that the key contribution that the United States can make to the effectiveness and usefulness of the organization does not consist of docility and deference, any more than it consists of the depositing upon the organization of burdens that the United States is no longer willing or no longer feels worthy to bear. Indeed, it is arguable that this country has contributed most to the organization in the past by what it has done—entirely outside the United Nations and sometimes more in defiance of it than in deference to it, more as a matter of by-passing the organization than of buck-passing to it—to shape and stabilize the global context within which the United Nations has had to operate. What the United Nations can become, and can do, in the future depends very heavily upon what the United States is willing and able to do to maintain an international environment conducive to the survival, the functioning, and the development of the organization. Somebody has to make the world safe for the United Nations before the United Nations can make much headway at making the world safe for mankind. The United States cannot do the job alone, but, unless this country continues to take the leading part, I see little prospect that the job will be done at all. It surely will not be done under the leadership of a United States that has become so preoccupied with the avoidance of mistakes that it makes a virtue of inactivity, or has become so guilt-ridden that it regards its own power as a liability for itself and for mankind, or has developed such a distaste for international responsibility that its zeal to drop burdens surpasses its concern about where they may fall, whether they will be picked up, and how they may be carried. In my view, the United States poses a severe threat to the future of the United Nations, a threat attributable not to the "arrogance of power," the rampancy of ambition, or the hypertrophy of pretension, but to their opposites—which add up to